Operations Management in
Service Industries and
the Public Sector

Operations Management in Service Industries and the Public Sector

Text and Cases

CHRISTOPHER VOSS
School of Industrial and Business Studies
University of Warwick

COLIN ARMISTEAD
The European School of Management Studies
Oxford

BOB JOHNSTON
School of Industrial and Business Studies
University of Warwick

BARBARA MORRIS
Department of Management Studies
Sheffield City Polytechnic

JOHN WILEY & SONS
Chichester · New York · Brisbane · Toronto · Singapore

Copyright © 1985 by John Wiley & Sons Ltd.

Reprinted January 1987
Reprinted April 1988
Reprinted November 1988
Reprinted October 1989
Reprinted May 1990

Library of Congress Cataloging in Publication Data:
Main entry under title:

Operations management in service industries and the
  public sector.

  Includes index.
  1. Service industries – United States – Management –
  Case studies. 2. Service industries – Great Britain –
  Management – Case studies. 3. Social work administration –
  United States – Case studies. 4. Social work administration –
  Great Britain – Case studies.
  I. Voss, Christopher, 1942–
  HD9981.5.64   1985   658   85 – 9339

  ISBN 0 471 90801 0 (paperback)

British Library Cataloguing in Publication Data:

Operations management in service industries and the
  public sector: text and cases.
  1. Service industries – Management
  I. Voss, Christopher
  338.4   HD9980.5

  ISBN 0 471 90801 0

Printed and bound in Great Britain by
Courier International Ltd, Tiptree, Essex

Contents

Preface

The study of the management of operations in most Schools and Departments of Business and Management has focused on the management of manufacturing operations. The disciplines of operations management are concerned with the design and management of physical operations so as to achieve efficiency, effectiveness, and profitable customer satisfaction. These objectives are equally applicable to service operations and over recent years it has become clear that application of operations management disciplines and concepts can achieve these objectives. This was first widely acknowledged after Theodore Levitt (1972) published his classic article: 'Production line approach to service'. In it he showed how application of production principles had radically increased the competitiveness of certain service operations. He illustrated this in particular with the McDonalds hamburger restaurant chain and the 'Engineered hamburger'. Any serious student of service operations should read this article and then visit a McDonalds or similar operation and observe it as a production process.

A significant fact was that the author of this article, Theodore Levitt, was a Marketing Professor. In service operations, consumption of the service and production of the service take place at the same time. Clearly production of a service is part of the marketing mix. Thus the marketing and operations functions clearly interact. It is difficult for the student of operations management in service industries not to get involved in market aspects as well.

The pioneer text in the service operation was that of Sasser, Olsen, and Wyckoff (1978). This for the first time brought together both a number of conceptual frameworks for the study of service operations and a collection of case studies.

A course on service operations management has been included in the curriculum of the London Business School since 1976. In teaching this course and using available texts and cases it became clear that there were a number of areas where concepts and materials needed to be developed.

First, most of the existing case material (with the notable exception of the Lex Garages series of cases which are included in this book) was US based. There are a number of substantial differences between the United States and the United Kingdom; for example, the context of site location, the public ownership of services such as health care, and cultural expectations of service. Second, existing textbooks either left out many important operations discipline considerations or assumed that they could be applied without adjustment to the service industry context.

In response to this a case writing programme was launched at the London Business School to develop case and other teaching material in the UK context. The case writing was funded by the School's educational development fund. At the same time operations management teachers at Manchester Polytechnic and Sheffield City Polytechnic were facing pressure to increase the service content of the operations management courses at their institutions. They responded with the development of specific material on operations management in service industries. This book is the result of the bringing together of the work at the three institutions by Chris Voss of the London Business School, Colin Armistead at Manchester Polytechnic, and Bob Johnston and Barbara Morris at Sheffield City Polytechnic.

This book is primarily a casebook with a linking text to provide an introduction to the description of the operations management concepts and issues in the study of service and public sector operations.

The book is structured as follows:

- Introduction to service operations
- Designing service operations
- Managing the workforce
- Capacity management
- Quality management
- Operations control
- Field service management
- Queue management
- Materials management
- Site location
- Strategy and the multi-site life cycle

Although the cases are placed in the section relating to these main issues, many of them reflect the complexity and diversity of business and cover other areas as well.

This book takes a broad view of service operations and includes not just service businesses but also a number of examples of public sector services and the field service operations of manufacturing companies.

This book is intended for students of management at all levels and for those who wish to increase their knowledge of operations management. In the classroom it can either be used as the basis of a course on operations management in service industries or to supplement the manufacturing based material in production/operations management courses.

REFERENCES

Levitt, Theodore (1972). Production line approach to service, *Harvard Business Review*, September–October **1972**.

Sasser, W.E. Olsen, R.P., and Wyckoff, D.D. (1978). *Management of Service Operations*, Allyn and Bacon, Boston.

Acknowledgements

I would like gratefully to acknowledge the contribution that many people have made to this book. I would particularly like to thank the companies who consented to be subjects for case research, the various people involved in the case writing process – in particular, Mark Law, Charles Pollard, and Elizabeth Kennedy – colleagues who have provided criticism and stimulation to parts of the book – in particular Charles Baden-Fuller and John Bateson – and my wife Carolyn who provided support and active help in suggesting sites for research and participated in the case writing programme. The London Business School has provided material support in funding part of the case writing and Alastair Nicholson has helped me find the time to complete the writing and provided me with much encouragement. Finally, I would like to thank my coauthors for the hard work that they and their colleagues have put into the making of this book.

C.A. Voss

I would like to thank the following:
* Those organizations who gave assistance in the preparation of the cases.
* Rosemary Napper and John Killeya for encouragement and helpful discussion on service operations.
* Students who have helped to refine the cases and texts by participating in their use.
* Coauthors who have worked hard to respond to the need for a service operations teaching book set in the UK context.

Colin Armistead

I would like to thank the people and organizations who provided help in the preparation of the cases, in particular, Roy Wildgoose and David Guile. I would also like to thank my wife, Shirley, for her help and encouragement and my colleagues at Sheffield City Polytechnic for their suggestions and support. Finally I would like to thank the coauthors for their efforts in the preparation of this book.

Bob Johnston

Chapter 1

Introduction to Service Operations

Colin G. Armistead

This book is concerned with the management of service operations in both the public and private sector.

What do we mean by the term 'service'? On a walk along a High Street in any town we are likely to see retail stores, banks, a town hall or council offices, police stations, building societies, insurance brokers, a post office, cinemas, schools, restaurants, theatres, electrical repairers, garages, doctors' surgeries and travel agents – not to mention builders working on yet another fast food outlet – and so on; to the man in the street they are all services. If we wish to know more about the different types of organizations from the standpoint of operations management we need to be able to make some separation and examine how the main resources are used in each case. Remember operations management is concerned with the design, planning, and control of the production function and the decisions which relate to the use of the main resources of materials, people, and machines (or facilities).

1. THE NATURE OF SERVICE

In manufacturing organizations there has evolved a classification for different types of manufacturers based on the way technology is used and on whether the company manufacturers to stock or to customer order. So far a similar method of classification has not been developed for services (Mills and Moberg, 1982). However, operations people do require some method of sorting different service businesses and identifying those operational aspects which are particularly important in an individual business if it is to be successful.

1.1 A Linguistic Approach

An interesting initial approach is to consider the use of the word 'service' (Zvegintzov, 1984) and how the usage has developed over time. Figure 1.1 shows three main elements – the right-hand stream indicates that the customer receives some benefit, the left centre shows the wide provision of capital infrastructure for public use, and at the bottom is the concept of catering for

2

Figure 1.1 Historical development of the connotations of the word 'service'. (From Zvegintzov, 1984. Reproduced by permission of Serge Zvegintzov)

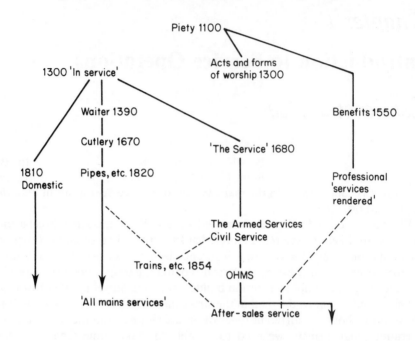

recurrent need. The word 'service' has in the course of time evolved a range of meanings which have a bearing on the way in which we see a particular organization which is termed a 'service'. We shall see that this is important in the context of the complete organization but it does not go a long way in assisting service managers to identify the activities they need to be good at doing. We will look at one approach which seeks to provide a framework for identifying the main operational activities.

1.2 Manufacturing to Service Continuum

The idea of being able to place any organization on a continuum between 'pure' manufacturing and 'pure' service is common. Pure manufacturing is considered to be associated with those organizations where there is a very low level of direct contact with the customer, as in mining, farming, and heavy engineering; 'pure' service is the reverse in there being a very high degree of direct customer contact as in medical services, legal practices, and dental practices (i.e. those categorized as professional services) (Chase, 1978). There are of course a large number of organizations which both produce goods and offer services; many manufacturing companies fall into this category through the provision of after-sales service. Such organizations would be placed somewhere along the scale between 'pure' manufacturing and 'pure' service.

1.3 Manufacturing/Supply/Transport/Service Grouping

We have already seen that the category of organizations which we might call service is very broad and varied. Further separation and grouping of organizations can be achieved by using a classification suggested by Wild (1971) according to the following definitions:

Manufacture: in which the physical output consists of goods which differ physically from the materials input to the system. Manufacture requires a physical transformation – a change in the *form* utility of resources.

Transport: in which the customer, or something belonging to the customer, is moved from place to place. Physical resources are not substantially changed in form – there is a change in *place* utility.

Supply: in which the ownership or possession of goods is changed without a change in form. The change is, primarily, of *possession* utility.

Services: in which the customer, or something belonging to the customer, is treated in some way. The state of physical outputs will differ from that of inputs by virtue of the treatment. The change is of *state* utility.

1.4 The Operations Tetrahedron

Attempts to rigidly categorize organizations into one of four groupings is bound to have severe limitations, especially when dealing with organizations which have a strong service component along with one or more of the other classifications. Examples abound like rail and bus services, which are a mixture of transport and service, retailing, which is a mixture of supply and service, and distribution, which is a mixture of supply and transport. Recognition of the shortcomings of a rigid classification leads to the idea of a series of scales or continua forming a tetrahedron with the corners representing theoretical 'pure' states for manufacturing, transport, supply, and service – an operations tetrahedron (see Figure 1.2; Armistead and Killeya, 1984).

The previous definitions for the manufacturing, supply, transport, and service functions can be extended to widen their scope in the following way:

Manufacture: is of course concerned with making things. This may involve making goods (i.e. traditional manufacture) or it may be the manufacture on paper (e.g. the package tour operator or the architect).

Supply: is concerned with the management of materials or information; this will include the operational activities necessary to give advice or exert influence.

Figure 1.2   Operations Tetrahedron. (From Armistead and Killeya, 1984)

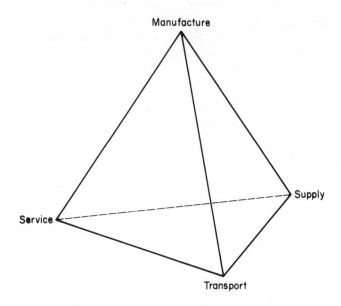

Transport: is concerned with moving people, things, or information (e.g. the telephone system).

Service: is primarily characterized by the customer/organization interaction.

Using the conceptual framework of the operations tetrahedron the main operational activities of the organizations seen in the High Street walk can be identified; these are shown in Exhibit 1.1.

An examination of those organizations and businesses which are termed services shows that in them there is a high degree of interaction between the organization and the customer and that this is a factor which in many services the operations people must manage at the same time as the other operational activities associated with the functions of supply, manufacture, or transport.

2.   THE CUSTOMER – ORGANIZATION INTERACTION

If it is the element of interaction between a customer or client and an organization which defines the organization as being a service, then it is important for those who are managing to appreciate the various types of interaction and for our purposes to see how these concern the operations people. We will in our consideration of the design of services see how the different types of interaction present a range of choices for the design and subsequent operation of the service business.

Exhibit 1.1 The main operational activities of High Street organizations. (From Armistead and Killeya, 1984)

Organization	Manufacture		Supply		Transport			Service	
	Material	Paper	Information	Material	People	Material	Information	Soft	Hard[1]
Supermarket				*					*
Shoe shop			*					*	
Bank			*	*			*	*	*
Town hall	*		*					*	
Police station			*					*	*
Building Society			*	*				*	
Insurance broker		*	*					*	
Post office – Counter			*	*				*	*
Mail					*	*		*	
Restaurant	*		*	*				*	
Cinema			*						*
Theatre	*		*					*	
Electrical repair	*							*	
Garage – repair								*	
sales			*	*				*	
School		*	*					*	
GP			*					*	
Travel agent			*					*	
Fast food		*		*				*	
Tour operator		*							*
Discotheque				*				?	
Public house				*				?	
Fire station	*	*							*
Hotel accommodation				*				*	
Dentist	*							*	
Coach operator					*			*	
Taxi					*			*	
Public library			*	*				*	*

[1] See Section 2.1

2.1 Personal or Non-Personal Interaction

The interaction between the service organization and the customer may be by way of a personal contact between the customer and a 'server' in the organization. Alternatively, the contact may be between equipment provided by the service organization and the customer. In both cases in the contact process the customer is participating; this customer participation in the service contact process is one of the most important features of services which for operations people distinguish services from manufacturing operations.

The personal and non-personal types of interaction have been called 'soft' and 'hard' (Levitt, 1972) or 'people based' and 'equipment based' (Thomas, 1978), which reflect in the first case the customer's possible perception of the way contact takes place and in the second the means by which the contact is performed. The personal interaction may be face to face interaction between the customer and the serving contact person or it could be contact by telephone or by letter, although each of these instances engenders a different level of contact and a progressive distancing of the customer from the server. The concept of level of contact has been applied to design of service operations as a means of removing the customer from the direct environment of the operations people (Chase, 1978).

The ultimate in reducing the level of personal contact is to substitute equipment to perform the task previously done by a person; this is the non-personal or equipment-based interaction. A bank cash dispenser and an automatic ticket machine are examples of non-personal contact placed close to the organization. Alternatively, the non-personal contact can be conducted at a distance (analogous to the telephone personal contact) through the use of a computer terminal and VDU.

Increasingly service businesses and organizations are choosing to use a mixture of personal and non-personal methods of dealing with the interaction with customers and clients. For example, see the use of automatic bank tellers (cash dispensing machines) described in the Baker Street Branch Case at the end of Chapter 8.

3. THE CUSTOMER IS PART OF THE SERVICE PROCESS

If the customer is participating in an interaction with the business in the main element of service, it follows that the customer must be regarded as part of the service process. This has definite implications for managers of services as it presents difficulties and opportunities both for marketing and operations people. Difficulties arise through people being individuals who will not always react in a consistent manner (this applies both to customers and service contact people) and the limited opportunity for mistakes to go unnoticed by the customer. Opportunities are in terms of being able to use the customer as a resource to do, to monitor, and to promote the service (Lovelack and Young, 1979). Furthermore service operations have to be capable of dealing directly with a large number of customers.

4. THE SERVICE PACKAGE

Consideration of the operations tetrahedron as a concept for looking at different service organizations illustrates that in many cases the business or organization is providing more to the customer than just the content of the direct interaction. For example, in buying goods in a shop we expect to leave the shop with some physical items as well as some impressions of the contact with the shop assistants. This leads to the idea of the 'service package'; this comprises any physical items which are provided to the customer, the environment in which the service takes place, the environment of the service contact, and the nature of the service contact. Thus in travelling on a particular airline the customer will be influenced by the comfort of the seat, the meals which are served in the flight, the attitude and competence of the cabin staff, and the boarding and embarking process, among others. This all makes for complexity in managing the operation, both from operational and from marketing standpoints, in terms of what the individual customer is buying. In the case of the airline, a customer may be on business and expects a comfortable journey with the opportunity to work or may be on holiday and thus wants to relax and to enjoy the in-flight entertainment.

In many cases it is difficult to establish just what an individual customer is buying. A consequence of this is that many businesses provide not just a package of one service but a range of service packages.

5. THE PRODUCTION OF THE SERVICE PACKAGE

As we have seen, the service package consists of a number of different features. Some of these are physical or tangible items which form part of the service package in that they are bought or hired or experienced in the service environment and others are ephemeral or intangible associated with the contact experience. The production of the service package often falls into two main areas: firstly, that part of the service-producing unit which produces the physical item (food in a restaurant, insurance schemes in an insurance company) and, secondly, that part which involves contact with the customer. In some services where something is done to the customer in the course of receiving the service (removing teeth, cutting hair, for example) the two processes tend to coalesce.

The involvement of the customer in the production process, as with the example of a haircut or with travel on a bus, illustrates that in services the production of the service package and its consumption by the customer tend to be simultaneous.

If the customer is to be involved to some extent in the service process, one operational consequence is that the service-producing unit must be accessible to the customer either through it being located near the customer (as with the examples in the High Street) or the service-producing unit must be taken to the customer (telephone, computer terminal, mail, and field service activities) or the customer must be taken to the producing unit (as with the ambulance service and package tours).

A second operational consequence of the customer being involved in the production process is that a service cannot be stored for future consumption in the same way as a manufactured product. A service business may approach this constraint by managing capacity either to accommodate fluctuations in demand or to manipulate demand to match capacity. Usually service businesses operate a mixture; so, for example, British Rail will stimulate low peak demand by reducing ticket prices and at the same time increase capacity by running relief trains.

The fact that many service packages comprise part which is produced without the customer (often physical items associated with the service package) and part which directly requires the participation of the customer leads to the idea of a 'back room' and 'front office' for the service business (Levitt, 1972).

6. FRONT OFFICE–BACK ROOM

Many service operations involve operational activities which are separated from the main customer–organisation interaction. This is the case for traditional manufacturing businesses where the goods for sale are made by production people who rarely, if ever, come into contact with the customer. The customer contact and interaction is with marketing and sales people. Looked at another way, the goods are made in the 'back room' (i.e. the factory or workshop) and sold through the 'front office' (i.e. the sales office). In the traditional manufacturing firm the operations people are insulated from the customer by the sales/marketing function and the interface between production and marketing (Figure 1.3).

Figure 1.3   Manufacturing and service operations

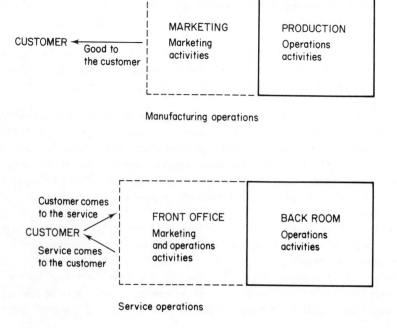

The same kind of separation of front office and back room will apply in many types of service operations, and especially those which are organized as traditional manufacturing operations. Examples are many types of repair services and catering operations.

The effect of having a back room content to a service operation is that this does to some extent de-couple this part of the operations from that which has the customer participating (Figure 1.3). The idea of isolating a 'technical core' is not new (Thompson, 1967); the advantages are that it is easier to control the operations in this more predictable environment and that it restricts the number of people who act as contact personnel. The operational management methods applied to 'back room' activities are very similar to those found in many traditional manufacturing operations; indeed, many of the activities in the 'back room' of service organizations are manufacturing in the terms of our definition of making goods (including repairing) and compiling on paper (or on a computer).

Another consequence of a back room activity is the need to manage the interface between the people in the back room and those in the 'front office' – again a situation analogous to traditional manufacturing with the divisions which often exist between operations and marketing personnel.

The 'front office' part of the service operation is where the customer contact takes place. This is the area which is more difficult to control and manage. The complexity of the interaction process, especially if it is personal, makes it difficult to produce a consistent level for this part of the service package. We shall see that attempts can be made to get consistency by a standardized approach to the service contact process (as exemplified by many fast food operations following MacDonalds' lead), although this can have the opposite effect of the customer perceiving the contact (and the service) as being impersonal and phoney. The management of the way a customer perceives a service experience is vital to the production of customer satisfaction with the service package. There is the idea that customer satisfaction represents the difference between the customer's perception of the service at the time of 'consumption' and the customer's prior expectation of what he/she would be like.

The part played by the service contact personnel in the front office obviously has an effect on the customer's perception of the service experience. It is often the case that they are performing both a marketing and selling activity as well as a production operation (Figure 1.3). A shop assistant not only performs the task of handling the goods and completing the sale but also a marketing activity in conveying an impression about the shop to the customers. Contact personnel also often carry out a wide range of activities for which they may not have been trained or authorized, as with medical receptionists performing diagnosis. Contact personnel often have more direct contact with customers than a sales force (especially in field service activities; Voss, 1984).

The more a service organization can increase the back office content of the operations the greater the degree of control it has. In the front office environment there is often a conflict of control between the customers, the contact servers, and the supervision or management (Bateson, 1984). Moreover, the presence of the customers makes it difficult to control the quality of the service encounter and mistakes which occur are often visible to the customers.

Consideration of the back room and front office concept has implications in the design of service operations, which we will examine in more detail in a subsequent chapter.

7. OPERATIONAL TYPES OF SERVICES

Service operations may be grouped into a number of different categories which reflect the organizational production of the service in relation to the service and the specific customers for the service.

7.1 Organizational Based

This is the form of most services where the customer either visits or makes direct contact with the service business or organization or the customer is brought to the service organization. The production of the service package and its consumption take place in the environment determined by the service business.

7.2 Field Service

A characteristic of field service activity is that the service is produced in the environment of the customer. The people who are performing the activity will be engaged in the operation process associated with repair or maintenance or installation (usually associated with back room activities) and at the same time they may engage in selling and marketing. There is a breakdown of the interfaces between the back room operations and the front office and the customer, as shown in Figure 1.3. The same model applies to any service which is produced with the customer participating so that the servers must be engaged in roles other than just operations personnel. This applies to many professional services where the front office with both marketing and operations activities is a much larger part of the whole than the back room activities.

7.3 Internal Services

A special category of services are those which exist within a larger organization independent of whether the organization is itself a service business or a manufacturer. The customers are then other parts of the parent organization. This relationship imposes constraints on the service department, but many of the management techniques and concepts which apply to other types of services are applicable to internal services. It is not uncommon for an internal service to start marketing its services outside of the parent organization and evolve into a service success in its own right.

Figure 1.4   Features of different service/manufacturing/operations. (From Maister, 1983. Reproduced by permission of Professor D. Maister)

	Value added mainly in the back room (out of client contact)	Value added mainly in the front office (during client interaction)	
Operating activities are highly proceduralized Standardized activities	'Factory'	'Mass service'	Programmatic control systems
Operating activites involve few routine procedures Customerized activities	Job shop	'Professional service'	Non-programmatic control systems
	Emphasis on technical skills	Emphasis on interactive skills	

8.   A FRAMEWORK FOR SERVICE ACTIVITIES

A further linking of the operations activities in service operations can be gained by considering the settings of what might be called 'factory', 'job shop', 'mass service', and 'professional service'. A matrix of these main environments is shown in Figure 1.4 (Maister, 1983).

Examples of 'factory' and 'job shop' might come from standard manufacturing activities where 'factory' activities correspond to manufacturing operations making goods by batch and flow production on a mass scale and 'job shop' activities belong with making to specific customer order and specification (probably on a small scale). We might also extend this classification to include what we referred to earlier as manufacturing 'on paper' and take as an example of 'factory' activity a market research programme to support a specific product launch and of 'job shop' activity the design of a computer-assisted stock control package. These two activities can be regarded as back room activities.

'Mass service' belongs with many of the businesses which we naturally refer to as service but which do not contain the same degree of personnel interaction as that typified by 'professional service'. Examples of 'mass service' will thus include fast food restaurants and transport services where the service element and the value added by that activity come mainly from the execution of the service in the customer−server contact. By contrast, in 'professional service' the added value of the service results mainly from diagnosis. The 'factory' and 'job shop' activities can be seen as back room activities with most of the added value from their execution coming from what is taken away from any interaction with the customer. On the other hand, 'mass service' and 'professional service' are front office activities with the added value being due to interaction with the customer or client.

'Factory' and 'mass service' activities are likely to be highly proceduralized as they are required to be repeated many times in a reproducible manner. 'Job shop' and 'professional service' are likely to operate with fewer routine procedures as they are suited to the individual needs of the customer (or client).

9. MANAGING SERVICE OPERATIONS

As production and consumption of service tends to be simultaneous, the service-producing unit or delivery system can be seen as part of the marketing mix. Thus the manager of a service organization needs to be both an operations and a marketing manager. It is unlikely that the manager of a shop, a bank manager, or a police inspector would describe themselves in these terms, but that is what they do in their jobs.

The management of services is complex – the functional areas which exist in manufacturing are not as distinct. There is clearly, in many cases, a great deal of overlap between marketing and operations management for both service managers and the service contact personnel.

10. CONCLUSION

Service operations have a number of unique features:

(a) Service production and consumption is usually simultaneous.
(b) Service is usually transient or perishable.
(c) The production of the service is part of the 'marketing mix'.
(d) People are part of the production system as customers or clients.
(e) Service operations deal directly with a large number of customers.

Managers of service businesses who forget the individual nature of people and regard them as inanimate items as in a manufacturing operation will not in the long run be as successful as those who design and operate their businesses to take account of the threats and opportunities offered by the participation of the customer. The subsequent chapters look at those aspects of service operations management which are important in achieving success.

REFERENCES

Armistead, C.G., and Killeya, J.C. (1984). Transfer of concepts between manufacture and service, *International Journal of Operations and Production Management*, **3**, No. 3.

Bateson, J.E.G. (1984). *Perceived Control and the Service Encounter*, Workshop on Research in Service Businesses: Institut d'Administration des Entreprises, Aix-en-Provence, France.

Chase, R.B. (1978). Where does a customer fit in a service operation, *Harvard Business Review*, November–December **1978**.

Levitt, T. (1972). Production line approach to service, *Harvard Business Review*, September–October **1972**.

Lovelock, C.H., and Young, R. (1979). Look to customers to increase productivity, *Harvard Business Review*, May–June **1979**.

Maister, D. (1983). *Research in Service Operations Management*, Proc. Workshop on Teaching and Researching Production and Operations Management, London Business School.

Mills, P.K., and Moberg, D.J. (1982). Perspectives on the technology of service operations, *Academy of Management Review*, **7**, No. 3.

Thomas, D.R.E. (1978). Strategy is different in service businesses, *Harvard Business Review*, July–August **1978**.

Thompson, J.D. (1967). *Organizations in Action*, McGraw-Hill, New York.

Voss, C.A. (1984). The service despatcher/receptionist role, *International Journal of Operations and Production Management*, **3**, No. 3.

Wild, R. (1971). *Production and Operations Management*, Holt, Rinehart and Winston.

Zvegintzov, S. (1984). Services: towards a unified view, *International Journal of Operations and Production Management*, **3**, No. 3.

Case Study: Morrell's Meat Limited

In common with most other parts of the food retailing industry, butchers have felt the effects of the growth in the ownership of domestic freezers over the last ten years. Nearly all butchers now will cater for freezer owners by offering a discount off large orders, but a few in the trade have totally changed their operations to cater for this new source of demand.

One such firm is Morrell's Meat Ltd. Until five years ago they were a conventional 'father and son' butchers shop on the east side of Leeds, close to the housing estates which serve the city's industrial area. In 1974 they moved to larger premises on the northern 'residential' side of the city, employed two more butchers, and changed their method of selling. Mick Morell explained:

> We could see the trend as far as bulk buying of food was concerned. It was becoming obvious that many people preferred to make fewer but bigger shopping trips, and the increasing number of home freezers meant that customers would now be able to do the same to buy their meat.
>
> We decided to go into bulk meat supplying because we hoped it would secure our future, but we were not satisfied with the way other butchers were doing it. The local Co-op butchers is typical. In their freezer meat centre the customer is faced with a large shop full of freezer cabinets — it's totally impersonal. We believe that the customer still wants personal contact with his butcher.

THE NEW SHOP

When the Morrells moved to their new shop they tried to reflect their concern for a more 'human approach' to bulk meat buying in the way they arranged the shop.

This case is based on a real organization and was prepared by Dr. Nigel Slack, Fellow of the Oxford Centre for Management Studies. The case is not designed to illustrate either the effective or ineffective handling of an administrative situation, but as a basis for class discussion.

The Author gratefully acknowledges the financial assistance of The Nuffield Foundation who supported the writing of this and other case studies in this series.

Figure 1

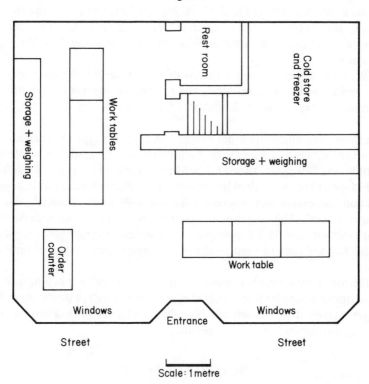

Scale: 1 metre

Figure 1 shows the present layout of the new shop. The selling area is 'L' shaped. In each wing there is a long butcher's table which can take up to three butchers. Around the shop there are storage racks which take the meat that is likely to be sold that day.

Generally the shop works in the following manner. The customer will come into the shop and give his order to a female assistant at the order counter. She writes the order down on an order sheet, costs it, and takes the money. When a butcher is free he comes over to the counter and takes the customer with his order sheet to his table. There he will discuss the customer's requirements and cut, weigh, trim, and bag the meat accordingly. The butcher then will carry the meat to the customer's car. Most customers seemed quite happy to pay for their meat before receiving it.

DEMAND

Since the move to the new shop demand in volume terms had more than doubled and the two Morrells now employed four other butchers. Demand varied through the week and also month by month, as Mick Morrell explained:

Both the week and the year are divided into two distinct parts. In the week, Monday to Wednesday's takings are low, while Thursday to Saturday are almost twice as high. In the year, Easter to mid-October is low with a pick-up in the autumn. This carries on to a high level through the winter.

We cope as best we can with this by taking our holidays in the summer months, which is no problem, and taking our one day a week off (other than Sunday) on either Monday, Tuesday, or Wednesday.

The shop sets a minimum order weight of 3 lb on any type of meat and sets its prices to encourage customers to buy whole pieces of meat such as whole legs of pork or lamb. This means that it is less likely to have odd cuts of meat left over.

The range of meats required by customers is broadly the same as in a conventional butchers except that Morrells will not usually prepare special joints such as 'crown roasts'. The company believed strongly in offering a service to the customer which is as close as possible to that which he would get at any smaller butchers and are keen to keep stocks of a comprehensive range of meats.

Occasionally we might run out of a particular meat, but as long as it's one of our less popular lines, such as rabbit for instance, I don't mind. I only get worried if we run out of a big seller like legs of pork. Fortunately this only happens about once a month.

BUYING THE MEAT

Generally retail butchers buy their meat from meat wholesalers who operate in wholesale meat markets. These wholesale meat markets are to be found in most large towns and cities.

The Morrells buy about 40 per cent of their supplies from Leeds meat market (which is the nearest one), about 20 per cent from Bradford (also relatively close), and the remaining supplies from several markets within an hour's drive – Huddersfield, Sheffield, Manchester. Furthermore, they will often use more than one supplier at each market.

This policy of buying from so many different sources is very unusual in meat retailing. Mick Morrell justifies it in two ways:

The main reason is that it spreads our business about so that if there is a shortage of a particular line or if I want something quickly, I have a lot of contacts to call on. It's the best way of guaranteeing supplies of what I want when I want. The other reason is that because I'm not big enough to be a very influential customer of a single supplier and get significant quantity discounts I have to shop around all the time to get the best bargains. Unfortunately it takes a lot of time.

The time it takes is one visit every working morning except Monday. Mick will take a van to the particular market and return one to three hours later, depending on where he goes. Some of these trips are made on a regular basis. On Tuesday and Fridays, for instance, he will 'top-up' his stocks of leg pork together with other purchases. Mick Morrell explains:

> I prefer to stock up my big selling items on a regular basis because then it's easier to organize and to keep in stock. With the slower moving cuts, I only stock up when I am down to my last few pounds.

FUTURE PLANS

By summer 1979 demand had increased to the point where the Morrells considered that the waiting time for the customers was getting too long (up to fifteen minutes on a Saturday morning). Since it was their firm belief that demand for their kind of service would continue to increase over the next few years they were considering the possibility of expansion.

The obvious way of expanding, by opening another shop, had already been considered and rejected by the Morrells. Mick justified this decision:

> If we opened another shop I would be spending most of my working day administering them rather than being a butcher, which is the work I enjoy doing. So, any expansion will have to be achieved by using the space we have more efficiently. I am convinced this can be done without destroying the quality of the service we give to our customers.

Case Study: Blood

This case describes the operation of a Regional Blood Transfusion Centre, of which there are fourteen throughout the country. Each is responsible for the collection of blood and supplying the hospitals within their region with blood and blood products.

Part One of the case describes the operation of the blood collection/storage/distribution network, while Part Two consists of verbatim extracts of comments by Dr. West, the Director of the Centre.

PART ONE – THE SYSTEM

Collecting

In the United Kingdom donors are not paid for the blood they give. Blood is collected by means of voluntary donor sessions organized by the Regional Transfusion Centre which keeps a register of blood donors. These donors are called twice a year to donor sessions which are attended by about 100 people. Generally there will be between ten and fifteen donor sessions scattered throughout the region on any one working day.

The Central Records Office at the Transfusion Centre keeps details of all donors and mails them as required. Not all donors turn up on the day, but the proportion who do is reasonably constant at about 51 per cent of those requested. Generally, donors are called to a session seven to ten days in advance of the date, so it is difficult to react to short-term changes in demand. If the demand warrants it, it is possible to use telegrams and phone messages to boost a donation session if a particular type of blood is low in stock.

In general, there is no great problem matching the number of donors to the demand for blood. Over the last few years there has been a levelling off in demand, while the number of donors has been reasonably buoyant. In spite of this, periodic campaigns are mounted to ensure that the supply of donors does

This case was prepared by Dr. N.D.C. Slack, Fellow of the Oxford Centre for Management Studies. This case is not designed to illustrate either the effective or ineffective handling of an administrative situation, but as a basis for class discussion.

The Author gratefully acknowledges the financial assistance of The Nuffield Foundation who supported the writing of this and other case studies in this series.

18

not fall off. London is probably the only exception to this. Here the combination of a relatively fluid population together with big demand from the Teaching Hospitals causes problems.

There is some flexibility in the supply of blood for times of emergency, since it is quite possible for donors to donate blood three times a year with no harmful effects, whereas the current policy is only to call upon them twice a year.

Testing

After collection the blood is tested. The testing laboratories are located at the Transfusion Centre itself, and they are primarily responsible for the testing of samples taken from each donation for certain diseases such as hepatitis and syphilis and for determining the blood group itself. This testing is very important for two reasons. Firstly, any blood that has traces of a disease could harm the recipient. Secondly, if blood of the wrong group is transfused into a patient very serious consequences could result.

Confusion is possible because the test sample is separated from the donation itself. After testing the information from the sample is reunited with the donation. These tests are performed by technicians using semi-automatic equipment.

Storing and 'Blood Products'

Up to a few years ago nearly all blood donated to the transfusion service was stored whole, but now much donated blood is split up into its constituent parts. In this way, one donation can be used on several patients, some of whom require the plasma only, others require concentrated red cells, etc. Of the 130,000 bottles of blood collected in the region each year about 65 per cent are split up into their constituent parts, the rest being stored whole.

When the blood is stored whole it has a shelf life of about three weeks. When blood is split up into its constituent parts the different constituents have different shelf lives. For example, platelet concentrate can only be kept under cool storage for forty-eight to seventy-two hours, whereas cryoprecipitate can be frozen indefinitely.

There is also some usage of fresh blood; this is blood that has not been treated, processed, or frozen. Generally the fresh blood is used in open heart surgery and is collected on the morning of the operation, or at most the day before the operation.

Blood can in fact be stored at very low temperatures in liquid nitrogen for a year or more. This, however, is an extremely expensive process. In this region very low temperature storage is used only on the rare blood groups.

Thus at any time the Transfusion Centre will have in stock fresh blood (although this is only collected to order for specific operations), whole blood (shelf life of twenty-one days), various blood products (cryoprecipitate concentrated red cells, platelet concentrate, etc.), or fresh plasma.

Issuing Blood

The Transfusion Centre delivers blood to the hospitals in its area either to replenish the hospital's blood stock on a regular basis (usually once or twice a week) or to meet emergency requirements. The hospitals' blood banks keep stocks of the major blood types and will also cross-match (check that the patient can receive the blood) and reserve blood for a particular patient. The majority of blood thus cross-matched will not in fact be used for that patient, having been set aside only as a precautionary measure. Once it is known that the patient will not require the blood it will be returned to the general blood store. In this way it is quite possible that blood could be cross-matched two or three times before it becomes too old to be used.

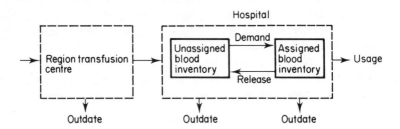

Any blood older than the twenty-one days shelf life is termed 'outdated blood' and is returned to the Transfusion Centre where the red cells are extracted and discarded, while the plasma is sent to the processing laboratory at Elstree for separation and crying. (Dried plasma is used in the treatment of haemophiliacs and in cases of shock and burns.) In this region more than 20 per cent of donated blood is eventually thrown away through outdating. This figure is not untypical of any region in this country.

If an emergency arises it is generally possible to bleed a donor at very short notice or to obtain blood from another region. In this way, and using the very high wastage margin, the Centre can offer a virtual 100 per cent service level.

The whole process from bleeding the donor to the blood getting into the Transfusion Centre's blood bank takes about forty hours. That is, blood taken today is likely to be tested tomorrow and banked the day after that.

PART TWO – THE ISSUES

This part reproduces some of the comments made by Dr. West when discussing the various issues he sees as being important at the time of writing this case.

... there is no doubt that a lot of blood gets wasted needlessly. We don't charge hospitals for blood, we don't pay donors for making donations, and I'm glad that we don't pay. In the countries where donors are paid there is obviously a financial motive for concealing previous disease and this results in a very high incidence of diseases such as hepatitis. We avoid that here, thank God . . . .

. . . mind you, at least where blood is paid for people do respect the blood and don't use it wastefully. I suppose we might charge hospitals a nominal figure, but this would take some time to organize, and would be a very contentious issue . . . .

. . . there is, after all, a moral obligation to be careful with people's blood of all things . . . to some extent we are using their goodwill to save expenditure for ourselves . . . .

. . . we could cut out all blood wastage totally: some parts of America have achieved this, but they do so at tremendous cost. It's quite simple really; all you do is process every drop of blood that comes to the Centre. So the concentrated red cells, the platelet concentrates, the cryoprecipitates, and the dried plasma are all stored at very low temperatures, and therefore stored practically indefinitely. When someone wants some blood all you do is reconstitute it. It would of course be hideously expensive to do it, but at least the wastage would have been reduced . . . .

. . . alternatively, we could reduce the wastage by getting an army of clerks to phone round the hospitals checking on how much blood has been cross-matched and temporarily allocated, and precisely what the stock levels were at any one time; that would give us better control . . . .

. . . of course, if we computerized the whole system, then that could be a very satisfactory alternative. In the USA computerization happened very quickly. Because blood is paid for over there, there is a legal duty to account for it, and computerization makes that particularly easy . . . here it is cheaper to pour it down the drain. It might be that we would reduce wastage by having better control, we would save some money by bleeding fewer people, saving in postage costs, and possibly achieve some staff savings. However, this would not outweigh the total capital cost of about £200,000 to set up the system in the first place. That amount of money out of our annual budget of £1.3 million is a lot to contemplate . . . .

. . . you see, we could spend our money on other things. For example, there is a new blood testing machine on the market which costs about £300,000 that is capable of about six or seven times the speed of the machine we are using at the moment. Mind you, the one we now use only cost £10,000. The advantage of the new machine is that, not only is it faster, but it is also capable of preparing bar-coded labels to be stuck on to the blood donation itself and printing out a record of all blood tested during the day. Of course, this makes a lot more sense when the whole system is computerized, but all this adds up to far too much money at the moment . . . .

. . . there are certain things that you can't control. For example, we have no say in the attitude of the hospital doctors when they request blood to be cross-matched and reserved for a particular patient. Obviously it is very convenient for them to have blood on hand in case it is needed, and often it has helped to save lives, but the more blood is cross-matched the higher the wastage rates. Who is to say if the reserving of blood is always necessary? . . .

. . . in general, I am sure that the future lies with improving our technical skill at physically storing the blood and improving our administrative procedures. The frustrating thing is that to do any of these things requires money to be laid out in the first place, and in the current climate there is not a lot of spare cash knocking around in the National Health Service . . .

Case Study: La Patisserie

La Patisserie is a small bakery and confectionery business operating from leased premises in a Thames Valley market town. The business is owned and managed by Mr. Arnold, a master baker, assisted by his son, and it consists of a shop, where all the bakery products are sold, and the bakery itself, which is at the back of the shop out of the sight of customers.

The production of bread, pastries, and confectionery is based on traditional methods, as Mr. Arnold explained:

> We use a big traditional oven and make large batches of the different products. The oven takes a long time to heat up and so we heat it to the right temperature for the bread, which needs the highest temperature, and bake the bread first. Then the other products are baked in the residual heat as the oven cools down.

This method is the most economical, but it is extremely time-consuming and expensive to have to go back through the cycle of bread, pastry, and confectionery and, therefore, once production of each product is complete, more of an earlier product cannot be produced. This method of operation means that it is necessary to decide in advance how much of each product is to be produced, and these amounts are fixed for each day's operations.

In addition to the traditional baking methods, the bakery employs traditional preparation and mixing. Three full-time bakers are employed, working overlapping shifts beginning at 4.30 a.m. and finishing at midday. Thus most of the products are ready for customers when the shop opens at 9.00 a.m. and the rest of the morning is spent preparing for the next day or making items which are only made less frequently, such as malt bread, which is only made twice weekly. The bakers have assistants to carry out routine work such as cleaning, tin greasing, and so on. Traditionally, master bakers do not carry out tasks of

This case was prepared by Barbara Morris, Lecturer in Management Studies at Sheffield City Polytechnic. The case is not designed to illustrate either the effective or ineffective handling of an administrative situation, but as a basis for class discussion.

The Author gratefully acknowledges the financial assistance of The Nuffield Foundation who supported the writing of this and other case studies in this series.

this nature, which are carried out by assistants learning the trade. None of the baking staff work in the shop.

The preparation and mixing of the various doughs is a skilled and time-consuming job. Bread dough, for example, takes three hours to mix properly and then has to be 'proved', which normally occurs overnight. High-speed mixers can be bought but the business does not have one.

The mixing and baking technology limits the rate of response to demand. It is possible to forecast demand reasonably well from past history, but once the day's production is decided it cannot be changed to cater for changes in demand. Because the goods are perishable, it is impossible in most cases to store them and hence the objective is to sell out. This can, however, mean failure to meet demand later in the day. It also means that it is difficult to allow for casual demand and since the town attracts a large number of tourists, casual demand can be high.

There is some fairly well-known fluctuation in demand for particular products throughout the week, and there is fairly well-known demand for seasonal products such as Christmas cakes. Hence the shop has a planned weekly production schedule, and production of seasonal times is added as necessary. Some items which are of a slightly less perishable nature such as malt bread can be held in stock for two or three days and do not have to be made daily. Malt bread, for example, is made twice weekly. Fruit bread is also made twice weekly because it requires a special oven temperature. This cannot be held in stock ready for sale since it is highly perishable, but it responds well to freezing and sufficient bread to meet daily demand is taken out for thawing and sale. Pastry is also made in large batches and much of the raw pastry frozen, with only sufficient for the day's production being taken out.

Items from the standard range can be ordered by customers, and the bakery will also produce items to customer demand. Normally all necessary stocks are held but special items will be bought in if required.

There is rigid demarcation between the jobs carried out in the bakery and those in the shop. Most of the counter staff work part time since the shop is fairly slack in the mornings and there are five boys and girls still at school who work on Saturdays and during holidays.

Being a small business, the quantities of materials consumed are fairly small and the shop does not have sufficient space to stock large quantities. In addition, the materials are perishable so that the length of time for which they can be stored is limited. Mr. Arnold, however, belongs to the London Bakers Buyers Association. This is a professional buying group owned by the bakers which buys in bulk, and hence gives the smaller bakers the advantage of a bulk-buying discount without having to carry excessive stocks.

At the time of this study Mr. Arnold had decided to purchase new premises in the town:

> You see, I'd like to update things a bit − buy some of the newer equipment. Finance is no problem: I'm my own boss and this is a good

business; the beauty of that is that I can please myself what I spend the money on, provided the Bank Manager is satisfied, and he is. The problem is that I don't want to put the new equipment in here. I've rented for years but over the last few years the rent has shot up and I can see the time coming when it's just not economical to carry on here. I'd be a bit silly investing a lot of money here under those circumstances.

Mr. Arnold believed there was enough business in the town to justify operating two retail outlets, but if the rent for the existing premises became excessive the entire business could be carried out from the new branch. He was undecided, however, about how to manage the two branches.

The new premises were about half a mile away and although Mr. Arnold wanted both outlets to be reasonably independent, he thought there might be some merit in a certain amount of interdependence.

The new shop will be managed by my son but we want it to have its own identity and customers, otherwise it will just take customers from the old branch and we shan't increase the overall business. On the other hand, the equipment we have at the old branch is capable of producing all the cakes and pastries for both branches and it seems silly to duplicate it at the new branch. What we'd like to do is buy a new high speed mixer and an electric oven for the new branch. That combination would give us far more flexibility than we have at present because if we baked in small batches we could respond to demand almost as it happens. The high speed mixer can produce a batch of bread dough in about an hour and we can change the temperature of the electric oven very quickly, so that we could bake small batches all day if demand seems to warrant it.

Mr. Arnold's proposal was that the existing branch should bake all the daily cakes and pastries for both branches whilst bread rolls and doughnuts should be introduced as new lines, baked at the new branch and taking advantage of the ability to respond flexibly to demand. Both branches would bake bread and seasonal products, such as Christmas and Easter cakes.

In principle this proposal seemed sound, but as Mr. Arnold said, there were a number of issues to be decided:

If we are going to be so flexible in meeting demand we want it to be obvious to people that we are baking all the time and that, within reason, there is little chance of us being sold out by the mid-afternoon. In addition, if we are going to bake small batches we want to sell them almost as they come out of the oven; if we don't, stocks will build up and we'll finish up in the same situation as at the other shop with a day's supply ready for sale, but without the economies of baking in large batches. We also want to attract new customers, and, in particular, the casual customers, because all this flexibility will be rather wasted if we don't. I think there may be something we can do with the layout of the bakery and the shop to attract people in.

Mr. Arnold is also well aware that his ideas are not compatible with the traditional working methods used at the old branch. Flexible response depends on the workers as well as the equipment and he is not sure how to get a flexible workforce.

Case Study: Ranmoor Car Hire

'Last year was terrible,' explained Jim Hubbard, 'we had cars stood in the yard unused even in the middle of August. At our end of the market we just can't afford to let that happen. You never know exactly how many cars you will need at any time but normally we guess pretty accurately. Last summer we had too many cars and paid for the mistake.'

Ranmoor Car Hire is one of the trading names for Ranmoor Car Sales Limited, a car sales and car hire company situated in an inner suburb on the south-west side of Sheffield. Jim Hubbard is one of the three director-managers of the company. Its turnover in 1977 was just under £¾ million. However, most of that came from the car sales side of the business rather than from car hire.

Jim was talking in July 1978 when the high season for car hire was well under way. In the high season, which was about fourteen weeks from June to September, the cars were usually out on hire for a very high percentage of time, about 95 per cent. In the low season utilization could get as low as 60 per cent, although demand would peak at holidays.

In the last ten years the car hire side of the business had trebled in size and was expected by the directors of the company to continue to grow steadily even though more small companies were entering the field in the area. Jim Hubbard explained:

In the car hire business every company is not fighting for a share of the same cake. It is very much a two-layer cake. One layer is the big national companies like Avis and Hertz; the other layer is the smaller privately owned businesses like ourselves. The Avis customer is normally on some

This case was prepared by Dr. Nigel Slack, Fellow of the Oxford Centre for Management Studies. The case is not designed to illustrate either the effective or ineffective handling of an administrative situation, but as a basis for class disucssion.

The Author gratefully acknowledges the financial assistance of The Nuffield Foundation who supported the writing of this and other case studies in this series.

Copyright © 1980
N.D.C. Slack

kind of expense account and hardly ever uses companies like us. Our customers tend to be people who do not own their own cars and hire them for holidays or people whose car is out of action but must remain mobile. This type of person very rarely uses the big companies. This means that the two markets are fairly separate.

HOW MANY CARS?

In July 1978 the company operated thirty-four cars: twenty-six Avengers, five Hillman Hunters, and three Ford Cortinas. The actual number of cars that the company operated was varied by buying cars when demand was high and selling the older cars as demand dropped off. During the previous winter the company had operated twenty-seven cars.

The low demand in 1977, mainly because of the weather, had caused the directors to rethink their policy on varying the number of cars they operated. In previous years the directors had made a rough prediction of average demand for a season and bought or sold cars to achieve that level. In other words, they had one 'big buy' in the Spring and one 'big sale' in the Autumn. The new policy which was being tried for the first time was to change the number of cars it operated on a week by week basis. For example, if they seemed continually to be short of cars they would buy an extra couple of cars to cope with this. Likewise as demand started to fall off in the Autumn they planned to sell the older cars as and when required. So far the directors were fairly pleased with the results of the new policy. Their major reservation was the increased amount of time and effort they were spending on finding the cars for purchase.

BOOKING THE CARS

Most of the company's customers booked their cars in advance, sometimes several weeks in advance in the summer period. Paradoxically, although summer is the busiest time, the car hire side of the business had in the past taken up less time than in the low season. Jim Hubbard explained:

> Most people hire cars on a Saturday to Saturday basis during the summer months. This means that we only have to turn the car round once a week. This involves doing the paper work, cleaning the car out, and checking the engine. In the winter the same car could be out three or four times a week and of course we have got to do all the checking, cleaning, and paper work every time we hire it. Mind you, the work is more evenly spread over the week in the winter, whereas in the summer everything tends to be concentrated on Saturday morning.

The company very rarely booked every car out, even in the summer, preferring to keep one car off the road for routine maintenance. This also gave the company some insurance if a customer was late returning a car or in the event of a breakdown, since the spare car could be made ready for a customer in about half an hour.

PURCHASING THE CARS

The company did not buy new cars, but tended to buy one year old cars, probably ones that had been used as part of a fleet, and consequently had a somewhat higher than average mileage for their age, normally about 23,000. They bought cars of this type because they had already depreciated considerably from their new value but their usage had not detracted from their performance. The company usually kept cars for about two years after they had done approximately 60,000 miles in total. The company would never keep a vehicle for longer than two years and sometimes sold cars off before that. Partly this was because the cars became more prone to breakdown but mainly the company felt that the appearance of the cars had deteriorated to the threshold of customer tolerance by this point. Normally cars were sold through car auctions.

Whenever they could the company bought Hillman Avengers. The only time they bought any other model was due to lack of availability. Jim Hubbard explained the choice:

> We use Avengers for several reasons. Many firms use them as their fleet cars so they are readily available and that's important when you want to buy cars quickly. We have found them very reliable, and they seem to need attention far less than comparable cars, for example, the Marina. Furthermore, they are very easy to maintain. For example, two men working on the car can change a slipping clutch, change the exhaust, and renew the brake pads in about an hour and a half. On a busy Saturday morning that's important. I know that they are a basic car but we feel that reliability is more important than a flashy image. Customer satisfaction with the dependability of our service is the best form of advertising we've got. In the last four years we must have had eight thousand lettings from our Avengers and only twice had a car not returned under its own power. Obviously the cost of the car is important and so is the ease with which we can sell and get a good price for the car when we eventually dispose of it.

Exhibit 1 shows the present 'bottom book' prices of the cars which the company would consider buying. The company probably bought at about 10 to 15 per cent below these prices, but they are a good guide to selling prices.

COST AND REVENUE

The directors were particularly anxious about their costs. For example, their 1978 insurance premiums had risen by 70 per cent over 1977 levels and were now running at £170 per car per year. Jim Hubbard explained:

Exhibit 1   Secondhand value of selected vehicles. (From *What Car*, July 1978)

		1974 £	1975 £	1976 £	1977 £
Avenger	L 1600	890	1,050	1,265	1,760
Escort Mk2	L 1300		1,340	1,580	1,860
Mk1	L 1300	1,000			
Chevette	L 1300		1,280	1,550	1,740
Hunter Super	1725	980	1,165	1,400	1,925
Cortina Mk4	L 1600			2,000	2,340
Mk3	L 1600	890	1,170	1,440	
Marina	L 1300	815	985	1,185	1,475

The business is getting very competitive these days which explains why we haven't increased our prices at all this year[1] yet out costs keep rising. Depreciation is the single biggest cost item and together with insurance, road fund licence,[2] and garage bills account for about 60 per cent of our total costs on the car hire side of the business.

Some costs, such as garage bills, were difficult to attribute specifically to either the car hire or the car sales side of the business but Jim estimated that each car would cost about £110 per year in maintenance and repairs.

Jim tried to summarize his attitude to his business:

It's twelve years now since we entered the car hire business and we certainly haven't regretted it so far. Admittedly more people are entering the field which makes things a bit tight, but the market is growing as people get more used to the hire of an occasional car. Our major problems are going to be in controlling the level of costs which means not only choosing the right types of vehicle but also ensuring that we have the right number of cars available at any time.

[1] Ranmoor Car Hire rates together with some of their competitors are shown in Exhibit 2.
[2] Currently £60 in the United Kingdom.

Exhibit 2   Car hire rates – Sheffield area, selected companies

Company	Vehicle	Basic Rate		Mileage
		Daily	Weekly	
Ranmoor Car Hire	Avenger Cortina Hunter	£8.20	£43.20	Unlimited
Avis[1]	Chevette Fiesta Escort	£9.50	£55.60	Unlimited
Godfrey Davies[1]	Chevette Escort	£9.95	£57.35	Unlimited
Wilsons Ltd.	Avenger Hunter	[2]	£49.73	Unlimited
Sheaf Motors	Honda Civic Fiesta	[2]	£49.75	Unlimited
Swan Car	Chevette Escort	£5.00	£30.25	6.0p per mile
Kennings Ltd.	Marina	£6.00	£32.50	5.5p per mile

[1] National based companies.
[2] Not offered.
All rates include insurance.

Case Study: Lex Service Group (A)

In January 1972, the management of the Lex Service Group was trying to define a policy for the implementation of the 'service concept'. Lex's growth had been very rapid over the past few years, with much of it due to acquisitions of service-oriented companies: car dealerships, travel bureaux, employment agencies, and hotels. Lex was committing itself increasingly to the service sector of the economy; the company had adopted the motto: 'Lex is in the service business. Service means customer satisfaction.' After several months of wrestling with the service concept, top management wanted to articulate a policy that would enable them both to measure and to manage the quality of service provided at the operating level of Lex.

COMPANY BACKGROUND

Lex was incorporated as Lex Garages in 1928, to build and operate parking garages and petrol stations in London. In 1945, Norman and Rosser Chinn bought control of the company and continued to expand Lex's activities in the parking, petrol, car repair, and motor distribution businesses.

In 1968, Trevor Chinn, the son of Rosser, became managing director and set about a programme to streamline and reorganize the company. Petrol stations and parking garages, which provided only small margins, were gradually discarded. At the same time it was decided to concentrate on a limited number of franchises and therefore the Renault, Ford, and Vauxhall distributorships were disposed of. The new strategy saw a concentration of Lex's resources in high-profit, high-growth areas, where existing management expertise was thought to be most beneficial. Motor distribution and service became the focus of company interests, and existing franchises of British Leyland, Volvo, and Rolls-Royce were consolidated through the acquisition of additional distributorships.

This case was prepared by Cliff Baden and Colin Carter, Research Associates, as a basis for class discussion rather than to illustrate either effective or ineffective handling of an administrative situation.

Copyright © 1972 by l'Institut pour l'Etude des Méthodes de Direction de l'Entreprise (IMEDE), Lausanne, Switzerland. Reproduced by permission.

LEX DISTRIBUTORSHIPS

Most British motor car companies had a two-stage distribution system, with cars passing from the manufacturer through an area distributor to a local dealer.[1]

Each distributor had an exclusive franchise for a geographical area, with the right to supply all cars from a given manufacturer to dealers in his area. The distributor received a 4 per cent commission on all dealers' sales in his area. The distributor could also retail cars to the public; Lex's distributorships tried to retail at least half the cars that they received from the manufacturers.

In 1971 Lex owned distributorships for Morris (9), Austin (8), Rover (6), Triumph (5), Volvo (4), Jaguar (2), and Rolls-Royce (3), as well as sixteen dealerships. As one London brokerage house noted, 'By following a policy of selective acquisition and using advanced management techniques in a relatively unsophisticated industry, Lex has now become the leading motor distributor in this country.'

All the Lex distributors and dealers had service garages attached to their new-car showrooms. A separate Parts Department provided parts to mechanics in the garages and also sold parts wholesale to other dealers; a small proportion of parts were also sold retail to the public. Each of Lex's car companies was thus in three different businesses: sales, service, and parts.

THE SHIFT TO THE SERVICE CONCEPT

In the summer of 1968, Trevor Chinn attended the six-week British–American Marketing Programme. On his return to Lex, he took a fresh look at the company and determined to develop an appropriate corporate strategy as a basis for future planning. Mr. Chinn wanted to run a company of considerable size; he realized that rapid growth could not entirely be internally generated, but much would have to come from diversification. After considering various sectors of the economy, he settled on the service sector as the one that showed the greatest promise of growth into the future. The choice of the service sector also fulfilled one of Mr. Chinn's principal strategic goals, that of not tying up Lex's capital in fixed assets of an inherently obsolescent nature.

The commitment to a service strategy was sufficiently well formed for Mr. Chinn to explain it to Lex's shareholders in the 1970 Annual Report:

> As the vehicle business is based on manufacturers' franchise arrangements, physical growth is not entirely at the sole discretion of a company such as Lex, and the strategic plans of the manufacturers concerned can impose limitations on our growth.

---

[1] Ford and Volkswagen had both changed to a one-stage system, with cars being sold through a few large dealerships.

While continuing to develop our existing motor vehicle distribution interests, we have, in order to meet our growth aspirations, started to diversify into other service businesses. We first moved into areas closely associated with existing activities such as vehicle leasing and retail distribution of tyres, oil, and accessories, and then moved further afield as we sought a broad enough horizon of opportunity to ensure the continuing development of the Company in the years to come.

It is our intention to become a diversified company operating in a number of major service industries. Each target industry will be selected on certain criteria:

(a) It must be large enough totally to allow Lex to establish a business entity complete in line and staff management of the highest calibre.
(b) It must have a growth potential in the coming decade which will enable us to maintain a rate of profit growth equal to that of our existing business.
(c) Lex must be able to establish itself among the market leaders of the industry.
(d) Lex must expect that within a reasonable time it will draw an important contribution to Company profits from that service industry.
(e) We will select industries that require a high level of service to customers that preferably are fragmented and operate on a decentralized basis and where accordingly profit improvement can be achieved through the exercise of modern management skills in the areas of planning, financial control, marketing, and personnel management.

By January of 1972, Lex owned interests in several service-related industries: passenger car distribution and servicing, commercial vehicle distribution and servicing, freight and transportation, hotels and tourism, and employment agencies. However, 80 per cent of Lex's profits were still derived from vehicle distribution and service. Mr. Chinn and his corporate staff believed that any steps taken to implement the service concept at Lex would first have to be proved effective in the motor side of the business.

ATTEMPTS TO DEFINE AND MEASURE SERVICE

At a corporate-level meeting in May 1971, the top managers of Lex discussed the service concept and the company motto: 'Lex is in the service business. Service means customer satisfaction.' Those attending the meeting were unable to come up with a definition of service beyond 'customer satisfaction'; nor were they able to choose any measures that would allow Lex to quantify the service it was providing. Measurements such as the number of complaints received were felt to be negative indices; management hoped to be able to measure positive results.

At this meeting, the following directive was given to all the divisional managers:

> Objective: to improve level of customer service satisfaction in every part of our company. Each General Manager is to report back to his Divisional Manager by 1st June outlining methods by which service to the customer is to be improved and causes of complaint eliminated. He is also to report specific steps which are being taken to improve communication between management and staff and management and customer to ensure that management is aware of customer complaints and can take speedy action to remove the cause.

Responses to this directive were received at company headquarters the second week in June. These responses varied in length from two to twelve pages; two of them are reproduced in Exhibit 1.

Exhibit 1   Sample responses to headquarters' request for service programmes

To: Group Headquarters, London   10th June, 1971
Subject: Customer Satisfaction

The Group's standard of Service to its Customers must be of the caliber to ensure that Customers return to the Group each and every time they require Service, and knowing that the Service received is of the highest standard we will acquire through the personal recommendations of our Customers, other Customers.

In order to achieve Customer Satisfaction, the following factors must be met:

1. Premises clean and businesslike and Reception points clearly marked so that the Customer can see exactly where he has to go to enquire for the Service required.
2. The Customer expects to be talking to a knowledgeable, helpful individual who shows complete interest in the Service requested and that at this particular moment the satisfaction of the enquiry is the most important task in the Employee's life.
3. Explain the operations or steps entailed in completing the service. After all the Customer has called upon us to satisfy an immediate need and we should treat this with the importance it warrants.
4. Make sure that completion time is reasonably accurate. If things go wrong, let the Customer know. We have had to amend our plans because something has gone wrong; give the Customer a chance to amend his.
5. If an Estimate of charges is requested and a firm one can be given, then give it, and stick to it. If you cannot say so – make it quite clear that charges you are giving are an estimate because of this or that – Explain why.
6. Make sure that the Service is performed correctly.
7. If a Customer complains and you cannot give him satisfaction, make it easy for him to see your immediate superior. Never leave a complaint unresolved.

8. Telephone answering:

    a. Upon the receipt of each call, state the name of the Company, followed by – Good Morning/Afternoon – can I help you.

    b. Ensure that you know the names and extensions of all Employees.

    c. Ensure that you know what type of Service is carried out by each extension.

    d. If the line is engaged, say so, and offer to ring caller back.

    e. If caller decides to 'hold on', keep advising him the line is still busy until it is free, or offer to ring back.

9. Invoice presentation of highest order; avoid padding to justify price charged.
10. Correspondence to be concise and businesslike.

I feel that appropriate Notices should be displayed at points of Sale informing Customers that our aim is to give a First Class Service and if the Customer feels that he has reason to be dissatisfied with the Service, he should write to a 'Customer Satisfaction' Department at Head Office. This would give Head Office an awareness and measurement of the standard of Service throughout the Group.

I believe that the quality of Service is remembered long after the amount charged is forgotten.

To: Group Headquarters, London   9th June, 1971
Subject: Service means Customer Satisfaction

To our customer service means friendly and professional attention, good availability of goods and services, completion of a supply or work contract within a specified period, and a good appearance of the finished product. The service has to be courteous, prompt, honest, and reliable in all Departments of the business which preferably should be carried out in clean, cheerful, and modern premises.

Any complaints should be given immediate attention with a fair and unbiased investigation at the highest company unit level.

WHY IS OUR SERVICE NOT ALWAYS AS GOOD AS IT SHOULD BE?

Service Department

1. Staff make promises which they are unable to keep or forget to take action.
2. They quote prices when they are not sure what the correct price is and without checking whether or not the repair is really necessary.
3. They do not check to see if the part is available.
4. They blame the Parts Department or the factory for problems rather than take a positive approach.
5. They do not always advise the customer in time regarding delays in completion of repairs.
6. They do not advise the customer at inception that we require payment on collection.
7. Telephone enquiries are not always answered as promptly as they should be.
8. Cars sometimes handed over dirtier than they came in.
9. Failure to advise Accounts Department of action taken after dealing with a complaint.

Parts Department

1. Area of weakness in supplying special order parts and the customer not always advised when parts are in stock.
2. The telephone service not always as good as it should be with customers being kept waiting too long either (a) before phone is answered or (b) while parts are being located.

SUGGESTED REMEDIES

Service Department

1. Re-name Tester by calling him Quality Control Supervisor; otherwise only cars with running faults get tested.
   Have check sheet specifying certain known failures in service in addition to the actual repair:

   a. Cleanliness of car
   b. Greasy sterring wheel
   c. Cleanliness of carpets
   d. Use of paper car mats
   e. Use of plastic seat covers (throwaway type)
   f. Use of wing covers
   g. Oil and water levels
   h. Tyre checks
2. The Foreman to constantly supervise all work as it progresses and notify either Reception or Progress Chaser of any delays and to notify customer.
3. Attach Customer Satisfaction card to all repaired cars and provide a handy receptacle for these, or send out regular mailing letters asking for comments on our servicing.
4. The retailing aspects of service and sales are complementary to each other and are better handled by one person in the Sales Department as they are stronger at this.
5. Service Managers to random check at least one car per day and report to General Manager on the quality of workmanship.
6. General Manager to check at least two cars per week to satisfy himself on the quality of work.
7. To ensure that all customers' complaints are dealt with promptly and sympathetically and if we are at fault to pass credit note immediately.
8. Notify customer of any work found and advise him or her while car is in workshop and not when the car is called for; they may have returned a hire car.
9. Display all customer complaints on notice board highlighting mechanic concerned. He would probably be more careful in future. Red label to be attached to works copy of repair order showing name of original mechanic.
10. Have all cars washed (with exception of very minor repair jobs).
11. Install dynamometers and brake testing equipment to minimize road testing.
12. Train staff to be clean and tidy in themselves and habits by providing good facilities, i.e.:

    a. Rubbish bins
    b. Clean toilets and washing facilities
    c. Clothes lockers and changing rooms
    d. Mess room

13. Advertise and give guarantee of service (we do anyway, why not say so).
14. Have a good level of investment in special tools and any labour-saving devices, i.e. power wrenches, diagnostic equipment, etc.
15. Have customer participation suggestion box in reception area.
16. Ensure that mechanics attend specialized factory training courses.
17. Offer incentive to fitters who carry out complaint-free repairs on monthly basis.
18. Offer incentive to Quality Control for returning cars with genuine faults in repair. (This way he will look for faults instead of disguising them.)
19. Train Receptionist to remember customers' names and their cars.
20. Return displaced parts to customer in plastic bag.

Parts Department

1. Ensure that the customer parts counter is always manned and ensure that customers know that they have been noticed.
2. Questionnaire mailing to all parts customers.
3. Parts Marketing Manager and marketing representatives to report back all complaints.
4. Give help and advice to all do it yourself customers.
5. General Manager and Parts Manager to make random checks as to the promptness with which incoming telephone calls are dealt.
6. One telephone Salesman to be responsible for provision of all parts required for urgent use which are not at the time in stock.
7. Compilation of non-availability record.
8. Separate counter for order telephoned in so that customers ordering by phone can have orders made up ready for collection to avoid waiting.
9. Investigate van routes, cut out non-paying, long-distance, time-consuming routes to give a better local service.
10. Ensure vehicles properly maintained to cut down 'off the road' time. Consider incentives for well-kept vehicles.
11. Employ women drivers, as it has been found that dealers prefer them to men.
12. Always try to reserve the last fast-moving item for workshop use.
13. Install interpretation section to retail parts counter, so that customers who know their part numbers can be dealt with more quickly, and so that those who need specialist help can receive it.
14. Improve the level of skill in the Parts Department and improve its image as the 'cinderella' of the business.

MEASUREMENT OF OUR SERVICE

1. Service complaints as a percentage against retail sold hours or as a percentage of number of repair orders issued monthly.
2. Sales as a percentage against vehicles delivered retail.
3. Parts as a percentage against turnover in retail terms. (These percentage targets to be set after a trial period in the light of experience.)

As examples of the efforts being made towards customer satisfaction, some of the Divisional Managers sent copies of public relations material that had been developed at the divisional or local levels. These included a 'Customer Satisfaction Card' (Exhibit 2) and an invitation to a free car inspection for vehicles over twelve months old (Exhibit 3).

Exhibit 2   Customer Satisfaction Card

CUSTOMER SATISFACTION CARD

Help us to provide the kind of service you want for your vehicle.
This is one of the most important aspects of our role as a Morris
Distributor, and to assist us in appraising our standard of service
and guide us in any improvements we make please put a tick in the
appropriate box and return this card to us at your convenience.

Does our reception engineer usually attend to you promptly
and courteously?   YES   NO

Are we good at diagnosing what is wrong with your vehicle? YES   NO

Are you satisfied with the quality of our work?   YES   NO

Do we usually complete the servicing on your vehicle when
promised?   YES   NO

Do we leave your vehicle in a clean condition after service? YES   NO

Name_____

Address_____   **LEX**

Exhibit 3   Invitation to free car inspection

Dear Customer,
   We are sure that you will be interested to know that we are running a Special Show and
Service Week at our premises for one week only from 22nd to 27th November, inclusive.
   For many years now Standard-Triumph have been organizing Show and Service
Weeks, and on the dates quoted, their Service Engineers will be available to carry out a
free inspection on all Standard and Triumph cars over 12 months old and which are no
longer enjoying the benefit of the Manufacturers Guarantee.
   If you would like a detailed report on the exact condition of your car, may we suggest
that you telephone our Service Reception Department, so that a convenient time and date
may be arranged.

In addition to the Engineer's Services, we shall also have our own Special Show of Triumph cars, both on exhibition and for demonstration. If you would like to wait while your car is being inspected, or come and see us anyway during this special week, our sales staff will be pleased to answer any problems you may have.

We look forward to the pleasure of your company during this special week.

Yours faithfully,

DIRECTOR

At the same meeting in May, it was decided to try simultaneously another approach to gauging the effectiveness of Lex's customer service. Questionnaires were sent to over 1,200 customers of two Lex garages asking them to evaluate the quality of service they had received. Responses were collected at the divisional level and sent to company headquarters for evaluation (Exhibit 4).

Exhibit 4   Report on customer service questionnaire

This report covers the results of a survey carried out during early May among customers of Cheltenham Car Mart and Lex TBC Kidderminster.

Background

A questionnaire was sent out, under cover of a personalized letter, to all customers who had used our service facilities during the three months period February–April this year. The covering letter stressed that it was our continued aim to seek complete customer satisfaction and to this end would they please complete the attached questionnaire, adding any suggestions which they thought might improve our customer service. A reply-paid envelope was enclosed.

At Cheltenham a total of 390 questionnaires were sent out, whilst at Kidderminster over 850 questionnaires were dispatched.

Findings

Question 1. Did you make a prior booking for your service?

	Cheltenham		Kidderminster	
Yes	152	95%	158	88%
No	7	5%	22	12%
Not completed	2		8	
Total	161		188	
Base for %	159		180	

Question 2. When did you last receive a service card or letter from us?

	Cheltenham		Kidderminster	
1 month	29	21%	113	66%
2 months	18	13%	24	14%
3 months	9	2%	10	6%
Never	85	60%	23	14%
Not completed	20		18	
Base for %	141		170	

Question 3. Has anyone from our Company ever contacted you by telephone about servicing your car?

	Cheltenham		Kidderminster	
Yes	20	13%	33	19%
No	131	87%	141	81%
Not completed	10		13	

Question 4. Were you satisfied with the reception you received from our staff when you arrived with your car?

	Cheltenham		Kidderminster	
Completely	140	89%	153	92%
Reasonably	16	10%	8	5%
Poor	1		4	2%
Bad	1		1	
Not completed	3		22	
Base of %	158		166	

Question 5. Was the work carried out to your satisfaction?

	Cheltenham		Kidderminster	
Completely	114	73%	112	63%
Partly	42	26%	55	31%
Not at all	1		10	6%
Not completed	4		11	
Base for %	157		177	

Question 6. Were they any grease marks on the steering wheel or seat when you collected the car?

	Cheltenham		Kidderminster	
Yes	4	3%	22	12%
No	156	98%	157	88%
Not completed	1		9	
Base for %	160		179	

Question 7. Was the car ready for collection when promised?

	Cheltenham		Kidderminster	
Yes	149	96%	146	84%
30 min late	6	4%	17	10%
1 hour late	—		1	
Over 1 hour late	1		11	6%
Not completed	5		13	
Base for %	156		175	

With the responses to the questionnaires and the directives in hand, Mr. Chinn and his staff hoped to define some measures of service that would provide workable guidelines for people at the operating level of the company.

Case Study: Lex Service Group (B)

In January 1972, Mr. Trevor Chinn, Managing Director of the Lex Service Group, was worried about the implementation of the service concept throughout the company.[1] Given Lex's emphasis on profit performance, there had been some uncertainty at the operating level over the added costs that increased customer service could involve. Mr. Chinn felt that clarification would be needed. He also wanted to give further thought to the type of local branch managers Lex would need to achieve the corporation's long-term growth objectives.

PERFORMANCE TARGETS FOR 1972

Lex had established an enviable growth record since 1966. Profits before tax jumped from £292,000 in 1966 to £4,382,000 in 1971. In the same period, fully diluted earnings per share grew at a compound average of over 50 per cent per year. Exhibit 1 gives relevant data from Lex's financial statement.

While 40 per cent of the earnings growth was attributed to acquisitions, 60 per cent was attributed to internal growth at Lex. Rationalization of existing operations and the introduction of effective management control systems were considered to be major factors in the company's growth. For example, Lex management believed that the car servicing and sales of spare parts offered at least as much profit potential as new car sales. This conviction, which was not shared by the motor trade generally, was supported by the information produced by Lex's accounting systems which carefully separated sales, service, and parts as profit centres. In the mid-1960s, Lex's emphasis shifted to active promotion of the car service and spare parts aspects of the business. Furthermore, because

This case was prepared by Cliff Baden and Colin Carter, Research Associates, as a basis for class discussion rather than to illustrate either effective of ineffective handling of an administrative situation.

Copyright © 1972 by l'Institut pour l'Etude des Méthodes de Direction de l'Entreprise (IMEDE), Lausanne, Switzerland. Reproduced by permission.

[1] See Lex Service Group (A) for background on the company and the origins of the service concept at Lex.

Exhibit 1 Lex Service Group six-year record. (From 1971 Annual Report)

	1966	1967	1968	1969	1970	1971
Turnover, £	23,756,000	25,539,000	32,614,000	45,179,000	85,016,000	111,325,000
Profit before charging interest on long-term debt, £	402,038	843,507	1,169,327	1,478,781	2,922,466	5,120,551
Profit before taxation, £	292,191	727,899	1,037,927	1,250,219	2,455,488	4,382,117
Net assets, £	4,541,380	4,815,205	6,586,633	10,619,626	21,575,401	36,290,540
Shareholders funds, £	2,484,152	2,612,695	3,431,042	5,950,443	10,810,858	25,392,481
Earnings per ordinary share:						
Basic	0.9p	2.4p	3.8p	4.2p	6.7p	9.2p
Fully diluted	0.9p	2.4p	3.8p	3.6p	5.7p	7.5p
Profit before interest on long- and medium-term debt as a percentage of net assets	8.9%	17.5%	19.7%	13.9%	15.2%	17.6%
Profit before taxation as a percentage of shareholders funds	11.8%	27.9%	30.2%	21.0%	26.5%	28.3%

management believed that the profits from servicing and sales of parts were less subject than new car sales to cyclical swings induced by the economy at large, the company adopted a 'service absorption' policy. According to this policy, the income from service and parts was expected to produce sufficient profit to cover overheads in all areas of the business.

Managers were expected to report 'service absorption' information each month to corporate headquarters, where it was viewed as a key measure of managerial performance. An English security analyst commented on the effects of the system:

> Service absorption obviously ensures that profits from new vehicle sales go straight through to the P & L account, and allow Lex to pass on increased overheads to the public relatively easily.

Rapid growth continued to be a prime objective at Lex. A 20 per cent improvement had been sought each year in both profits and earnings per share. Management also looked for a 35 per cent return each year on current assets.

In October 1971, Mr. Chinn issued the 'Corporate Targets of Performance for 1972'. The first of these targets called for each division to improve its profits by at least one-third over 1971. Division Managers were further advised that:

> ... particular emphasis should be paid to Net Profit before tax expressed as Return on Sales as a key financial ratio through control of trading margins and detailed control of all expenses. Specific targets for this ratio have been allocated to each Business Group.

For the first time, one of the targets in 1972 was concerned with the quality of service provided by Lex. The Managing Director called for:

> ... a dynamic commitment to the improvement of the level of customer satisfaction in each location through the implementation of the 'Customer Satisfaction' programme. The level of customer satisfaction is to be improved by 25 per cent in each location as measured by:
>
> (a) the number of complaints,
> (b) repeat business,
> (c) sample questionnaires on customer satisfaction developed and administered by the Publicity Department.

By including service as one of Lex's targets and by calling for improvement in this area, Mr. Chinn hoped to impress upon Lex's employees at all levels of the company the seriousness of his commitment to the service concept. Now, as the company moved into 1972, he began to hear, through the Divisional Managers, that some local managers were finding it difficult to reconcile the profit targets with the goal of improved service.

PERSONNEL PLANNING

In his original statement outlining Lex's strategy for becoming a service-oriented firm, Mr. Chinn had spelled out the kinds of businesses where he thought Lex would be most effective:

> We will select industries that require a high level of service to the customer, that preferably are fragmented and operate on a decentralized basis, and where accordingly profit improvement can be achieved through the exercise of modern management skills in the areas of planning, financial control, marketing, and personnel management.

Travel agencies and employment agencies were thought to fit this description, as were Lex's local car dealerships and distributorships. The hope was to turn each operation at the local level into a profit centre.

Accordingly, Mr. Chinn and his corporate staff decided that a professional manager should head each local operation wherever possible. Traditionally in the motor industry the manager of a distributorship had come to that position from a job as car salesman, or as head of the Service or Parts Departments. Some local managers had previously worked as mechanics on the shop floor. While people at Lex's head office acknowledged that these local managers were usually able to deal adequately with day-to-day operating problems, they felt that personnel with graduate-level qualifications and professional managerial experience would be better able to run each distributorship as a profit centre and to do the kind of analysis that would make most effective use of Lex's management accounting systems.

One member of the corporate staff explained:

> Knowledge of the motor trade is not a prerequisite of motor trade management. A good manager should be able to work with our accounting systems and our budgeting and planning systems. That is what a manager's job is: analysing, planning, and controlling. He should not be out there pumping gas.

People at the corporate level hoped eventually to be able to transfer these professional managers from one Lex business to another (e.g. from managing a car distributorship to managing an employment agency).

In November 1971, Lex was advertising in the London newspapers for general managers for its car distributorships (Exhibit 2).

INTERVIEW WITH A MEMBER OF THE CORPORATE STAFF

In an interview at Lex's head office in London, a member of the corporate staff expressed some of his concerns about implementing the service concept.

Exhibit 2   Advertisement for general managers. (From *Sunday Times*, 14th November 1971).

GENERAL
MANAGERS

Motor Vehicle Distributorships
up to £4,000

The planned growth of the Lex Service Group is creating a number of opportunities in various parts of the Country within its car and commercial vehicle distributorships. The appointments to be filled involve complete responsibility for the planning and direction of operations of businesses having annual turnovers of between £1m and £4m.

Applicants should be agred between 28 and 40 with graduate or equivalent professional qualifications and with at least two years' experience in a profit-responsible post in a sales or marketing orientated environment. Such experience need not have been in the motor trade since full training will be given prior to appointment.

Salary will be negotiable up to £4,000 p.a. and, in addition to excellent career prospects in an expanding and progressive company, benefits include non-contributory pension and sickness schemes, a company car and assistance with relocation expenses where appropriate.

Applications in writing, giving brief details of age, qualifications and experience, should be sent to:

S.D.E. Dunford, Management
Development Manager,
Lex Service Group,
18 Great Marlborough Street,
London, W1V 2BL.

It was relatively easy to shift the company's emphasis to service. The hard part comes afterwards, when you have to define service – what does it mean in operational terms?

We are prepared to give that issue a lot of attention because anybody should be able to run the business from a cost-control viewpoint as well as we are. Therefore, the only way to set ourselves apart is by the quality of our service, by what our people do.

We need to develop better measures of service – and positive rather than negative measures. Criteria for performance should be positive. We also have to recognize that the measures must be implementable by relatively unsophisticated managers. We want them to help identify positive measures, but how do you get them to think that way without having to come down and flog them all the time?

In any case, we are not certain where in the company structure is the leverage to implement the service concept. Can we do it at the corporate leve? Or is it at the divisional or local levels? We can design training programmes to try to shift the emphasis to providing service, but will people believe them? There is a traditional sales orientation in the motor trade and this is coming into conflict with the more open-minded service orientation of some of the non-motor people who are now entering the organization. We are not sure if we should encourage this conflict and thereby speed up a change in orientation, or if we should let change take place slowly, one case at a time.

That raises the question of management. Our greatest problem is going to be finding people to manage our local operations. People tend to think that garage work is low level or that you have to be a travel agent to run a travel agency.

It is not true, of course. We want to be able to find people who can run a unit by themselves and who can shift from one Lex operation to another. On the other hand, it may be more important than we suppose that the manager maintain close customer contacts over time with his customers. Some people argue that we are putting too much faith in corporate systems without recognizing the harmful effects that these might have on the operating routine in the front line. I do not think this is right, but we have still to prove our case conclusively. We are just beginning.

INTERVIEW WITH THE MANAGER OF
A LOCAL DISTRIBUTORSHIP

The manager of one of Lex's local distributorships discussed his perceptions of the service concept. His comments seemed typical of those of other branch managers.

You know we have Management by Objectives at Lex. We used to express our objectives in terms of financial objectives, like sales, or turnover per year, or ROI. Now Lex is telling us to express our objectives in terms of the issues that are behind the selling of cars – things like improving the existing customer retention rate or evaluating the cost effectiveness of better service shop equipment in terms of customer satisfaction. They tell us that the arithmetic on the financial performance of the company is only part of a job description or a profit plan. It's not an objective. I do not know if that is right or wrong.

They have a new corporate objective to increase the level of customer satisfaction by 25 per cent, and there are some very positive things about this. First of all, we are defining customer satisfaction as an objective. We always try to provide customer satisfaction, of course, but making it an official company objective gives just that much more weight to it. And it's a common-sense thing to say, anyway. It is not contrary to operational things. So, it should enable us to grow.

On the other hand, we have got some problems with the service concept. We are in a very vague area. Defining customer satisfaction and measuring it is a task which the average man is not going to be capable of achieving. Is any objective good if we cannot measure it? Do we need to measure everything? Management theory is that you should be able to measure something if it is an objective. I cannot help thinking that some things — like loyalty — cannot be measured.

There are basic conflicts, too. There is the obvious one between short-term and long-term profits. We are not measured on profits three years from now, but in the car business that is when you reap the benefit of a satisfied customer who returns to buy a car. Maximizing our profit on today's dealings with him may lose him next time.

The pressure to raise customer satisfaction as well as current profits gives difficult trade-offs. The temptation, if you worry about the first in the case of a demanding customer, is to squeeze more money out of another customer to make up for any loss.

There are lots of delicate problems that are difficult to resolve, but they are important if you decide that customer satisfaction is a paramount objective. For example, what do you do when a little old lady comes to buy a car and is too timid or does not know enough to ask for the normal discount? Should we tell her? Give her a big discount she did not ask for? If we want to get this year's profits up, we'll charge the full price. But what happens when she goes home and finds out that she could have had a discount? That is one customer we'll never see again. So, the customer satisfaction idea really runs head on against the pressure for profits.

Or take another fairly common example. We have serviced a man's car, and he comes back a week later and claims that the work we have done is not satisfactory, and he wants a refund. Should we give it to him? Even when we know we have done the job properly?

And then, there is a contradiction in the way we price our service and our parts, in taking different profits on the same deals. Or in following service manual suggestions saying it's necessary to replace parts when, in the particular instance, they do not really need to be replaced. Do we have a moral obligation to tell the customer that parts do not need replacing until x-thousand miles?

There is a problem of people, too. You have seen that Lex has placed advertisements in the papers for new managers. Now the Personnel Department is sending around university graduates. These are long-term people; you know, thinkers, cold, intelligent planners. But they do not fit the needs of our existing businesses. Personally I believe that we are engaging, for a majority of our companies, the wrong kind of people.

If I have to choose between the entrepreneur and the planner, I'll take the first. We are engaging thoroughbreds to pull a cart. They are all right for the Derby, but not for pulling a cart.

Only a really mature company can afford to take on a profit planner. Most of our businesses — these car and truck distributorships — are not mature yet. They need entrepreneurs running them: people who have excellent relationships with customers, who enjoy a beer with them after

work, and inside the business are prepared to jump in and help sweep the
– off the floor. And how many university graduates would want to go to
the Road Haulage Dances? Not too many, I would guess, but you have
got to do that sort of thing if you want to sell commercial vehicles in a
tough market.

I agree, though, that long-term objectives are improtant even if the
management performance measures are biased against it, and I might
have to say that you would want a different person in the long run to the
present.

Chapter 2

Design of Service Operations

Colin G. Armistead

The design of a service operation must take into account the special features which are characteristic of services and which result from the participation of the customer or client at some point in the service-producing process. Provision cannot therefore be made to stock a service, although capacity can be made available in anticipation of demand. The participation of the customer in the production operation means that there must be access to the service operation for the customer, either physically or through more indirect means like postal or electronic communication.

Although the customer is an integral member of some part of the service-producing unit (called the 'servuction system' – Eigler and Langeard, 1984 – or 'service delivery system' – Sasser, Olsen, and Wyckoff, 1978 – by other writers), in most service organizations there is part of the service package which is produced out of sight of the customer (the back room activities) and part where the customer must participate (the front office activities). There is a choice in the design of a service operation as to the extent to which there is high contact with the customer (front office) or low contact (back room). Generally back room activities are more easy to control operationally than front office because of their greater predictability (Mills and Moberg, 1982); although the extent to which customers will accept a restricted contact must be a consideration in the design process.

The design of any service operation is dependent on a number of factors:

(a) What is the 'service package' or 'service packages'?
(b) Who are the customers for the 'service package'?
(c) What are the standards for the 'service package'?
(d) How can the 'service package' be given to the customers?

When designing a service operation, the designer needs to encompass areas and interests normally defined by marketing, operations management, and behavioural science; there is not the same distinction between marketing and operations as exists in a manufacturing operation. A service operation which satisfies customers and conforms to financial measures of success must be an

51

integration of the skills from the various discipline areas, reflected in the design and the subsequent management of the business. Success will also entail being able at least to match customers' expectation of the service package with what is given by the service organization.

1. THE SERVICE PACKAGE

The design of any service depends on there being a concept of the aims of the service package with regard to customers and other organizational measures of effectiveness. The service package which is offered in most cases consists not of a single service but a number of services (Eigler and Langeard, 1984). A visitor to a hotel, for example, may use the service organization for a bed for a night, and a meal, have a haircut, have clothes cleaned, and use the swimming pool. In this case the use of the hotel room would be the 'core' service with the other services being peripheral. However, another customer may come to the hotel just to use the restaurant, when the meal would be the core service. In a service operation it is often difficult to identify which is the core service, so consequently in the design of services it is dangerous to ignore the importance of any one service (Eigler and Langeard, 1984).

The service package will consist of a mixture of physical items which are part of the package and the more subjective and intangible part of the service interaction.

1.1 The Physical Items

The physical items in a service package fall into four groups:

(a) Those *items which are purchased by the customer directly* (e.g. meals in a restaurant, goods bought in a shop) or *items which are supplied free* as samples.

(b) *Physical items which are changed in the course of the service process.* These can cover repair activities carried out both on physical items owned by the customers and can also include changes to the customers themselves. Examples include hairdressing, weight-reducing clinics, solariums, and medical services.

(c) *Other physical items which are associated with the service package in the operational sense but which may not be part of the main service package.* These include admission tickets, cheque books, and appointment cards which are not purchased for their own sake but form part of the service operation.

(d) *Physical items which form part of the environment of the service operation.* Taking the example of a hotel, these will include decoration of rooms, types of furniture, size of beds, uniforms worn by the service personnel, and landscaping.

1.2   The Elements of Service

The elements of service in a service package are often referred to as the intangibles associated with:

(a) The *nature of the service contact*; this may be personal (soft) or non-personal (hard) and have a high or low predictability of outcome.
(b) The *atmosphere of the service environment* created by the sights and sounds and comfort.
(c) The *feelings created in the customer* of the sense of security, status, and wellbeing.

The mixture of the physical items and service elements in service organizations will differ. In the service package represented by a self-service supermarket most of the price reflects the goods and far less the service element. On the other hand, for professional services or an orchestral concert the position will be reversed. In the latter there are few if any physical items received by the customer and the price charged arises from the service element. Midway would be a service package which is half physical items and half service elements, such as a take-away food outlet. We can categorize different service organizations by the proportion of the service package that is physical items and service elements (see Figure 2.1).

Figure 2.1   Comparison of different service packages. (Adapted from Sasser, Olsen, and Wyckoff, 1978, 1982)

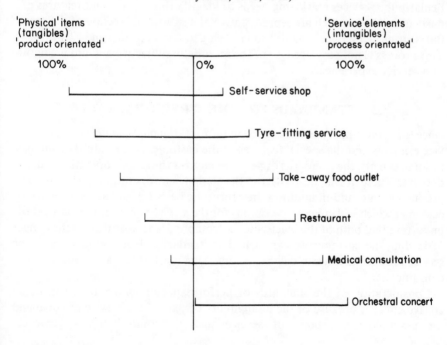

It is more important that the part played by both the physical items and the service elements are appreciated when designing and operating a service operation. A restaurant which has good food but is dirty and has rude waiters is in the long term not going to be any more successful than one that serves poor food with pleasant surroundings: both factors are important. Often attention is paid to the physical items to the exlusion of the service elements.

2. THE CUSTOMER AND THE SERVICE PACKAGE

Chapter 1 highlighted the importance of the customer in the operation of the service organization. It is obviously important from a marketing standpoint to identify the characteristics of potential customers for the service, and many of the same characteristics are important for the designer and operations manager of the service.

A service which is intended primarily to attract retired people needs to be different from one which is directed towards the young. Examples exist from package holidays with holidays for the young, families with children, and for the retired, which have different physical contents of the service package in terms of accommodation and entertainments and also different 'service' contents to reflect the differing needs for security, comfort (Sasser, Olsen, and Wyckoff, 1978), and control (Bateson, 1984).

All customers come to a service organization with some expectation of what is likely to occur, based on past experience, advertising, or hearsay. This may be fear of flying or of dentists, or past experience of friendly company in a particular pub. Services marketing needs to identify those important features of a particular service which are representative of a substantial section of the potential customers a service organization is trying to attract (Lewis and Klein, 1984). This process is not easy because of the essentially subjective and unique nature of a service experience.

3. STANDARDS FOR THE SERVICE PACKAGE

Once the service package is designed in terms of the physical items and the service elements and the special features of the customers are established (at least to some extent), the standards of performance for the service operation must be defined. These form the basis for the design and operation of the service-producing unit, and in addition they form the basis for any advertising to the customer which will create expectations for the service package. It is particularly important that both of these activities correspond, otherwise there is the danger of leading the customer to expect higher standards of performance than the service-producing unit can deliver — something most of us have experienced as consumers.

Consideration of the standards of performance or service level can be an elusive concept because of the intangibility of part of the service package and the psychological aspects of service such as atmosphere, convenience, friendliness, and security. The perceptions of the service will vary from one customer to the next. Setting standards for the 'service' contact element in the service package is much more difficult than setting standards of performance and quality for manufactured goods. The individuality of the 'service' encounter and the intangibility of the 'service' contact make it more difficult to lay down concrete standards. Further consideration is given to this important aspect in the chapter on quality.

When dealing with the physical items in the service package, quality control techniques can be used in a similar way to those common in manufacturing.

4. SERVICE-PRODUCING UNIT

The design and operation of a service organization to meet the performance standards of the service package will reflect the scale of the operation and choices which are made associated with the level of contact of the organization and customers. The participation of the customer to a greater or lesser extent in the production process of the service requires that the service-producing unit be designed in terms of the total service package. There is a tendency for production and consumption of the service package to occur simultaneously. In a restaurant the food, drinks, and atmosphere are produced either just prior to or during consumption, and the customer is intimately involved in the production of a haircut, medical examination, game of tennis, or class lesson. The presence of the customer imposes constraints and opportunities for the service designers and managers.

The effective management of a service operation requires an integration of the four elements:

(a) the service package,
(b) the service package standards,
(c) the service-producing unit,
(d) the customers' expectations (as far as they can be established).

All elements of the service package must fit together to form a successful service operation (see Figure 2.2).

5. FACTORS IN THE DESIGN OF SERVICE OPERATIONS

The design of the service-producing unit follows from the definition of the service package. In its design a number of factors should be taken into account:

(a) The *service package* mix of the physical items and the service intangibles. These will effect the choices for front office—back room activities and the type of contact between the customer and the service organization.
(b) The *service package standards*. These must be achievable by the service-producing unit.

56

(c) The *degree to which the customer needs to be involved in the production activity* (i.e. to what extent are production and consumption simultaneous). This consideration is important in those cases where the customer needs to be physically present.

A consideration of these factors presents the designer of a service operation with choices to achieve the best design for a particular service operation. The main choices are the following.

Figure 2.2 Framework for producing the service package. (Adapted from Sasser, Olsen, and Wyckoff, 1978)

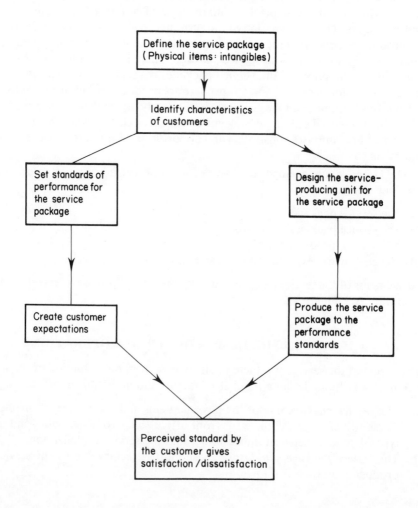

5.1 Organization

5.1.1 Back room to front office mix

The choice as to which tasks are to be performed in the back room and the front office will be influenced by the degree to which there exists the need for the customer to be involved in the production activity. If the choice rests with the service operation managers there are suggestions that the increase in the back room content leads to greater control of the service operations (Chase and Tansik, 1983) by the creation of a 'technical' core (Mills and Moberg, 1982; Thompson, 1967). However, there is the danger that if the service operations management is driven by the need for operational efficiency this may be at variance with the customers' needs and expectations (Morris and Johnston, 1983).

5.1.2 Personal or non-personal contact (between the customer and the service operation)

The choice will be a function of the need within the service package for personal contact and the willingness of the customers to accept alternatives to a high level of contact where it is operationally possible. Non-personal contact can often lead to higher levels of efficiency of delivery; personal contact can lead to customerization of the service and possible differentiation.

5.1.3 Mass (standardized) or customer-specific (professional) service

The choice will to some extent be a function of the nature of the service package and the extent to which it is capable of being delivered to the customer in a mass (standardized) form or whether it must be customer specific (like medical services). Some of the characteristics of the service organization and the service package for the two alternatives are shown in Exhibit 2.1.

5.2 Facilities

5.2.1 Sequencing of activities

The aim for arriving at a sequence for a particular service operation should be to arrange the sequence of activities in logical stages which minimize customer inconvenience and, if appropriate, allow flexibility for the individual customer to miss a stage.

5.2.2 High and low customer contact points

It is important for the designer of a service operation to know where the high and low contact points are in the service operation. This may result from the organizational choices made in the mix of the front office and back room activities. It is then possible to decide on the best methods to be used to manage a particular contact.

Exhibit 2.1 Characteristics of 'mass' and customer-specific 'professional' services. (Adapted from Chase and Tansik, 1983; Eigler and Langeard, 1984; Mills and Moberg, 1982; Morris and Johnston, 1983; Sasser, Olsen, and Wyckoff, 1978)

	'Mass' service	Customer-specific ('professional') service
Service package		
1. Number of services	Few	Many
2. Volume	High	Medium/low
3. Price	Low	Medium/high
4. Standardization	High	Low
5. Customization	Low	High
6. Front office/back room ratio	Low/medium	Medium/high
Service-producing unit		
1. Physical items	Standardized	Varied
2. Service environment	Specialized (standardized)	Varied
3. Service contact	Standardized	Flexible
4. Contact personnel	Low qualification Unskilled/semi-skilled	Medium/high qualification Semi-skilled/highly skilled
5. Reproducibility	Easy	Difficult
6. Flexibility	Little	Medium/high
7. Control of quality	Structured (difficult)	Varied (difficult)
8. Control of technology	High/medium	Medium/low

The use of a flow diagram is a useful method to assist in the design and analysis of a service operation. It allows the designer to:

(a) Identify the information and physical flows.
(b) Identify the different stages (and then maybe seek to eliminate stages).
(c) Ensure that the stages are in a logical sequence.
(d) Identify those stages where there is direct contact with the customer.
(e) Calculate the capacity of the service-producing unit.
(f) Identify the bottlenecks in the flow.

A flow diagram for a car rescue operation is shown in Figure 2.3. It identifies those stages at which there is personal contact with the customer (where the customer's perception of the service will be created) and to which the service operation people need to direct attention.

5.2.3 People based or equipment based

The choice is linked to the choice of personal (soft) or non-personal (hard) contact between the service organization and the customer. The choice of equipment-based service is a way of reducing costs for the service operation unless alternative sources of cheap labour are available. The introduction of ticket franking by travellers themselves on buses and the barriers operated by the introduction of tickets on the London Underground are examples of a

Figure 2.3　Flow chart for a car rescue service

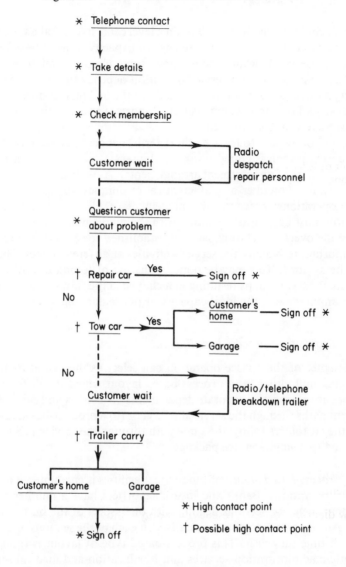

switch from personal to non-personal contact. In these cases the customer is required to make a greater contribution to the operation of the service. A continuum has been suggested (Thomas, 1978) for different kinds of people-based and equipment-based services related to the skill level of the service people. For people-based services there is a range from highly skilled professionals to unskilled cleaners and ticket collectors and for equipment-based services a parallel range from services operated by skilled people like airline pilots to those services which are fully automated, like cash dispensers.

5.2.4 Capacity strategy

The main choice is whether to maintain a level capacity and take steps to control demand or to have flexibility in the level of capacity so as to be able to follow changes in demand. Many service operations choose a mixture of the two strategies; the success of a service operation depends to a great extent on the capacity strategies being followed because of the inability to store all of the service package. Forecasts are particularly important to determine the level of service coverage which is required.

It is not always easy to forecast short-term changes in demand or the amount of time each person is going to take in the service-producing unit (one of the causes of failure of appointment arrangements). As with all types of forecasting there are a large number of mathematical techniques which can be applied to service operations; however, the judgement of those managing the service operation must be considered along with the mathematical forecasts.

Once the overall level of capacity is established for a service operation, it is still important to balance the service activities at different stages if bottlenecks are to be avoided. This may be done by the use of techniques of work study, queueing theory, perhaps resulting in a change in the flow of the service operation or an increase in the local capacity at particular stages.

5.2.5 Product- or process-based layout

The designer of the service operation can select as the layout of the service-producing unit either (a) a process-based layout where the different types of facilities are arranged in separate departments or sections and customers follow different paths through the service facility, or (b) a product-based layout where all of the customers follow the same path through the service facility, which is dedicated to a single-service package.

(a) *A process-based layout* of the service facilities is encountered in many service operations. Banks and insurance offices have a number of different departments or sections dealing with one aspect of the business.

All customers do not necessarily visit each of the sections or departments each time they visit. This process-based type of layout is found in many public administration services and in education and medical services. An example of the layout of a clinic is shown in Figure 2.4. The use of the layout by process maintains greater flexibility and is often used where there is the requirement to provide an individual customer-specific service package as exists for many professional services.

(b) *A product-based layout* has the activities arranged in a set sequence and all customers move through them in that sequence. The layout is often adopted for a highly standardized service package associated with 'mass service'. An example of product layout is shown in Figure 2.5 for the flow through a selection process for entrance to an education course. A product-

Figure 2.4   Process-based layout

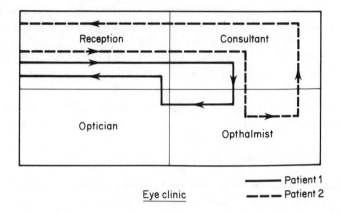

Eye clinic

———— Patient 1
— — — Patient 2

Figure 2.5   Product-based layout

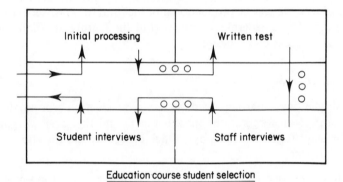

Education course student selection

based layout is often adopted by many transport organizations carrying passengers.

In a particular product-based layout it may be possible for the customer to miss a stage. Therefore in a self-service cafeteria a customer may join part way along the line or miss out several stages.

The *choice between a product- or process-based layout* for a particular service operation will depend on a number of considerations:

(a) The potential for the *reduction in the cost* of the service through the introduction of capital equipment. Product-based activities allow more opportunities for this to be done.

(b) The need for *reproducibility* or the *consistency* of service. A product-based layout offers greater opportunity for this to be achieved.

(c) The need for *flexibility* for *changing demand*. Process-based layouts are normally better able to accommodate such changes.
(d) The need for *flexibility to produce a wide variety of services*. Process-based layouts are usually more able to accommodate a wider variety as they are not dedicated to a single-service activity.
(e) *Service personnel*: the nature of the work in a product-based layout may be repetitive and it may be difficult to maintain the same level of service.

In practice many service operations will use a mixture of product- and process-based layouts.

5.2.6 Mass (standardized) or customer-specific ('professional') services

As indicated earlier, the choice will be dictated partly by the nature of the service package and the capability for the service package to be standardized. It will also be a function of the size of the service organization in terms of the number of outlets. As an organization grows and increases the number of service outlets, there are benefits to be gained from standardization. Some of the characteristics of the service production unit facilities for mass service are given in Exhibit 2.1. These generally correspond to the feature associated with the product- and process-based designs.

5.2.7 Type of access

As the customer has to participate in the service production process, this means that for most service operations the customers and the service organization must be brought together. The ways of achieving this and the choices for the service designer are:

(a) Locate the service facilities near to the customer (e.g. food and general shops).
(b) Take the customer to the service facilities (e.g. package tours, ambulances).
(c) Take the service facilities to the customer (e.g. field service repair operations, travelling libraries).
(d) Provide other means of linking the customer and the service organization by telephone, mail, and increasingly by electronic information transfer (e.g. home shopping and banking services).

6. PEOPLE

In all service operations, whether predominantly people based or equipment based, there will be some parts of the service activity where there is participation by the customer in the service process and contact with service people. The manager and designer of any service operation needs to take account of the requirements of these two groups if the business is to be successful.

6.1 Service Personnel

The mix of service personnel in any service operation will depend on the nature of the business or organization. Those organizations which may be considered as providing 'mass' service have a higher proportion of lower qualified and unskilled personnel than 'professional' services (Exhibit 2.1); e.g. when comparing retail organizations with providers of legal and medical services.

A major choice is in the separation of the contact and non-contact personnel. Non-contact or low contact personnel will usually be employed in a back room environment where the recruitment and training will concentrate more on the production of the physical aspects within the service package. High contact people have to be skilled in the process of interaction with the customer. The training of service people in this aspect of the provision of the service is particularly important.

One of the main difficulties of managing service operations is the attainment of standards of performance for the interaction between the customer and the service personnel. Problems arise through differing perceptions of the customers and the varying attitudes of the service personnel. One important aspect governing the attitude of service personnel may be the degree of control that they perceive themselves to have in the service encounter (Bateson, 1984). If the outcome of the service encounter is highly unpredictable this effect may be exacerbated (e.g. police control of a demonstration).

6.2 The Customers

Customers may be seen by a service organization as takers from the service operation. More positively they can be marketers and promoters for the business as well as providers of a resource for producing part of the service package, and monitoring standards.

Many of the expectations of customers visiting a service operation are developed from word of mouth contact with friends and relatives who have previously been customers (Sasser, Olsen, and Wyckoff, 1978). The use of existing customers to market services can be of special importance because of the intangible nature of much of a service package.

If the customer is in the service-producing unit there is the opportunity to use the resource in the provision of the service package rather than using the operations people in the service organization. This may involve the customers carrying, form filling, or using machines instead of dealing with contact service people. Introduction of new methods may cause difficulties and resistance by the customers to change, which may be minimized by (Stanley, 1979):

(a) Understanding customer behaviour relating to such features as perception of control in the service environment and expectation from the service operation.
(b) Training the customers how to participate to improve the effectiveness of the service operation.

(c) Promoting the benefits of changes in terms of price reductions or faster service times or increased customer control.

(d) Monitoring and evaluating performance as changes are made.

One particular feature of service operations is that customers often have to wait in queues for the service. The way in which queues are allowed to develop and are then managed by the operations people is dealt with in a subsequent chapter.

7. CONCLUSION

The design of the service-producing unit to deliver the service package must be seen in the context of the overall design of the service package of physical items and service elements. Analysis of the service operations will allow those parts requiring a customer–service organization interaction to be identified and catered for in the service operation. The satisfaction of the customer with the service package will depend on his or her perception at the time of the service. The part played by the intangible aspects of the service interaction may be the dominant one. Service operations managers must be aware that concentration on only one part of the service package can lead to the failure of the enterprise.

REFERENCES

Bateson, J.E.G. (1984). *Perceived Control and the Service Encounter*, Workshop on Research in Service Businesses, Institut d'Administration des Entreprises, Aix-en-Provence.

Chase, R.B., and Tansik, D.A. (1983). The customer contact model for organization design, *Management Science*, **29**, No. 9, 1037–1050.

Eigler, P., and Langeard, E. (1984). *Offering Services: Concepts and Decisions*, Workshop on Research in Service Businesses, Institut d'Administration des Entreprises, Aix-en-Provence.

Lewis, R.C., and Klein, D.M. (1984). *Taking Off on Service Intangibles: Theoretical and Practical Implications for Marketing Services*, Workshop on Research in Service Businesses, Institut d'Administration des Entreprises, Aix-en-Provence.

Lovelock, C.H., and Young, R.F. (1979). Look to customers to increase productivity, *Harvard Business Review*, May–June **1979**.

Mills, P.K., and Moberg, D.J. (1982). Perspectives on the technology of service operations, *Academy of Management Review*, **7**, No. 3, 467–478.

Morris, B., and Johnston, B. (1983). *Perspectives on Processes in Service Industries*, Workshop on Service Operations, Manchester Polytechnic.

Sasser, W.E., Olsen, R.P., and Wyckoff, D.D. (1978). *Management of Service Operations*, Allyn and Bacon, Boston.

Shostack, G.L. (1982). How to design a service, *European Journal of Marketing*, **16**, No. 1.

Stanley, T.J. (1979). Marketing self-service banking, *Journal of Retail Banking*, **1**, No. 3, 23–29.

Thomas, D.R.E. (1978). Strategy is different in service businesses, *Harvard Business Review*, July–August **1978**.

Thompson, J.D. (1967). *Organizations in Action*, McGraw-Hill, New York.

Case Study: Wimpy International (A)

In December 1978 Ian Petrie, the Managing Director of Wimpy International, was reviewing the operating results of the new counter service restaurant at Notting Hill. This was their first venture into high volume fast food and was the lynchpin of their strategy to compete with the invasion of US hamburger restaurants led by McDonalds. Despite continued improvement, the Notting Hill restaurant was still experiencing serious operational problems and was running at a loss.

BACKGROUND

Wimpy is a fast food franchise based on the Wimpy pure beef hamburger. The name Wimpy was originally developed from a hamburger eating character in the Popeye cartoon series. This name was adopted by an entrepreneur Eddie Gold for a hamburger bar in Chicago. Gold developed his chain until he controlled thirty-six branches in the United States. In 1954 J. Lyons Ltd. bought the UK rights (reputedly for an agreement which gave him six months holiday a year and an unlimited expense account). They also purchased the franchise rights for Wimpy worldwide except in the United States.

Lyons opened their first restaurant in Coventry Street, London, in 1955. They called it a 'Wimpy Bar'. Wimpy bars were successful and Lyons soon received requests from people wanting to operate Wimpy bars on a franchise basis. The first franchised operation was opened in May 1957 in Ramsgate. In 1958 Lyons formed a subsidiary, Pleasure Foods Limited, to develop the franchise operation, and in 1970 Wimpy International (WI) was formed. WI was responsible for coordinating the activities of the UK outlets and a considerable number of overseas outlets.

By 1974 WI operated 640 UK outlets, of which only two were company operated, one of which was used as a training centre in Chiswick not far from WI headquarters. WI was also responsible for franchising the Golden Egg chain (up-market from Wimpy bars, serving a range of meals from omlettes to steaks) and Bake 'n' Take (a take-away service of pies and chickens, both of which had developed in the late 1960s and early 1970s).

This was written by Charles Pollard under the direction of Chris Voss, London Business School. Some of the names and figures may be disguised.

Lyons had expanded rapidly in the late 1960s and early 1970s by takeovers and had borrowed heavily to do so, much of the money coming from abroad. The falling pound and the high interest charges forced Lyons to sell assets to meet its interest bill. In December 1976 J. Lyons sold the entire operation to United Biscuits. In the financial year ended March 1976 net assets amounted to £1.3m, and a sales turnover of £6.1m and pre-tax profits of £1.4m.[1] United Biscuits, who already operated a successful chain of franchised Wimpy bars in Scotland, paid £7 million. Ian Petrie was appointed Managing Director at the beginning of 1977.

THE MARKET IN 1978

Fast food is a loosely defined, fragmented, and unstructured market. *Catering News* tried to answer the question 'What makes fast food?' as follows:

(a) Limited menu choice
(b) Fast service of the entire meal
(c) Low unit cost of meal
(d) No booking, or advance warning of custom
(e) Often some element of take-away

A company analysis of the size of the fast food industry is shown in Exhibit 1. In the hamburger segment, the leading US chains had begun to penetrate the UK market.

Exhibit 1   Market share in United Kingdom 1978

Company	Number of outlets	%	Estimated retail turnover	%
Wimpy	603		£46.5m	34.7
McDonalds	20		£13.0m	9.7
KFC	245			
Golden Egg	100		£8−10m	6−7.5
Pizzaland	45		£5−6m	3.7−4.5
Tennesee Pancake	12			
Old Kentucky	22			
Quality Inn	60		not known	
Strikes	23			
Happy Eater	23			
Others	447			
Total	1,600	100	£134m	100

[1] The system-wide sales of Wimpy franchises was estimated at £35m.

McDonalds

Turnover in the United States for 1978 in McDonalds' 4,200 outlets was expected to be £2,000m. They had a mix of both company-owned and franchised stores. In the United Kingdom they were firmly established with twenty stores, all company owned, and were expected to be operating fifty by 1980. They had expanded in the London TV area and had a current turnover of around £13 million, forecast to rise to £37m by 1980. Their average turnover per store was £720,000 and their average investment in shopfitting and equipment was £250,000. The total capital per store averaged £650,000.

Other US Corporations

Many of these such as Burger King were already established in Europe, but their expansion in the United Kingdom was slower than expected, probably due to lack of financial resources. Wimpy expected this expansion to be by franchising.

OPERATIONS

Operations were controlled from the Chiswick head office. In 1978 there were about 600 franchised and two company-owned table service restaurants, and one company-owned counter service restaurant (discussed later). Table service restaurants were the traditional Wimpy bar. Hamburgers and other hot food were cooked to order on a griddle and served at the table by a waiter or waitress. (Wimpy bars also did take-out food.) A sample menu is shown inExhibit 2.[1] A counter service restaurant was one where a customer ordered and was served at a counter. Fast service was ensured by maintaining stocks of fresh hamburgers.

WI revenues came primarily from a product loading or markup system. This was different from the more usual method of a levy or royalties on retail turnover. Franchisees were obliged to purchase their 'frozen goods', i.e. hamburgers, fish products, and pork products, from WI at a price which, after a deduction for distribution costs, gave WI an average 40 per cent gross margin. This was roughly equivalent to a 8.5 to 9 per cent levy on retail turnover.

Other products, 'dry goods', such as condiments, ketchup, coffee/tea, etc., were provided by major national manufacturers. For example, a single firm supplied serviettes with the Wimpy logo printed on them. However, franchisees tended to purchase their own serviettes and other goods and food from various sources, and these were of extremely variable quality.

The system of product markup on Wimpy-supplied hamburgers was easier to administer than royalties on turnover. WI did not need to know an outlet's

---

[1] WI set maximum prices for only two items on the menu. The menu was determined by WI and prices were similar, with local variations. A commonly used rule of thumb was that the price charged in the restaurant was three times the cost of the product.

Exhibit 2   Wimpy table service menu

Maxi Quarterpounder   66p

*Quarter pound pure beef hamburger steak served in a toasted bun with fried onions and lettuce.

with chips 86p

Wimpy Kingsize   80p

Two Wimpy pure beef hamburger steaks with fried onions, in a toasted bun with lettuce and tomato, topped with melted cheese.

with chips 100p

Wimpy Hamburger   35p

The pure beef hamburger in a toasted bun served with fried onions.

Wimpy Cheeseburger   45p

Wimpy Eggburger   48p

Egg 'n' Baconburger   48p

A delicious Baconburger with a fried egg served on an open toasted bun.

Portion of Chips

(Served with above)   20p

Wimpy Brunch   78p

Two pure beef hamburger steaks served with fried onions and a portion of chips.

Wimpy Salad   80p

Two Wimpy hamburger steaks with fried onions served with lettuce and tomato, and a helping of vegetable salad.

Wimpy Grill   78p

Wimpy hamburger steak with a Bender frankfurter served with fried onions, tomato, pickle and a portion of chips.

Wimpy Special Grill   90p

Wimpy hamburger steak with a Bender frankfurter and fried onions, a fried egg, tomato, pickle, and a portion of chips.

The International Grill   112p

One pure beef hamburger steak, a Bender frankfurter and a delicious Baconburger, served with fried onions, a portion of chips, tomato, lettuce and pickle.

Baconburger Grill   78p

A delicious Baconburger, and a Bender frankfurter served with tomato, pickle and a portion of chips.

Baconburger Special Brunch   90p

Two delicious Baconburgers and a fried egg served with a portion of chips.

Bender Brunch   78p

Two delicious Bender frankfurters served with fresh tomato, pickle and a portion of chips.

Shanty Fish Brunch   83p

Two golden fried fish portions with tartar sauce and a portion of chips.

Shanty Fish Salad   85p

Two Shanty fish portions with tartare sauce served with lettuce and tomato, and a helping of vegetable salad.

Children's Brunch   48p

One Wimpy hamburger steak or Bender frankfurter or Baconburger or Shanty fish portion with a portion of chips.

Soup   17p

CHEESE EGGBURGER	58p
WIMPY EGG BRUNCH	60p
TWO EGGS AND PORTION OF CHIPS	48p
SOFT ROLL AND BUTTER	12p

*Approx. uncooked weight   All prices include VAT

Our Guarantee

Wimpy hamburger steaks are made entirely from pure beef with spices.

Soft Ice Cream Portion   18p

Chocolate Nut Sundae   26p

Soft ice cream covered with smooth chocolate sauce, topped with chopped nuts and a wafer biscuit.

Strawberry Sundae   30p

Strawberries, soft ice cream and wafer.

Fruit and Nut Sundae   30p

Soft ice cream with fruit cocktail, topped with chopped nuts and a wafer biscuit.

Brown Derby   33p

A doughnut ring smothered with soft ice cream, covered with chocolate sauce and sprinkled with chopped nuts.

Knickerbocker Glory   45p

A long luscious combination of strawberries, fruit cocktail and soft ice cream – the summit sprinkled with chocolate vermicelli.

Banana Long Boat   45p

A whole banana, split lengthwise, with fruit cocktail and a jumbo-size portion of soft ice cream topped with chocolate vermicelli.

Whippsy   22p

Thick tasty milk shake made with soft ice cream; strawberry, lime, chocolate, pineapple and vanilla flavours.

Ice Cream Float   22p

A refreshing cola with soft ice cream.

Sweets

DOUGHNUTS	10p
APPLE PIE	20p
APPLE TURNOVER	20p
PORTION OF ICE CREAM with above	
	extra 12p

Hot and Cold Drinks

TEA	10p	HOT CHOCOLATE	18p
COFFEE	18p	COLA	16p
MILK	12p	SPARKLING	
HORLICKS	18p	DRINKS	16p
		ORANGE	16p

WIMPY PERCOLATED COFFEE	24p
GATEAU	24p

All prices include VAT.
Ice cream contains non-milk fat

---

retail turnover (which owners were often reticent at disclosing). For some years, however, there had been numerous occasions where franchisees were caught by visiting field staff using non-Wimpy or 'alien' hamburgers. If franchisees were found to be using 'alien' hamburgers they were given a warning. On the second occasion their franchise agreement could be terminated.

THE FRANCHISEES

Ian Petrie had described the franchisees as coming in all shapes and sizes, but with the common factors of entreprenurial spirit, self made, keen to make big profits, and understanding buying but not selling. Fifty per cent of Wimpy turnover was in the hands of ethnic groups (particularly in south London). These groups were closely knit and very powerful. They generally had good sites and were prepared to work efficiently for long hours in hot conditions.

THE FRANCHISE PROPOSAL

A new franchisee paid around £1,000 for the right to trade under the name 'Wimpy'. He could then expect to make an investment of between £10,000 and £25,000 for shopfitting carried out to Wimpy's standard specifications. Wimpy provided free, on loan, equipment for griddling and toasting together with point of sale advertising.

WI did not grant 'master' franchises which would allow a franchisee to sub-franchise, but it was possible for an individual (or group) to own several outlets. (In 1977 eight franchisees accounted for 25 per cent of Wimpy turnover.) The minimum length of the franchise agreement was five years. Franchisees did not have an exclusive right to a territory but might be given first refusal on a new site if WI decide to open one nearby. Franchisees wishing to sell out could do so to any buyer approved by WI. A contract could be terminated prematurely by WI for serious or continuous default.

FRANCHISE ASSOCIATION

A franchise association had been formed just before the takeover. Its stated objective was to enable franchisees to buy on better terms than those offered through Wimpy's recommended suppliers. They were concerned that Wimpy used only suppliers such as Telfers (for meat) and Lyons Maid (for ice cream) which were J. Lyons subsidiaries. For example, they could often buy the Lyons Maid ice cream cheaper in their local supermarket.

The franchisees felt that Head Office did not listen to them and were not influenced by what they had to say. On the other hand, Ian Petrie felt that on operational matters Wimpy often lacked sufficient expertise to exert any real power over the franchisees. At the end of 1977 Wimpy had decided to implement two national dealer meetings a year at which franchisees would be consulted about menus, training, advertising, standards, etc.

OPERATIONAL CONTROL AND TRAINING

Operational control was achieved through the catering advisor. Each advisor was responsible for the control of twenty to twenty-five outlets, visiting each one eight to twelve times a year. One of the prime tasks was to ensure that outlets were purchasing Wimpy products, particularly hamburger patties. The advisor was also responsible for carrying out store audits and checking standards.

WI had always required that new franchisees received training, but this had not always been possible. Training consisted of five days of instruction in an outlet. Catering advisers had recently begun to take films around to the outlets to help train staff. Frequently franchisees, rather than discuss problems with operations supervisors, would phone up a head office manager or even the managing director.

OPERATING RESULTS

For the purpose of management accounts, sales were described in two ways: firstly, by 'piece sales', which was the total number of individual food items sold on which WI obtained a gross profit, and, secondly, by extrapolating Wimpy's gross profit to give an estimate of the franchisee's turnover. Franchisees were not obliged to reveal their turnover to WI. Exhibit 3 shows the last seven year's annual results.

Exhibit 3   Wimpy operating results

Year	1970	1971	1972	1973	1974	1975	1976	1977	1978
Total number of *four-week periods that outlets were* trading during year	6,434	7,055	7,588	8,076	8,309	8,177	7,837	7,940	7,878
Million pieces total sales	66.6	72.2	80.1	80.4	79.2	72.8	64.6	66.0	76.0
Estimated retail turnover 'systemswide', £m	13.1	15.8	19.9	24.8	28.0	28.8	32.2	37.8	48.6
Gross profit margin on product loading, %	28.4	26.0	28.6	30.5	33.7	37.9	41.5	41.1	39.3
Gross profit, £m	0.70	0.78	1.08	1.44	1.78	2.09	2.56	2.93	3.62
Wimpy trading profit, £m	0.41	0.45	0.81	0.98	1.33	1.29	1.55	1.63	1.50

BUYING AND DISTRIBUTION

Until 1978, WI had no buying department as such. Frozen products (hamburgers, fish, pork, etc.) on which WI charged a markup were supplied to WI by various manufacturers, most of whom were also Lyons subsidiaries. Other products were sold direct to the franchisee's outlet by the supplying company.

Some thirty bakeries around the country supplied outlets with buns for the hamburgers, some to as few as three outlets. WI tended not to negotiate special prices for franchisees on dry goods; franchisees made individual contracts and the national supplier would then deliver to the outlet. Less than 50 per cent of dry goods were bought from WI-recommended suppliers.

Frozen goods (i.e. hamburgers, etc.) were delivered by Alpine distributors for Wimpy International. Hamburgers would be delivered to Alpine's central depot at Greenford and, from there, redistributed to its forty UK depots around the country. Dry goods were not delivered for WI; the franchisee had to contact the supplier direct. Often, franchisees did not know the contact address of a supplier. Naomi Arnold, the new buying manager for WI, had related that when she arrived in early 1978 and wanted to talk to one long-standing supplier of coffee to Wimpy bars she was obliged to find a box of coffee, note down the address, and use directory enquiries to obtain the telephone number.

Within the last few weeks, Spillers French, who were a major supplier of Wimpy's buns, had decided to pull out of baking due to losses, leaving a large plant at Crawley vacant. WI were therefore considering purchasing the site, continuing to bake buns, and possibly using the space as a central dry goods distribution centre.

MARKET IMAGE

Under the Lyons Management the standard of quality of Wimpy outlets had fallen, with many examples of restaurants of exceptionally poor standards of cleanliness, service, and decor. Despite some tighter operational control and allocation of additional funds to help franchisees refurbish premises, the situation was still poor and Wimpy had a very poor market image.

Recent market research suggested that only 20 per cent of people questioned felt that the name 'Wimpy' was a positive asset. However, it was a name as well known as Hoover or Heinz, with a recall rate of 95 + per cent (see Exhibit 4). It was felt that the public had negative feelings towards Wimpy which they did not have towards McDonalds, and that they might forgive McDonalds a lapse in standards but would not do so for Wimpy.

FUTURE DIRECTIONS FOR WIMPY

John Servent who had been with Wimpy for four years, having previously run the Golden Egg chain, said of the pre-UB takeover days:

Until 1976 the Wimpy franchise was a licence to print money. There was no competition, outlets were highly profitable, and even a bad franchisee

Exhibit 4   Prompted awareness of name

	1977, %	1978, %
National		
Wimpy	95	94
Kentucky	74	79
Little Chef	66	73
McDonalds	18	28
None of these	4	4
London TV Area		
Wimpy	98	95
Kentucky	92	93
Little Chef	74	79
McDonalds	57	78
None of these	1	4

would make good money, whereas a good franchisee would make very good money. Wimpy was living in a fool's paradise. When challenged operationally by the franchisees they usually lost because they had no operating experience. While they had the respect of the franchisees in a professional sense, it was lacking in the operational sphere. Moreover, the lack of controls led to accusations of favouritism and the multiple franchisee (who might be absent) wielding power.

While competition began to flourish rapidly, he felt that apathy had reigned in recent years at Lyons and in the Wimpy management. For example, management had believed that McDonalds would never catch on (or that if it did, it would only be in London).

Ian Petrie was also worried and had initiated an evaluation of the outlets in order to understand them and improve them. In August 1977, Ian Petrie gave John Servent a free hand and six months in which to produce recommendations about 'how we keep Wimpy in the forefront of the market over the next few years'.

Servent formed a small team of four, and after several visits to the United States and Europe (where they received enormous cooperation from fast food outlets) they drew up a report (extracts are given in Appendix 1). This report proposed that Wimpy should move immediately into the McDonalds style of counter service restaurants. Counter service restaurants promised, if successful, to yield higher revenues from a given area and per square foot (although the minimum size for a counter service was much larger than for a table service restaurant).

The proposal had been accepted and an immediate search was begun for a site. The initial proposal was for a 'flagship' site somewhere in London's West End, but the only available site fell through at the last moment when the building's owner decided that Wimpy was not a 'suitable tenant'. By chance a large table service franchise in Notting Hill Gate, in West London, came up for sale, and it was decided to put the first counter service restaurant there. The restaurant was opened on 12th July 1978 (see Appendix 2).

THE SITUATION IN DECEMBER 1978

Despite a successful launch, the Notting Hill restaurant was not running smoothly. Operational problems were being experienced in all areas and the latest operating results (see Exhibit 5) were disappointing. US experts had been called in but they did not seem to be able to adapt to UK conditions. Despite these disappointing results, Ian Petrie maintained a strategy of focusing managerial effort on counter service, both debugging Notting Hill and finding new sites. He believed strongly that 'there is no greater joy in heaven at the return of one sinner who repenteth than for all the ninety-nine good people who don't need salvation' and he was determined to take Wimpy, the sinner, by the scruff of the neck, screaming into the eighties.

Exhibit 5 Notting Hill Gate operating results

		Budget period 1978				
		8^2	9	10	11	12
Net turnover	Week 1	11.0	8.3	7.1	6.6	6.5
	2	8.4	7.9	6.8	6.7	6.7
	3	7.1	7.5	6.9	6.9	6.5
	4	8.4	7.5	6.9	6.9	6.4
	Period	34.9	31.2	27.7	27.1	26.1
Less						
Food cost[1]	£'000	18.2	15.4	11.7	12.0	11.3
	%	52.0	49.5	42.3	44.4	43.2
Franchise charge[1]	£'000	2.9	2.7	2.4	2.3	2.2
	%	8.5	8.5	8.5	8.5	8.5
Wages	£'000	21.7	11.6	9.1	7.7	7.2
	%	62.2	27.2	32.9	28.4	27.6
Operating costs	£'000	5.6	4.0	4.4	4.2	3.4
	%	16.0	12.8	15.9	15.5	13.0
Rent and rates	£'000	1.0	1.2	1.5	1.0	0.9
	%	2.8	3.9	5.4	3.6	3.4
Depreciation	£'000	3.5	2.1	2.1	2.6	2.6
	%	10.0	6.7	7.6	9.6	10.0
Store operating profit	£'000	(18.0)	(5.8)	(3.5)	(2.7)	(1.5)
	%	(51.5)	(18.6)	(12.6)	(10.0)	(5.7)
Less						
Pre-opening costs	£'000	15.2	(2.2)	1.1	0.1	—
Net profit	£'000	(33.2)	(3.6)	(4.6)	(2.8)	(1.5)
	%	(95.1)	(11.5)	(16.6)	(10.3)	(5.7)

[1] Food costs contained no product loading. A notional franchise charge was made although the restaurant was company owned.
[2] The restaurant opened at the start of period 8.

Appendix 1

Extract from Report on the New Counter Service Proposals

From: *John Servent*   To: *Ian Petrie*

OBJECTIVES

1. Customer profile target: – 16–24 age group, prime targets
   – strong representation in all groups up to 35 years old
   – C_1 and C_2 income groups extending to B and A.
   – emphasis on children and family groups

2. New improved image (in terms of product quality customer service and operational standards) to offset 'yesterday' image and 'modest expectations' of current Wimpy users.

3. Achievement of the following cost structure at outlet level:

Food (including WI royalty)	38%
Wages (including manager)	28%
Rent/rates/overheads	20%
Depreciation	5%
Profit before tax	9%

4. Minimum profit (before tax) of £20,000 per outlet and return on capital of 33% p.a.

5. Sales per £ of investment in shopfitting and equipment should not exceed 40% of 1st year retail turnover and should average around 33%.

CONSUMER PROPOSITION

Ideally, the counter service outlet should enable the following response from our target market group:

If time is short and I want something to eat, I can go into one of the new Wimpy's — they don't just serve good hamburgers; they have some specialities that other places don't sell. It's a great place too; my friends and I go there quite often.

In developing the concept and its communication to the target market, areas of difference from competitive outlets will be highlighted where they are of advantage to us. These differences will be essential to overcome their current image advantages in terms of hygiene, staff, environment, quality, and value for money.

THROUGHPUT

The target for the time from the customer entering the premises to receiving his food will be four minutes maximum and an estimated fifteen minutes total time (at peak hours) from the customer entering and eating his meal. It is assumed that take-away will account for approximately 35 per cent of total business.

PRODUCT AND SERVICE

Disposable materials to be used to provide 'hygenic alternative to dirty or chipped crockery'. It is vital that the leading product — the hamburger — should be of a high perceived quality.

ECONOMICS

The required cost structure for three new counter service outlets of £250,000, £350,000, and £600,000 turnover together with the cost structure for two new table service outlets of £150,000 and £200,000 turnover are attached.

COMMENTS

Our objectives will bring WI head on with McDonalds and WI must therefore create or maintain major points of difference which could assist in outweighing unfavourable image comparison.

Our US consultants advise us that real growth in fast food is due to people believing it is as cheap to eat out in a fast food restaurant as it is to cook at home, and to support this belief the real cost of food should eventually rise to 35 to 40 per cent of the retail turnover (excluding franchise payments, notional or actual).

Evidence obtained from a survey in our outlets suggests that no volume change occurs when Wimpy price rises match the retail price index. However, it appears that a 0.7 per cent decline in volume takes place for every percentage point rise above the RPI. Our consultants advise that these global figures may be correct.

The success of our plans will depend on us meeting head on the advertising challenge of major competitors. We must therefore aim to spend 3 per cent of retail turnover on advertising.

The aim will be to grow by TV regions.

Revenue and cost estimates

Start-up costs (£'000)	Counter service			Table service	
	1	2	3	1	2
Property					
Fees − estate agent	3.5	3.0	3.0	2.0	2.0
− surveyor	.5	.5	.5	.3	.3
− solicitor	2.0	2.0	1.0	.8	.8
Stamp duty	1.0	.5	.5	.6	.6
Freehold price	—	—	—	—	—
Lease premium	—	—	—	—	—
	7.0	6.0	5.0	3.7	3.7
Construction					
Fees − design	5.0	4.0	3.0	—	—
− architect					
− franchise	10.0	10.0	10.0	5.0	5.0
Equipment	75.0	50.0	35.0	15.0	15.0
Shopfitting including ventilation	225.0	175.0	92.0	75.0	75.0
	315.0	239.0	140.0	95.0	95.0
Pre-opening costs					
Wages	2.5	1.5	1.0	.5	.5
Operating costs	.5	.5	.3	.3	.3
Other costs	3.0	1.5	1.0	.6	.6
Rent	10.0	6.1	4.4	2.5	2.5
	16.0	9.6	6.7	3.9	3.9
Total start-up costs	338.0	254.6	151.7	102.6	102.6
Less loan (repayable over 5 years at 18% p.a. interest)	150.0	100.0	65.0	35.0	35.0
Net investment by franchisee	188.0	154.6	86.7	67.6	67.6

Trading (before tax and depreciation), £'000 p.a.

	Counter service						Table service			
	1	%	2	%	3	%	1	%	2	%
Turnover	600.0		350.0		250.0		200.0		150.0	
Food cost including packaging	228.0	38.0	133.0	38.0	95.0	38.0	80.0	40.0	60.0	40.0
Gross profit	372.0	62.0	217.0	62.0	155.0	62.0	120.0	60.0	90.0	60.0
Franchise contribution	51.0	8.5	29.8	8.5	21.2	8.5	—	—	—	—
Wages	126.0	21.0	73.5	21.0	52.5	21.0	50.0	25.0	37.5	25.0
Operating costs	54.0	9.0	31.5	9.0	22.5	9.0	16.0	8.0	12.0	8.0
Rates	12.0	2.0	7.0	2.0	5.0	2.0	3.0	1.5	2.5	1.7
Rent	40.0	6.7	24.5	7.0	17.5	7.0	12.0	6.0	12.0	6.7
Operating profit	89.0	14.8	50.7	14.5	36.3	14.5	39.0	19.5	28.0	18.6
Interest on loan	27.0		18.0		11.7		6.3		6.3	
Loan repayment	30.0	9.5	20.0	10.8	13.0	9.9	7.0	6.3	7.0	8.8
Cash flow	32.0	5.3	12.7	3.7	11.6	4.6	25.7	13.2	14.7	9.8
Whole project	*£'000*		*£'000*		*£'000*		*£'000*		*£'000*	
1. Total start-up costs	338		254.6		86.7		10.26		102.6	
2. Operating profit	89		50.7		11.6		39.0		28.0	
Years pay back	3.8		5.0		5.0		2.6		3.7	
Franchisees share	*£'000*		*£'000*		*£'000*		*£'000*		*£'000*	
1. Net investment by franchisee	188.0		154.6		151.7		67.6		67.6	
2. Cash flow	32.0		12.7		36.3		25.7		14.7	
Years pay back	5.9		7.0		4.2		2.6		4.6	

Appendix 2
Counter Service Operations

COOKING

Buns and hamburgers are cooked in a broiler. Frozen burger patties are placed on one of two slowly moving belts (depending on their size − 2 oz or 4 oz). Cooking time is 1 to $1\frac{1}{2}$ minutes.

Chips, fish, chicken bits, and apple pies are deep fried in a computer-controlled frier. As baskets of frozen chips are automatically lowered into the hot fat, the computer registers the drop in temperature and adjusts the cooking time automatically. At least 12 lb of chips can be cooked at any one time.

ASSEMBLY

Toasted buns are laid out on a stainless steel surface and garnish and sauces squeezed onto them. The cooked hamburger is added, (with cheese if required) and the product is then normally wrapped in special thermal paper or placed in a box.

Checken bits are placed into cardboard boxes and the chips into paper bags (large or standard).

STORAGE

Chips are stored separately under a hot lamp, otherwise the wrapped products are placed onto a sloping storage area under heat lamps. Hamburgers are kept up to 15 minutes if they contain lettuce, otherwise up to 20 minutes. Freshness can be established by pressing the top of the wrapped hamburger. Chips are kept up to 7 minutes, and chicken and fish up to 20 minutes.

SERVICE COUNTER

Customers enter and are directed to a vacant till. Staff enter details of the customer order and when complete they press the total button which displays the cost and prints out a receipt itemizing by name the product requested in the order in which they should be collected.

The till also acts as a staff checking-in device, and gives daily or weekly sales analyses and stock records.

Between one and four staff usually attend the tills, at peak times; they use 'runners' to assemble the order with the help of management.

CONTROLS

All waste is placed in a bin during the day; at night, the duty manager sifts through it itemizing each product.

Staff can be rewarded (or admonished) for their standard of work at management's discretion (e.g. extra half hours pay).

Kitchen floor plan

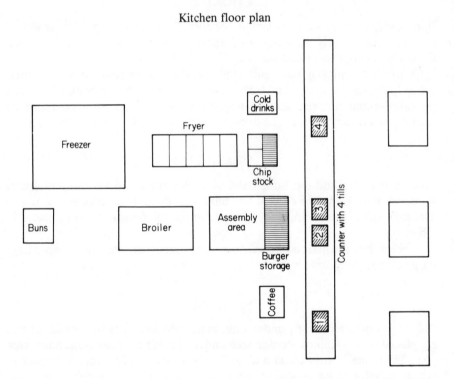

Chapter 3

Human Resource Management

Barbara Morris

This chapter is concerned with the problem of organizing people and work. Obviously, using people effectively and making the most of their skills and abilities is important in any organization, whatever its type, but in service operations human resources have an added importance for a variety of reasons:

(a) Service operations are normally labour intensive, and the human resources are prime contributors to the success of the operation, as well as being a major cost element.

(b) As discussed in Chapter 1, the behaviour of the worker is often an integral part of the service product. If service contact personnel create a poor impression, then customers may well not return, no matter how good the physical attributes of the service.

(c) Even if the behaviour of contact personnel is only a minor part of the service it usually has a major impact on the customer's view. For example, when buying consumer goods, a disinterested or rude assistant may cause the customer to buy elsewhere even though the after-sales support or the price may be superior to competitors. As Davidson (1978) asks, 'Think how many times you have heard people say, "I'll never deal with that outfit again. The employees are rude and indifferent." How many times have you said something like this yourself?'

(d) Not only is managing the human resource important because of the key part it plays in normal operations, but it is also important because of the simultaneous nature of service production and consumption. Services cannot be stocked and so, unless the customer is prepared to wait or has no alternative but to wait (as, for example, for medical treatment), any disruption caused by the human element (whether employee or customer) causes an immediate problem. Strikes by the operators can have a major impact. Striking bus crews, for example, have an immediate impact on the customer, whereas the coal industry can satisfy its customers for a considerable time if miners strike. A similar problem occurs, of course, in manufacturing operations where output stocks are not held, but demand for services is often more transitory than demand for manufactured goods, and in these circumstances, the demand is less likely to be held over. For example, strikes by air traffic controllers often lead to an absolute loss of flights rather than a postponement, because if the demand cannot be met when the customer requires it, there is no point in meeting it at all.

(e) As well as the task of managing the workforce, there is the additional task of managing the customer, who often provides some, or all, of the labour required to produce the service. An obvious example of this is the customer in a supermarket who selects and carries his/her own goods to the checkout.

Even where the customer does not provide a labour input, his/her behaviour usually has to be managed. In some service organizations, the customer has to pass through a number of stages in a prescribed manner, almost in the same way as material has to flow through a manufacturing system. Examples of this are hospital outpatients, who often have to visit a number of different departments in a set pattern (clinic, X-ray, back to clinic, etc.), or customers in a hair dressing salon, who have to move from one work station to another. While this is often necessitated by the technology or the desire to make the best use of skilled resources, customers are not materials and often resent being treated in this way. In other service organizations the customer has to be 'trained' to take the appropriate action to gain the required response. Typical of this kind of situation is the need to know whether to sit at a table and wait for service or to go to the counter to order in a snack bar, or understanding that the appropriate way to see a doctor in a particular practice is to make an appointment. People familiar with the situation often fail to recognize that this is a problem for new customers. Some customers can feel quite anxious about changing suppliers for a particular service, or may even not purchase a service, because they do not know the routine.

Hence, the customer has to be managed as a labour resource, and as a resource which has to flow through the system, and also has to be trained to behave appropriately. This is an aspect of human resource management which is unique to service operations.

(f) The behaviour of customers and operators varies considerably, which makes it very difficult to define standards and ensure consistency of the service. This means that in a service operation quality is likely to be more variable than in a manufacturing operation. However, because of the immediacy of the production and consumption referred to above, it is impossible to operate the kind of quality control system used in manufacturing operations, where defective items can be screened out before reaching the customer. Because of this, managers in service operations are very dependent on the labour force to try and maintain quality and consistency in the face of variability in both their own and the customer's behaviour. (The issue of quality management is discussed in more detail in Chapter 8.)

Given these factors it is fairly clear that the labour-intensive aspect means that human resource management is important in service operations, but the presence of the customer adds a further dimension. It is particularly important at the operator–customer interface, where relatively minor factors can have a major impact and unwittingly operators can create a bad impression. Tea breaks in offices, for example, can irritate customers. Staff are entitled to their breaks, but often they are taken in the office, and where this is visible to the customer it can cause problems. Customers who have to wait usually become annoyed at the sight of tea-drinking staff! Aspects like this, though apparently trivial in the light of all the other tasks involved in managing human resources, often have consequences which are not appreciated by either the operators or their managers.

1. TASKS INVOLVED IN MANAGING THE LABOUR FORCE

Managing the labour force is not just a task of man-management; it involves the design of jobs, recruitment, selection and termination, training and development, promotion, motivation of the workforce, payment, manpower planning, health and safety, and industrial relations. There is a clear interaction here with the personnel function and in many organizations the operations manager will not be directly responsible for all of these aspects; however, even where personnel specialists exist the operations manager needs to understand what is involved in order to work effectively with the personnel department. In smaller organizations, the operations manager often has responsibility for most of these tasks but unfortunately, while generalists of this kind are often very effective at working with people, they usually have neither the time nor the expertise to cope with all the other aspects of managing the labour force and often do not make the best use of their staff. In this text we can give only a general discussion of the tasks involved in managing the labour force; a more detailed treatment is available in specialist texts (see, for example, Torrington and Chapman, 1984).

2. PROVISION OF HUMAN RESOURCES

The task of providing an adequate workforce usually falls to personnel specialists, where they exist, and the provision of sufficient and appropriate customers is normally the task of the marketing specialist. However, in both areas operations management has a major impact. In the case of the worker, the operations manager is directly responsible for the tasks the worker does, and the conditions under which they are done. In the case of the customer, the operations manager is responsible for ensuring that needs are satisfied and that where a labour input is provided it is managed appropriately. In addition, in high contact services, the operations manager needs to be aware of the marketing aspect because the operation is part of the selling process. Understanding what is involved in providing and retaining both labour and customers is therefore essential for the operations manager.

2.1 Manpower/Customer Planning

Manpower planning is needed to ensure that the organization has the right number of people, with the appropriate skills, in the right place, at the right time. Meeting the skill and timing requirements is often left far too late in the planning process and insufficient time is allowed. For example, a supermarket chain may be planning an expansion programme but its programme may be severely hampered by the lack of adequate manpower planning; checkout staff and shelf-fillers may be easy to recruit and train in a short time, but store managers, who need much longer training, may not be available when required. An analogous, market planning process is needed to ensure customers are available. It is pointless developing a highly efficient operation if there is insufficient demand for it.

Manpower and customer planning has five basic steps:

(a) *Analyse the organization's future plans.* The labour requirements are determined by what the organization intends to do in the future, e.g. open a new department store or change from a personalized service to one where everyone receives the same service package. Failure to develop manpower plans as part of the operational plans can cause severe problems, as can failure to identify and plan marketing, advertising, and sales efforts.

(b) *Carry out an audit of existing manpower and customer base.* This is necessary in order to provide base information from which predictions can be made about future manpower availability and customer changes.

(c) *Identify probable losses.* Manpower losses occur because of retirements, terminations, transfers within the organization, and sometimes deaths or disabilities. Often these can be predicted with some accuracy from past data, and in some cases improvements can be made to reduce the rate. Better selection or training, for example, may reduce the rate of termination due to unsuitability or inadequacy. Customer losses can also occur, for example, because of competition or local economic changes.

(d) *Make short- and long-range manpower forecasts.* Forecasts of future requirements are based on operational plans and the current manpower availability, adjusted for losses, and require not only an estimate of future skill requirements but also an estimate of labour capacity. This in turn requires an estimate of the work involved and the number of people required to carry it out. Such forecasts, of course, need to take account of the customer input.

(e) *Take action to meet the plan.* A plan is useless unless action is taken to achieve it and to monitor the activity and correct it if necessary.

Manpower planning requires a lot of fairly detailed information, and it is important that the operations manager is able to supply it. This means that he/she has both to collect the information and to communicate it to whoever is doing the manpower planning, so that problems (which will ultimately fall on the operations manager) can be avoided as far as possible. For example, an assumption made by the personnel department that certain people will remain in their post, when in fact the operations manager knows that they will be leaving in the near future, can result in manpower shortages which could have been avoided if the operations manager had communicated this knowledge to the personnel department. Similarly, changes to the operation which affect the customer need to be communicated to the marketing department. Promises made by the marketing or sales staff which cannot be met by the operations staff can only have an adverse effect.

2.2 Recruitment and Selection

These tasks are concerned with the whole process of acquiring new labour resources and putting the right person into the right job. In essence, the tasks are the same as recruitment and selection in manufacturing operations, but often slight differences are introduced by two factors which seem to have more impact on service operations than on manufacturing ones. The first of these is the professional nature of many service operations, e.g. legal and medical services, where the skills, and many of the job requirements, are prescribed by professional bodies. The second is the part-time or temporary nature of many service jobs.

(a) *Recruitment* is the process of attracting a range of applicants for a job so that the organization can choose the most appropriate candidate. Generally, the organization defines the job to be done and then appropriate advertising is carried out in order to make the right kind of people aware that the job is vacant. Where professional services are concerned, the organization is often constrained by restrictions or conditions imposed by the appropriate professional bodies, and this can limit the freedom of choice the organization has over working conditions, salaries, and duties. This simplifies recruitment in some ways, because there is a common understanding of job titles and a limited range of qualifications, but it also means that the organization has to provide the necessary working conditions and salaries.

The approach to recruitment varies considerably according to the economic climate. Wide (and consequently more expensive) advertising may be needed to attract interest if unemployment levels are low, while limited, local advertising may be adequate if there is high unemployment. Whatever the overall focus, however, good recruitment should result in attracting the most appropriate applicants and discouraging others, and in the retention of the people subsequently appointed. It is expensive to recruit, select, and train a worker, and then have him/her leave because the job was not what was expected. This means that it is usually a mistake to overglamourize a job or to recruit ambitious people into routine jobs, although it is often tempting to make the job sound more attractive than it is if applicants are in short supply or to recruit more ambitious or better qualified people than are needed if there is high unemployment and such people are available.

General inducements, such as high salaries, pleasant working conditions, fringe benefits, etc., are necessary to attract people into the organization but these are not always sufficient to keep them. Generally, people require things like good salaries to prevent them becoming dissatisfied with the job, but these alone are often not enough to make them enjoy the job. Job satisfaction tends to come from the challenge and responsibility in the job, from personal recognition, and the opportunity to develop oneself. (See, for example, Herzberg 1966, and Maslow, 1943, for a fuller discussion of motivation.) Few managers are in the business of providing satisfying jobs for their own sake, but over the last twenty years, research applying these ideas has shown that factors such as these can have an effect on productivity. The implication is that commitment and involvement, and hence productivity, derive from factors such as challenge and responsibility. (For a useful summary, see Bailey, 1983.) However, it is inadequate to generalize. Some people are very happy doing mundane, repetitive jobs all day long, because they derive satisfaction at work from other things, like talking to their friends or thinking about their own interests, while other people could not stand this type of work. It is therefore important that not only is recruitment aimed at the type of people most likely to apply for, and stay in the job, but also that the selection procedure is effective in choosing appropriate people.

(b) *Selection* is the process of ensuring that the candidate has an accurate picture of what the organization is offering, so that he/she can make a sensible choice, and that the organization adequately evaluates and appoints the best possible applicant for a particular position. It is important that both parties make the right decision, because the worker may leave if the job is different from what was expected and the whole procedure will have to be repeated, while the organization obviously wants someone who is going to fit in and do the job well.

Selection procedures vary enormously, both in terms of their effectiveness and their cost, ranging from very brief interviews to two or three day procedures involving written and practical tests. Fairly obviously, the choice will depend on the costs and benefits to be gained, but it is worth mentioning that the interview, the most common technique, can be extremely ineffective unless carried out by someone who is trained in the use of selection interviews.

The key input to good selection is a clear job description. If the job requires someone who will perform a fairly standard, routine task, then this implies that the person needed is someone who can learn and follow a prescribed set of routines. On the other hand, such a person is unlikely to be appropriate if discretion and judgement are needed. A job description makes explicit what is to be done and provides an indication of the kind of person required.

Recruitment and selection are closely interrelated, both depending heavily on an adequate description of the type of worker required. This is often not done well in service organizations because the real skills needed in a job are not always recognized sufficiently clearly for the person doing the recruitment to be effective. For example, receptionist and telephonist skills are often described by the rather all-embracing phrase 'pleasant and friendly personality who enjoys meeting the public'. The problem with a description like this is that often a receptionist or telephonist has to be very highly skilled at diagnosing exactly what a customer wants, at screening out the trivial from the important, at knowing when something is urgent and when it is not, and at knowing who to contact (and where to find him/her) in a given situation. He or she often has to be fairly knowledgeable about the service itself, because the job may actually involve elements of selling the service, or turning away inappropriate business (Voss, 1983). Failure to specify this can result in advertisements aimed at the wrong kind of applicants and inappropriate appointment. Attractive young ladies with high social skills may not be the most appropriate people to advise a worried mother that it is not necessary to ask a doctor to make a house call for a child with a temperature, for example. Similarly, it is essential to be clear about whether social or interactive skills are needed at all. Young people often say they would like a particular type of job, such as shop work or social work, because they like dealing with people, yet many of the jobs in organizations like these have no contact with the public and may involve very little interaction with other workers. Stock-room staff in large department stores, for example, require skills far more akin to similar staff in manufacturing than to their 'front office' counterparts performing the selling jobs.

It is usually well worth the effort of trying to determine not only what qualifications and experience are required, but also what are the characteristics of someone who is already doing the job successfully. These provide a guide to what is needed. However, they should not be treated as a blueprint because the service may suffer if a new employee tries to imitate the successful style of an old one rather than finding his/her own style. A good example of the problems of trying to imitate a successful provider of a given service is the stand-up comedian. It is possible to try and identify what makes a particular comedian successful in entertaining his audience, but attempts by a newcomer with similar characteristics to use the same style are often a failure.

The 'blueprint approach' can be successful where standardization is needed, but total reliance on such a list where personal style is important may be inappropriate. This is particularly true of the customer-specific or professional service described in Chapter 2, where it is difficult, if not impossible, to define and standardize the nature of the service and its quality, and where the success of the organization is usually highly dependent on individual employees.

A similar 'recruitment and selection' process applies to customers, although it is rarely recognized as such. In Britain there appears to be a tendency to believe that any customer will do, but as the manufacturing industry discovered in the days of Henry Ford, specialism and standardization lead to efficiency, and this approach appears to work well for service operations like McDonalds (see Levitt, 1972). This does not mean that all services should be standardized, but often more discrimination about the type of customer to be served can lead to great savings in operating costs. Many British service organizations attempt to serve all customers. This demands flexibility, which inevitably means that excess resources are needed. Less flexibility will certainly lead to a loss of some customers, but any resulting benefits passed on in the form of higher efficiency or lower cost may well attract more customers. Careful consideration of the 'ideal customer' and of methods to attract and keep him/her involve similar tasks to those of recruiting and selecting the workforce.

2.3 Training and Development

Training is concerned with the acquisition of skills, experience, and education, and no matter how well qualified the worker or how low skilled the job some training is always needed to prepare the worker for a particular position. Training is also needed for customers, to persuade them to do the things the organization needs. For example, training is needed to persuade customers to use automatic cash dispensers, instead of taking the time of bank clerks to cash routine cheques, or to dissuade them from doing other things, like going to a doctor's surgery without an appointment. Development means the on-going training or improvement of the worker, either in order to do the existing job better or to fit him/her for promotion or transfer. Unfortunately, this is the area most likely to be reduced when cost-cutting exercises are undertaken, and it can often be a false economy; not only does existing performance not improve but often the organization has to recruit and select new staff because it does not have suitable people in its workforce.

(a) *Training for employees* can vary from the absolute minimum of describing where the various facilities are and how things are normally done to long-term training courses on either a full or part-time basis. Most organizations provide some kind of 'orientation', either formally, through films or talks by key staff, or informally, by assigning an existing employee to look after the new member for a short time. In low-skilled jobs or in very high-skilled jobs where staff are recruited directly from outside, the amount of formal job training provided by the organization will usually be low. Rather more investment is needed for semi-skilled people or for skilled people if the organization decides to develop its own staff.

Training for operators who have direct contact with customers is often ignored, particularly where experienced staff are recruited, or is limited to the operational aspects of the job – e.g. cash register operation. Given the importance of the customer-contact employee, this seems inadequate. By comparison with American companies, or British companies who seem to take the customer–operative interface seriously, such as Marks and Spencer PLC, many British organizations are poor at handling customers. Operatives are often rude, or seem to regard the customer as a nuisance, and have little interest in satisfying him/her. This is annoying for the captive customer (like the patient in a hospital outpatient department) and can result in loss of custom where the customer has freedom of choice. Attitude training and training in social skills are particularly important in this respect. Such training is probably best carried out in-company, using the company's own staff, since it is very dependent on the culture and attitudes of the company. It does, however, require the company to identify clearly what its attitude to customers is and what it regards as good customer service; in many companies it is assumed that operatives know what constitutes good service and this is by no means an assumption which is always justified.

Skill training can be carried out in many ways: on-the-job training, classroom training provided either in-house or through educational establishments, apprenticeships, etc. On-the-job training is the cheapest and easiest from the organization's point of view, but it may be totally inadequate for the type of skills required or may serve to perpetuate a not very satisfactory status quo. The fact that a job has always been done in a particular way is not always a good reason for continuing to do it that way. In-house training can be exactly matched to the needs of the organization, but is expensive for small numbers, and unless the trainers are able to develop their own knowledge and are exposed to the latest thinking it can suffer from the same problems of stagnation as on-the-job training. External courses are often cheaper, especially for the organization which does not have its own training and development staff or all the resources necessary, but as they are normally not intended for a specific organization they are often only partially relevant. Training programmes, no matter whether internal or external, which keep new employees away from the job for which they were appointed for too long may well bore them and make them lose interest. They do, after all, want to do the job for which they were appointed.

Training of new employees is important in service organizations, particularly where customer contact is involved, because it is one way of trying to instill the attitudes and standards needed in dealing with the customer and of trying to provide some consistency. This latter is particularly important for part-time or temporary staff, who do not have the same exposure to the organization as full-time staff and may not have the same commitment. If such staff are employed in the back room, they may not be so productive as full-time staff, and where they have direct contact with the customer they may create a poor impression. The customer who calls in on a busy Saturday is unlikely to be impressed with being told, 'Please would you call back later on .... I'm only a part-timer and can't help you.' Unfortunately, many service organizations regard such staff as 'fill-in' resources, and not worth investing in.

Even where training is provided, there is no guarantee that the training programme will produce the desired results. All training programmes should be evaluated. Evaluation immediately after the event is needed to find out if they are achieving what was intended and whether the trainees find them suitable, and on-going evaluation of the employees' performance is needed to ensure that they continue to perform as intended. This serves both as a means of checking the long-term effects of training and to determine if re-training is needed. Again this is particularly important for employees who have contact with customers, and a simple technique is to use checkers posing as customers (as many insurance companies do). The aim is to find out if customers are being treated correctly; while supervisors *may* detect weaknesses, staff generally perform correctly in front of them and so total reliance on supervisors may not be adequate. Where problems are discovered, it may simply require correction for an individual employee, but sometimes it may require changes to the training methods.

(b) *Customer training* is equally important, but different methods are needed. The simplest way to train customers is to explain how things are done by the use of notices or pamphlets. Many organizations ignore or forget the fact that new customers may well not be aware of how the system operates and this causes frustration for everyone as well as disrupting the system. A typical example of this was observed in a small video rental shop, where a new customer who had spent some time selecting three video films was highly incensed at being told on going to the rental desk that only two could be borrowed by new customers, and a considerable queue of other customers built up while the matter was dealt with. Nowhere in the shop or in the introductory notes given to each customer was this fact made clear, and the failure of the shop to create the correct customer expectation resulted in annoying not only the customer concerned but also several other customers.

Another method of training customers is to provide some incentive for preferred behaviour, such as the lower charge which is made by some banks for cashing a cheque through an automatic dispenser rather than through a bank clerk. Yet another method is discouragement, such as extra charges for non-standard services if the organization prefers to provide a standard service or obvious reluctance to comply with a particular request. If these are practised as a regular routine, the customer will either adjust to the preferred or normal mode of operation or will go elsewhere. It does, however, require the organization to be clear about what it wants; advertisement of a personalized service accompanied by treatment which clearly discourages anything which is non-standard can only result in loss of custom, while training which encourages the customer to accept a standardized service package when staff are available to provide a customized service results in wasted resources.

Another method of 'training' is to limit customer discretion or flexibility so that he/she is made to behave in a particular way. Supermarkets are particularly good in this respect, in that in most supermarkets customers are encouraged and constrained by the layout to move through the system in a particular way.

Customer training can be extremely difficult if the customer sees no advantage in adopting the behaviour preferred by the organization. A simple example of this is the case of post codes introduced by the postal service in the United Kingdom. These codes are intended to improve the sorting of mail (and hence to provide a more efficient service), yet despite efforts to persuade customers to use them, a significant proportion of customers do not.

Successful training and development, like recruitment and selection, depends on careful identification of the skills required (of both the customer and the employee) and can be wasted if this identification is inadequate. It also depends, however, on the person being trained seeing some advantage (or the avoidance of a disadvantage) in it. This is not a major problem where employees are concerned, although some employees do refuse training because they do not share the organization's view of the advantages, but can be very difficult where customers are concerned. Inevitably any action taken by the organization to provide customer-recognized incentives or disincentives will be seen as part of the total service package, and it may have the effect of driving customers away rather than training them into a desired behaviour pattern.

2.4 Promotion

Promotion is an important issue for service organizations because the change of skills required in operators and supervisors and managers can be far more marked than equivalent changes in a manufacturing organization, resulting, as it often does, in a separation from dealing with customers.

The choice of whether to promote internally or to recruit from outside is always a difficult one. The advantage of 'home-grown' management is that it provides a source of people who know the organization and the jobs, as well as providing a career structure for the employees. However, it can also result in stagnation, because unless training and development and exposure to new ideas is provided, the existing situation is perpetuated. External recruitment, on the other hand, may result in resentment, and will certainly require time for the new manager or supervisor to settle down and get to know the organization.

There is, however, a further problem where the person promoted moves from a high customer-contact job to a managerial position which does not have very much, if any, direct customer contact. Even where he/she is now managing the customer-contact part of the operation a new approach is usually needed. In a customer-contact job, the needs of the organization are met by satisfying the customer. However, at higher levels in the hierarchy, other needs, such as efficient use of resources, have to be taken into account and may sometimes have to override individual customer satisfaction. Successful management or supervision usually involves the reconciling or balancing of often-conflicting objectives, yet far too often it is assumed, for example, that a good shop assistant will make a good supervisor or that a good bus conductor will make a good inspector.

In high customer-contact operations most direct contact personnel are trained to put customer satisfaction high on their list of priorities. Where people like this are promoted they may well miss the customer contact and become frustrated in the new job, or may allow the satisfaction of one customer to override organizational effectiveness. It may well be appropriate for a shop assistant to spend time trying to satisfy an individual customer but the supervisor needs to be able to decide when it is more effective to accept the loss of an individual customer who needs time and effort which might be better spent on other customers. Readjustment to this type of attitude, where individual customer satisfaction may not be appropriate, is difficult, and without training may never happen, yet service organizations often do not provide managerial or supervisory training and just assume that the necessary skills will somehow develop.

3.   JOB DESIGN

Job design in any organization involves far more than merely identifying what is to be done. It requires the determination of how it is to be done, how it is to be subdivided, and how it fits into the organization, and it also requires consideration of how best to make the personnel involved productive and to remain with the organization. In simple terms, it is the process of not only deciding how the job is to be carried out but also getting the people who do it to do it well. There is usually a small core of people in any organization who want to do their jobs as well as possible, but the majority work because they have to and, while not shirkers, need to be induced to be interested and to work well. Pay plays an important part in this, but it is not the only thing which motivates people.

An easy answer would be to say jobs should be interesting, but the reality of work is that a far greater number of jobs are boring and repetitive, and usually will remain so no matter what is done to try and improve them, than are interesting and challenging. Even with customer variability, jobs involving customer contact can be monotonous, and this is particularly the case where attempts are made to reduce variability by the production line approach advocated by Levitt (1972). This does not mean that this approach is inappropriate, but it does mean that it may be necessary to look for interest and challenge outside the job itself.

The traditional way to organize work and jobs in manufacturing for many years was directed towards rationalization, using techniques such as method study; the aim was to specialize and subdivide work so as to minimize and standardize the skills required and take advantage of the efficiencies which this approach undoubtedly generates. This approach has not been used particularly widely in service operations, though, as Levitt's (1972) report of McDonalds shows, there is much to be gained from it in appropriate circumstances. The relevance of adopting a more 'manufacturing' attitude to the design of jobs is increasing with the change of so many jobs to a machine-based, rather than manual, technology. For example, with the increasing use of computers, particularly in the office environment, many traditional clerical and intellectually skilled jobs are being de-skilled in terms of their labour input, and such jobs are in many ways similar to manufacturing jobs.

The rational approach has much to recommend it in terms of efficiency and productivity, and it can certainly reduce immediate operational costs. The problem with this approach is that it can lead to a lack of involvement and commitment on the worker's part, and this in turn can lead to greater costs in the long term. Some of these costs are visible, in that absenteeism and labour turnover may well increase, but others are less obvious, resulting, for example, from lack of labour flexibility and resistance to change. The difficulty is knowing where to draw the line. There is no doubt that efficiency in service operations can be improved by this approach, and indeed it is to some extent inevitable given the rapid change to machine technology which is taking place. Equally inevitably, however, it will reduce the job interest in many cases, as well as bringing a number of problems associated with machine-based jobs which are only just beginning to be recognized in service operations.

One way which has been adopted in manufacturing of overcoming the problems associated with the rational approach to job design is to incorporate the lessons learnt from the wealth of research on motivation which have been applied to job design by, for example, Hackman *et al.* (1975) and Wild and Birchall (1973). The general approach is to build into the work attributes which make it more attractive, challenging, and interesting. Research suggests that work needs to provide variety, meaning, some scope for setting standards and feedback on whether they are achieved, and some scope for individual or group autonomy. It should include some of the preparatory and auxiliary tasks needed in the job, some degree of care, skill, or knowledge which earns respect or prestige, and should make an identifiable contribution to the utility of the product to the customer. Following these ideas, a variety of techniques, such as job rotation, job enrichment, job enlargement, and group working, has been adopted, which does seem to overcome some of the disaffection, although evidence of improvement in productivity is somewhat dubious.

Ideas like these have been applied in service operations. Hodgeson and Burden (1979), for example, describe work done in a local Department of Health and Social Security Office in Swansea, and later at Wallsend and Wakefield, where the aim was to give a better service to the public and greater job satisfaction to the staff. The staff and the public were involved in analysing the problems and attempting to find solutions. Improved working methods, more sensitivity to the service provided and to customer reactions, and better relationships with the social services are reported. The changes made involved the combination of jobs which had previously been separate, the bringing together of different specialists who deal with the same type of client, more contact between working groups, and more reliance on the staff's sense of responsibility, with correspondingly less time spent in supervision.

The difficulty of advocating techniques like this on a large scale in service operations is that many of the existing jobs are already interesting and challenging and productivity is probably a more meaningful aim in these situations. The danger lies in going too far down the efficiency route and losing sight of the fact that the search for standardization and rationalization may result in a service product which is vastly different from what the customer thought he/she was buying. Where a standardized service is acceptable, however, there is still the danger of introducing the problems associated with lack of involvement and commitment, because standardization usually results in a reduction in worker discretion, closer supervision being needed to maintain standards, and a reduction in variety in the job.

Efforts to improve efficiency can also produce a further problem in that there is a tendency to analyse and define to the finest possible level of detail, and thus to remove as much discretion as possible. This may well be appropriate in mass service operations, where low skills and high standardization are needed, but is highly inappropriate in a personalized service where the server needs a fairly high degree of autonomy.

The type of job carried out by the worker will obviously have a major impact on the supervisory and managerial tasks. Where employees need to be self-motivated, as in professional or personal services, the supervisory/managerial aim in managing such employees is to discover what their needs are and to provide means of achieving them. Such individuals usually need responsibility or challenge, and a manager is required who can facilitate, rather than be authoritarian, and can delegate authority and responsibility without feeling undermined or that he/she could do the job better. Close supervision in this type of situation is inappropriate and may demotivate the employees. By contrast, in a mass service the low skills and the need for standardization means that supervision needs to be close, and the task involves a far higher degree of employee checking and evaluation.

The whole area of job design in services is relatively unexplored. During the last twenty years considerable attention has been paid to shop floor problems, but comparatively little attention has been paid to service jobs, and in particular to office jobs, which represent such a large proportion of jobs in service organizations. Yet, while this attention has been focused on manufacturing, there has been a dramatic change in the balance of employment, from about 48 per cent in each sector in the late 1950s to about 57 per cent in services and 40 per cent in manufacturing in the late 1970s. Given this shift, and the need for service organizations to reduce overheads and indirect costs, together with the rapidly growing impact of new technology in service jobs, it seems likely that considerably more attention will be given to job design in services in the future (Bailey, 1983).

4. THE IMPACT OF NEW TECHNOLOGY

Machine technology has for many years been the domain of manufacturing operations, but the so-called 'micro revolution' has accelerated a trend towards automation and mechanization in service operations. This development can be seen in the progression from carbon copies to photocopies, from handwritten receipts to electronic tills, from the simple typewriter to the word processor, from the hand-carried message to electronic mail, from cardex record systems to computer data bases, and from barter to electronic money.

The so-called electronic office is not yet with us, but it is technically feasible; widespread buying from home does not yet exist but home sales through television and telephone are increasing; automatic vending is increasing; automatic warehouses already exist. One could be forgiven for assuming that technology has a life of its own!

However, while we may be aware of what is technically possible, its implementation depends heavily on people. Yet, despite the obviousness of this, it is very often overlooked. Usually, the sellers of high technology products stress their economic and operational advantages, and considerable money is spent in advertising the technical advantages of one product over another, but very little attention, so far, has been paid to their effect on people. As Steven Roberts remarks, 'Magazine ads show smiling secretaries blissfully inserting diskettes into drives, while worry-free executives beam from across the room', and, as he succinctly comments after several remarks in this vein, 'Nonsense!' (Roberts, 1984, p. vii). The change from traditional techniques to microtechnology, while potentially having great benefits, is by no means as simple as such advertisements suggest.

It is difficult to forecast accurately the impact that such technology will have on the people employed in service operations. Various opinions exist, ranging from those who claim it will lead to widespread unemployment and the same kind of problems we have had in manufacturing for the last twenty years, to those who see it as the solution for all business problems and problems concerned with human inefficiency. As yet we have very limited experience and knowledge on which to base long-term forecasts. It is, however, possible to identify lessons which need to be considered if such technology is to be implemented in a given situation.

We shall briefly outline the issues which concern the human operator and new technology. For a more detailed treatment of new technology, there are a number of useful texts available (see, for example, Birchall and Hammond, 1981; Roberts, 1984), a rapidly increasing number of articles in professional and academic journals (see, for example, Bird, 1980; Jessup, 1978; Sell, 1980), and a proliferation of popular journals, which are the most up-to-date source of information about the technology itself.

The most significant issues of relevance to managing human resources are trade union reaction, ergonomic factors, and the impact on the job itself:

(a) *Trade union reaction.* The TUC has made a clear statement of how it views new technology (TUC, 1979). It feels fairly positive about new technology, in that it presents the opportunity to improve the competitiveness of business and industry, to improve the quality of working life, and to provide benefits for working people. However, it also sees threats in that the new technology will lead to the loss of more jobs and to social dislocation. Trade union reaction to employment issues, in the widest sense, has been, on the whole, rather quicker than management reaction. A number of unions have issued guidelines which recognize both job security and working condition issues. Typical of these are NALGO and APEX. APEX, for example, have issued as part of their guidelines booklet (1980) a model agreement which covers not only the security of employment but also terms and conditions, health and safety aspects, and stipulates that the effects of the new system on job content and satisfaction should be fully analysed through joint management and union committees.

(b) *Ergonomic factors.* Ergonomic factors, which can improve or impede employee performance have been well investigated and reported (see Meister, 1971, for example), but since much of this work is concerned with the man—machine interface it has not been an issue of major concern for service operations. However, the advent of the microcomputer in particular is changing this, and many jobs in service operations, such as word processing, point-of-sale operations, and airline bookings, are becoming very machine dependent.

One of the consequences of this is that many employees spend many hours working at visual display units. This in turn can impose environmental stress, which is all the more difficult to accept for being totally new to the operators. There can be constant noise, from fans, disk drives, and printers, which can get on people's nerves, and sometimes the working temperature increases. However, more important is the fact that employees who previously were probably fairly active, moving around the work area, talking to people, going to and from filing cabinets, etc., now spend considerable periods of time in front of a screen, with their hands in one position over a keyboard. If problems with backache, eyestrain, headaches, and so on, are to be avoided, then attention needs to be paid to seating, lighting, and screen design. Even where computers are used in high customer-contact jobs, which involve far less time just sitting in front of a screen, good ergonomic conditions are necessary. Yet very often one sees sales assistants trying to use electronic tills which are poorly lit and positioned at the wrong height for comfortable use, or travel agents trying to read a screen which has been put on some convenient shelf or table with little thought for the user.

Hardware manufacturers are now aware of the problem, following a series of studies carried out by the National Institute of Occupational Health and Safety in the United States, and considerable improvements have been made in the design of the actual machine. However, the buyers of new technology seem less aware of, and appear to give little consideration to, the working environment. Some unions have technical specifications for the equipment which are designed to alleviate some of the problems, but these rarely deal with the conditions in and around the job.

Sensible approaches to adopt, based on the wealth of research in ergonomics, seem to be mandatory rest periods of about fifteen minutes after two hours of continuous screen/keyboard use, eye tests annually, adjustable work stations which allow the operator to modify the layout, screen and keyboard height, screen angle, foot position, and so on, and a reduction in lighting intensity in the normal office environment or an increase in the lighting intensity in many other environments (such as the fairly subdued lighting found in some department stores and many hotel reception areas).

(c) *Impact on job content.* Adequate ergonomic design in the job is important, but even more important is the impact on the job itself. Most service operations have until recently employed fairly limited technology, such as the typewriter, the telephone, the copying machine, and for many employees just paper and pencil and the normal fixtures and fittings of the trade. A change from this to a machine-aided or machine-dependent job can have a major impact on what the employee actually does, and though it may speed up operations, or relieve them of repetitive tasks, it may also result in a de-skilling of the job or degradation of working conditions. It may be efficient in terms of productivity, but may lead to precisely the kind of conditions which have generated problems in manufacturing – boredom, wasted skills, feelings of being controlled by the machine, assembly-line conditions, and loss of motivation (Roberts, 1984).

The kind of impact technology can have is illustrated in Figure 3.1. Some

Figure 3.1 Summary of advantages/disadvantages of microtechnology in job design and work organization

Organizational	**Individual**
	Advantages
Potential reduction in manning/staffing	Elimination of repetitive typing jobs
Improved accuracy	Pride in speed/accuracy
Greater potential for control (through	Learning of new skills
the availability of extra information)	Ability to provide better service (where
Potential reduction in operating costs	information processing is required)
	Disadvantages
Capital cost may be high	Waste of existing skills
Organizational change required	Potential de-skilling
	Potential unemployment
	Increased machine control
	Monotony/boredom (where the job
	changes to one of machine operation)
	Loss of personal contact and job
	interest where the machine totally
	replaces existing methods

Figure 3.2   A comparison between a secretary and a word processor operator.
(From Damodaren, 1980)

	Secretary/PA	**WP Operator**
Skills	Motor skill (keyboard)	Organizing skill and WP skill
Speed	35–50 w.p.m. intermittently 10 w.p.m. effective speed	50–80 w.p.m. effective speed
Equipment	Typewriter, dictating machine	Automatic typewriter, dictating machines, copiers, facsimile transmitters, VDU
Relationship to originator	Likely to know originator Established relationship Shared understanding/language	Less likely to know originator Impersonal relationship Little knowledge of work and language of originator
Sources of reward:		
(a) Intrinsic	Pride in high speed/accuracy/ attractive presentation Visible productivity Knowledge of context of document	Machine control of speed, accuracy, and presentation Intermediate effort not visible Little knowledge of context of document
(b) Indirect	Appreciation/feedback from originator	Little contact/feedback
Sources of dissatisfaction	Repetitive copy typing of successive drafts/author changes/ Poor personal relationship with originator	Repetitive typing virtually eliminated Little involvement with business activity Isolated machine minding

of these effects are, of course, highly subjective, and some may not be realized. The most uncertain effect is that of staff reductions; very often, no reductions are achieved, either because just as much work is involved in using the new system as the old (e.g. data entry into computers instead of manual systems) or because the benefits come from dealing with more work with the same number of staff. The view of whether an effect is an advantage or a disadvantage depends on the perception of the observer. Some employees, for example, may regard the need to learn new skills as a disadvantage, while employees who are bored with the existing job may find the new technology adds interest. In general, though, it appears that the organization has more to gain than the employee from new technology. This is demonstrated particularly well by a comparison made by Damodaren (1980) between a secretary/PA and a word processor operator, as shown in Figure 3.2.

In addition to these potential problems with employees, there may also be job-related problems with management when new technology is introduced. The usual argument for introducing computer technology, particularly, involves some reference to 'improved management', but the reality is that the only thing the new technology can do is provide easier and faster access to information. Unless management sets out to use the information appropriately, no improvement will result, and there may be complaints about extra paperwork. In addition, there may well be difficulties with issues like confidentiality and management prerogative. For example, the technology exists for internal electronic mail, electronic diary keeping, telephone conferences, and so on, but many managers are reluctant to adopt these techniques because they make many managerial activities highly visible. Most managers rely on a secretary to keep their appointment books, but few are happy at present with the idea of these being available on a VDU for other people to be able to see them.

Some managers have accepted the idea of electronic mail and use a keyboard and screen for sending/collecting messages, but others still prefer the telephone and a memo pad. More fundamentally, many managers have no keyboard skills and are unwilling to learn them.

Yet a further problem can arise, particularly in large companies which have separate departments. This is the 'territorial' issue. Where new technology resources provide a centralized resource, disputes can arise over who has control of it and who has priority. This can be even more difficult where, as so often happens, one individual has invested a lot of time and effort in investigating and acquiring the new technology and, when available, everyone wants to use it.

Many service operations discover after the introduction of new technology that there has been a shift in the balance of power in the organization. In many instances, tasks which were once visible are no longer visible, or information which was available at departmental level is now only available through centralized information-processing systems. For example, the change from normal cash registers to point-of-sale terminals in a department store removes the visibility of stock recording, and the supervisor has to rely on the accuracy of the shop assistants in entering the data correctly. In this case, the operator has more power than previously because there is no way of checking the work very easily. On the other hand, the introduction of centralized computer systems for personnel records and wage payments means that very often it is difficult for departmental personnel to obtain quick answers to questions. Here hostility and resentment can be generated, and local management may feel that power has been removed from them. These issues are not obvious to the new user, but can have a major impact on the way he/she feels about the resulting job.

Most of these problems can be overcome to a large extent by measures which sound simple and obvious, though they are often difficult to apply in practice.

(a) Involve the employees who will be working with the new technology in its selection and in planning for its implementation. They will often have very good ideas about how it can best be done, but, even where this is not the case, at least they are aware that their opinion matters, and this can, at least in part, overcome any resentment.

(b) Try to avoid the worst aspects of machine minding by making the technology fit the people instead of the other way around. Attention to ergonomic factors and the selection of equipment which is easy to understand and operate or computer software which is user-friendly contribute a great deal here.

(c) Use training and exposure to the new technology, say through visits to exhibitions or to other companies using the proposed technology, to try and overcome fear of the new equipment and to promote understanding. Learning by rote is generally inadequate, as is evidenced by the occasional department store assistant who has to ask for help in putting a particular transaction through her point-of-sale terminal and is obviously scared of 'breaking' the machine.

(d) Be prepared for many employees, particularly the longer-serving ones, to distrust the new technology and to maintain their own manual systems. One example of this observed by the writer is in a group of opticians, where manual records are maintained in parallel to a computerized accounting system and are used to check the computer output, and where after the use of an adding machine to total figures, a manual check is made of the addition! Checks like this are certainly necessary in the early stages to ensure that the new methods are working correctly, but again education is needed to help employees to trust it and to abandon both their checks and manual methods.

5.   CUSTOMER REACTION TO NEW TECHNOLOGY

Finally, of course, there is the problem of customer reaction to new technology. Even though automatic cash dispensers are now common, many customers prefer not to use them, and there is still reluctance to exchange real money for plastic cards. It is not only the direct interaction of the customer with new technology in the customer-contact part of the operation which needs to be considered, but also the impact on the customer of back-room technology. The change to a computerized accounting system has no direct impact on the customer, but will almost certainly affect any paperwork sent to him, and any problems encountered will affect the customer.

It is difficult to involve the customer in the decision to invest in new technology, but informing him/her about it, and giving clear, easy to understand instructions about how to use it, if necessary, are important steps to take.

6.   SUMMARY

The basic aim of managing the human resources in service operations, which are increasingly changing their nature as new technology and new demands for efficiency have an impact, is concerned with making efficient and effective use of employees and with managing customer behaviour so that it is appropriate for the organization and acceptable to the employee. These demands are often conflicting, and a trade-off is often required between what is efficient in resource-utilization terms and what is effective in terms of customer satisfaction. There is also the problem of determining what the customer wants and ensuring that operational changes do not change the product the customer thinks he/she is buying. In parallel is the need to control factors which influence customer satisfaction as well as those concerned with operational efficiency (Johnston and Morris, 1985). All of these issues can present a conflict between efficiency and effectiveness, and there are no rules which remove the essential management task of reconciling them.

However, provided decisions are made which take account of conflicting demands, the task of managing human resources becomes slightly easier. It will always remain a key issue, though, because human behaviour is unpredictable, and as long as human beings are a part of the system there will be elements of uncertainty. With good planning, recruitment and selection, and training the appropriate resources should be available, but good job design is needed to motivate them to work effectively and customer cooperation is needed for a successful operation. Fundamental to all of these is the need to be clear about precisely what service product is being offered and what is needed to provide it successfully.

REFERENCES AND BIBLIOGRAPHY

APEX (1980). *Automation and the Office Worker*.

Bailey, J. (1983). *Job Design and Work Organization*, Prentice-Hall.

Birchall, D., and Hammond, V.J. (1981). *Tomorrow's Office Today – Managing Technological Change*, Business Books.

Bird, E. (1980). *Information Technology in the Office: The Impact on Women's Jobs*, UK Equal Opportunities Commission.

Chase, R.B. (1978). Where does the customer fit in a service operation?, *HBR*, November/December **1978**.

Damodaren, L. (1980). Word processing: occupational and organisational effects, *Management Services*, June **1980**.

Davidson, D.S. (1978). How to succeed in a service industry: turn the organization chart upside down, *Management Review*, April **1978**.

Hackman, J.R., Oldham, G., *et al.* (1975). A new strategy for job enrichment, *Californian Management Review*, **xviii**(4).

Herzberg, F. (1966). *Work and the Nature of Man*, World Publishing Co.

Hodgeson, A., and Burden, D. (1979). In *Working on Quality of Working Life*, Nijhoff.

Jessup, G. (1978). *Technology As If People Mattered*, Department of Employment Work Research Unit Occasional Paper No. 2.

Johnston, R., and Morris, B. (1985). Monitoring and control in service operations, *International Journal of Operations and Production Management*, **5**(1), 32–38.

Levitt, T. (1972). Production-line approach to service, *HBR*, September/October **1972**.

Lovelock, C.H. (1984). *Services Marketing*, Prentice-Hall.

Lovelock, C.H., and Young, R.F. (1979). Look to consumers to increase productivity, *HBR*, May/June **1979**.

Maslow, A.M. (1943). A theory of human motivation, *Psychological Review*, **50**, 370–396.

Meister, D. (1971). *Human Factors and Theory of Practice*, Wiley.

Roberts, S. (1984). *The Complete Guide to Microsystem Management*, Prentice-Hall.

Sell, R.E. (1980). *Microelectronics and the Quality of Working Life*, Department of Employment Work Research Unit Occasional Paper No. 17.

Shostack, G.L. (1977). Breaking free from product marketing, *Journal of Marketing*, April **1977**.

Torrington, D., and Chapman, J. (1984). *Personnel Management*, 2nd ed., Prentice-Hall.

Trade Union Congress (1979). *New Technology and Employment*.

Voss, C.A. (1983). The service despatcher/receptionist role, *International Journal of Operations and Production Management*, **3**(3), 35–39.

Wild, R., and Birchall, D. (1973). Means and ends of work restructuring, *Personnel Review*, **2**(4).

Case Study: Wisewood Chemicals PLC

I'm fed up! That's the fifth time he's told me to change the layout of that report. Doesn't he think I've got enough to do without him changing his mind all the time about what paragraphs he wants where. And it's no use asking Bob to do anything — he's too busy playing with his machine.

The outburst came from Margaret, one of the three girls employed in the typing pool at Wisewood Chemicals. The 'he' referred to was the Marketing Manager, and Bob was the Office Manager. The occasion was the receipt of a note from the Marketing Manager telling Margaret to change around some of the paragraphs in a report he had been writing for several days. What made it even more annoying was that she was convinced that one of the changes only put two paragraphs back to where they had been in the second (or was it third?) draft. Still, at least it was on the word processor.

Six months ago, the Company had moved its executive and general offices into a new building and at the time it had seemed like a good idea to try and make the secretarial and clerical services more efficient. Prior to the move all the Heads of the various Company departments and several of the more senior managers had their own secretaries as well as small clerical sections. It was well known, however, that many of the secretaries were not fully occupied. The work of many of the senior staff took them away from their offices for two or three days at a time visiting the Company's other plants, and during their absences their secretaries often had little to do except deal with incoming mail, distribute it to other members of the department, and take telephone calls. In theory, they were supposed to help other secretaries and the typists when they had time, but in practice that never happened.

When the idea of centralization of the secretarial and clerical services had been put forward some two years earlier, there had been a lot of resistance from both the managers and their secretaries, and many of the clerical staff did not like the idea, though it was thought they would go along with it. The Company was going through a difficult period financially, however, and senior management felt it was not a good time to pursue the idea, given the very negative response.

The move to the new offices seemed the ideal opportunity to change the existing practices.

Bob Jenkins, head of the invoice preparation section, was given the task of investigating where savings could be made and planning for a new centralized secretarial and clerical services department. He was to become the Office Manager when the move was completed.

Bob spent a lot of time visiting other companies and also investigating the use of computers and word processing equipment. He thought that a lot of time spent producing standard documents could be saved by using word processing and that a number of the clerical services could be improved by using a micro-computer. He thought this would be particularly useful for budgeting and costing exercises.

In the event, most of his recommendations were accepted. The secretaries of the senior executives were to remain with their current bosses, but all other secretarial work was to be carried out in a central typing and word processing office. A number of clerical workers, whose duties were specialized in particular departments were to stay with those departments, but the rest were to be central-ized in a new clerical services office. The new arrangements should result in the saving of two secretaries and five clerical workers in the long term, though he thought they would need to be kept on in the short term until the new offices were working correctly and he had set up the various computer packages he needed.

A supervisor was needed for each of the two new offices and it was decided that the appointment should be made from the existing staff. This would serve to 'sweeten' the changes a little.

Time was getting short at this point if the necessary staff training in word processing was to be carried out and Bob felt it had to be done before the move so that the new working practices could be adopted right from the start. He therefore decided it was time to tell the staff who were to be affected.

He called all the secretarial and clerical staff together and announced the changes planned. The announcement was received with little enthusiasm. The situation was made even worse because he had assumed that the general manager had discussed the changes with the managers involved but the planned briefing with the managers had had to be delayed and, in fact, the secretaries and clerical staff learned about the proposed changes before the managers did.

However, he was philosophical about it. He had expected the managers affected to feel resentful. He knew many of them would look on it as something of a status loss, but they would have the good of the Company at heart and would get over it as the benefits from the new, improved service were realized.

He was more concerned about the secretarial and clerical staff. Some of them preferred to work for one boss rather than doing work for 'all and sundry', as one of the older secretaries remarked. Others said they could not stand the idea of working in a noisy office full of typewriters. Two or three said there should be extra pay for using word processors. Several said that being 'stuck in a general office' would mean there was no opportunity for promotion to senior secretarial status and working for one of the senior executives. Most of them were anxious about the word processor and the computer, which they had never used before, and all of them were worried about possible redundancy.

Bob knew he had to get their cooperation, but he also knew he could not set the precedent of giving more pay for using new technology or to buy in the changes. He set out to reassure them and point out the advantages of the new technology and the reorganization.

He explained that, although he expected to make staff savings, no redundancies were planned in the immediate future because all the staff would be needed until the new systems were working properly. He also anticipated that there would be other openings within the company so it was unlikely that there would be any redundancies at all. As far as the new technology was concerned, he described the situation he had seen in other companies and told them that all the staff he had seen using word processors and microcomputers were delighted with them and would not go back to the old methods. He also pointed out that the company would train them in the use of the new technology, which would, of course, make them far more attractive to new employers should they decide in the future to look for new jobs – though personally he would be unhappy to see any of them leave and he hoped they would be just as happy working for Wisewood in the future as they had always been.

Opportunities for wage increases in the new offices would be just as good as they were at present and when openings for secretarial work occurred in the senior executive offices they would be eligible for them. Additionally, he pointed out, two more senior posts had already been created, and he explained about the two new office supervisors, who were still to be appointed. This in turn would mean they were still only working for one boss – the office supervisor – and through her, himself. There would be far more work variety, because they would now be doing work for a number of departments, but that was an advantage not a problem, because the work would be much more interesting.

He did not envisage that noise would be a problem. Most of the work would now be done on word processors so there would be no noise from keyboards. The only noise from a word processor was when the finished document was printed out, and that could be reduced by using a printer silencer, which he promised would be provided. The word processor itself would be an enormous help to them. It was easy to correct mistakes without retyping; it would allow them to produce well laid out documents easily, and, the biggest advantage of all, it would get rid of the drudgery of typing up the same old things time after time.

On the strength of these reassurances, all but one of the girls decided to cooperate with the move. 'After all', one of them said to a friend, 'what else can we do? There aren't that many good jobs around.'

Several of the staff volunteered for training in word processing and two of the clerical staff asked for computer training. Their comments to other staff who thought they were letting the side down summarized how they felt:

> If that's what they're going to do, I don't want to know about it. The sooner I'm out of here the better and it'll be easier to get a job if I can use a word processor.

If they do make anybody redundant, it won't be the people they've just trained.

It'll be much more interesting using the word processor than just typing.

The computer will do all the routine stuff − no more paperwork!

Everybody's getting them. You can't stick your head in the ground.

You're just old-fashioned.

There's nothing we can do about it anyway. If we say we won't go along with it they'll just get rid of us and get someone who will, so we might as well make the best of it.

Given this agreement, albeit less than enthusiastic, Bob pressed on with his plans. The secretarial and clerical staff would adjust after all, and in time the managers and supervisors would accept the reorganisation. Those who did not would just have to put up with it because senior management was backing the changes.

He interviewed staff for the jobs of office supervisor and made the appointments. One he was not entirely happy about, but she was the best of the available candidates, and he felt it would be a mistake to bring in someone from outside. He also selected staff for training. This caused him a problem, because they all had to go at once if the training was to be completed by the time the move was completed and their absence would cause difficulties. He explained the problem to the managers concerned and when they complained, agreed to bring in temporary staff to cover the absences. He also completed his investigation of the equipment and ordered three word processors and a microcomputer together with software packages (a spreadsheet and a data management package). He knew he would have to spend time learning to use them, but that would have to wait until the move was over.

In the event, the move itself went smoothly. The staff training was completed successfully and the new equipment arrived as promised. The offices were not quite ready when it arrived, so the suppliers could not set it up for him. They promised to return when the offices were organized and set up the machines but he felt certain he and the staff could cope and so he did not bother to call them back. He set up the machines himself one weekend, and when the suppliers contacted him a few weeks later to enquire when they should come and install the machines, he told them they did not need to come.

Despite the ease of the actual move, things did not seem to work as he had expected. There were a lot of complaints from both managers and secretarial and clerical staff, but he had expected that in the early days. However, the complaints seemed to increase as time went on. He found that learning to use his own computer and set up all the things he wanted to do with it took far more time than he had anticipated, and that did not leave him with much time to deal with all the complaints. Still, that was what the supervisors were there for, and, in any case, once he had put the office budget and details of the office staff onto his computer, he would have much more time.

After twelve months, things were still not quite right. Bob still had a few more things to put onto the computer to help him manage better, and there were still complaints. He was looking forward to the day when everything he needed was on the computer and he did not need to spend so much time on it. When everything was set up, he would be able to use one of the clerks to do the routine work and that would free him to sort out the complaints and make the new system work properly.

People clearly did not understand how the new system operated, despite the memos he kept having the word processor operators produce for him and send to the managers and supervisors.

The office staff were complaining that managers were using their own clerical staff in secretarial capacities and only sending the routine, uninteresting work to the central office. They also complained that some of the managers were taking advantage of the word processor capabilities – particularly John Robson, the Marketing Manager, who kept on changing the layout of his reports. Bob did not understand why they were complaining about that. After all, it was easy to change the layout of a report with the word processor; it did not have to be re-typed every time.

The managers were also complaining. They said that were far more errors in work sent to the central office, because the girls were no longer familiar with the work, and that the staff were very slow in returning work sent down to them.

The clerical staff were complaining that they still had to do all the clerical work manually and they had been promised they could use the computer. Two of them had even been trained to use the packages Bob was so busy with, but he would not let them use the machine until he had set it all up.

It was at this point that John Robson sent his fifth request for an amendment to the secretarial office.

Chapter 4

Capacity Management

Colin G. Armistead

The objective of capacity management is to match the level of operations with the level of demand so as to find the best balance between cost and service levels. This involves the service operations manager in the consideration of medium- to long-term demand and the development of strategies for the use of resources to accommodate changes in demand in the short term. Some of the factors concerning long-term demand are covered in the chapters dealing with site location and the multi-site life cycle. The present chapter deals with the issues of medium- and short-term capacity management.

Service operations present a particular difficulty for capacity management because of the special features of services, namely:

(a) Service cannot be stored. As services are perishable they cannot be stored as a buffer to cope with future demand.
(b) Services require the participation of the customer at some stage in the production of the service. This creates uncertainty about the arrival of customers for the service and the processing time for the service. There is, however, the opportunity to utilize the customer as a resource to increase the capacity of the operation. Also the establishment of capacity levels must be evaluated in respect of the quality of the service which is of itself often difficult to quantify.

1. CAPACITY PLANNING

Capacity planning involves the service operations people in the task of providing answers to the following questions:

(a) How much capacity is required?
(b) When is the capacity needed?
(c) Where should the capacity be located? (See Chapter 10.)
(d) What strategy should be adopted to cope with fluctuations in demand?

2. HOW MUCH CAPACITY AND WHEN IS IT NEEDED?

Capacity is measured in units of output per time period. Some examples of capacity measurement are:

> Patients treated per month
> Customers served per day

The determination of the required capacity in the short to medium term is made difficult by two factors:

(a) The variability of the demand for the service may be large over relatively short periods of time (hours, minutes). This is typically experienced in retail outlets and restaurants in the course of a day.
(b) The time taken to perform the service may itself vary from customer to customer.

In some cases the use of a service is characterized by the random arrivals of the customers, when the determination of capacity may be dealt with by the application of queueing theory (see Chapter 8). If the demand for the service follows a pattern, or is expected to follow a pattern, historical data or marketing research data may be used in mathematical models to establish an estimate for demand in the future. The resulting trends in demand will be either constant, rising, or falling. Choices relating to capacity may be thought of as managing the gap between the required and the available capacity.

3. STRATEGIES TO COPE WITH FLUCTUATION IN DEMAND

There are two basic capacity management strategies for service operations which can be used independently or in combination.

Strategy 1: Vary capacity. The capacity is changed to follow changes in demand (referred to as the 'chase' strategy by Sasser, Olsen, and Wyckoff, 1978).
  This may be accomplished by:

> * Changing the number of service people
> * Changing the hours worked
> * Using subcontractors
> * Utilizing the customers
> * Sharing capacity with other service operations
> * Transferring resources from one part of the operation to another

Strategy 2: Manage demand. Influence demand to minimize the need to make changes in capacity.
  This may be accomplished by:

* Price changes
* Advertising and promotions
* Developing non-peak demand
* Developing complementary services
* Using reservation or appointment systems
* Making the customer wait or queue

A service operations manager may choose to implement either of the strategies, or, as is more common, use a combination of the two. This may be done as follows.

3.1 Strategy 1: Altering Supply by changing capacity

3.1.1 Personnel and Hours changes

The use of part-time people is very common in service organizations. They may be employed for part of the year, as in the tourist and holiday industries, or they may be used to cope with peaks which occur over times ranging from weeks to days to hours. The use of part-time people in this way is especially common in retailing and is a way of reducing costs for the organization while maintaining a high level of service if the scheduling of people is effective.

The use of longer working hours for full-time employees is also a means of coping with short-term fluctuations in demand.

Scheduling of people to start at different times in a day is one of the most effective ways of coping with demand patterns in service operations which show pronounced peaks and troughs.

3.1.2 Customer Participation

If the consumer can be persuaded to do some of the work, this reduces the demand on the existing resources of the service operation. This may be by the consumer helping with the handling of physical items as with self-service super-markets, restaurants, petrol stations, and baggage handling on airlines.

3.1.3 Resource Transfer

Another way of dealing with peak capacity is to transfer resources from one part of the service system to another. This requires that people need to be trained in a number of tasks.

3.1.4 Subcontracting

One of the means of expanding the capacity of a particular service operation is to use the capacity of others. The possibility of using the capacity of others is commonly seen in transport service operations. This may be done to cater for short-term fluctuations in demand or as a way of satisfying a constant level of demand without having to stand the risks of expenditure associated with increasing the capacity by purchasing planes or coaches and employing additional staff.

A danger with adopting the strategy of using other organizations to handle peak demands may be that at these times the subcontracting organizations may also be busy and thereby not available.

3.1.5 Share Capacity

If the cost of holding additional capacity is high but there is the need to cover peak demand on the service there may be the opportunity to share capacity with other service operations. This is often done with the emergency services of fire, ambulance, and police where neighbouring organizations make their resources available for use if an emergency in one area makes excessive demands on the existing capacity.

3.2 Strategy 2: Manage Demand to minimize the need to change Capacity

3.2.1 Pricing, Advertising, and Promotion

One method of shifting demand from peak to non-peak periods is to use a differential pricing scheme (which might also create primary demand for the non-peak time). There are very many examples of this happening such as telephone off-peak charges, travel, entertainment, and pubs and restaurants. Such changes may be accompanied by advertising and promotions. Alternatively, pricing may be used to limit the use of the service so as to maintain the same level of service for existing customers as with banks making a charge for withdrawals by people who are not account holders.

3.2.2 Developing Non-peak Demand

Service operations which are designed to provide a certain level of service for most of the operating time often find that there are periods when demand is much lower. City hotels at the weekend and country hotels out of season are examples of this. If the times of low demand are prolonged it may lead to a closure of the service for that time (country hotels) or if this is not appropriate alternative uses may be sought by the managers; the use of public schools for summer education and recreation camps is an example.

There are dangers for the management of a service organization introducing new service activities. The new activities may involve skills and other resources which are not available and divert management attention from the main service activity. It may prevent the non-peak time for the main service being used to train staff, carry out maintenance, and generally prepare for the next peak.

3.2.3 Developing Complementary Services

Demand may be shifted from peak periods by developing complementary services which attract the consumer or provide a diversion while waiting for the primary service. The use of automatic cash dispensers by the banks has increased the time over which customers are able to withdraw money, thereby reducing the demand on the counter service staff. The provision of bars in restaurants and cafes at stations are examples of services which ease the wait for the main service.

3.2.4 Customer Reservation or Appointments

The use of a reservation or appointments system effectively books the capacity of the system ahead of actual use. This may have the effect of also filling low peak times (theatre booking) or transferring demand to another service operation (hotel booking and travel agencies).

Problems can arise with reservation and appointment systems for the operations management. These are usually associated with the customer not turning up. Unless the organization makes a charge in advance there is a tendency to anticipate a number of customers not appearing and to overbook. When all customers do appear this leads to either a reduction in the level of service or some customers being forced to wait for long periods. If overbooking is not done, low capacity utilization can result. This is one of the classic service management trade-offs.

3.2.5 Customer Waiting or Queueing

If there is insufficient capacity to cater for peak demands customers can be made to wait or to queue. The adoption of this course of action may lead to loss of the customer because of an unwillingness to tolerate the delay in the provision of the service. There are strategies which can be used to increase the tolerance of the customer to waiting.

4. SCHEDULING

An important aspect of capacity management in service operations which choose to vary capacity to chase demand rather than to maintain a level capacity is that of scheduling. In service operations this usually concerns the scheduling of people to be available to perform the service. The aim of the scheduling process is to keep the waiting or queueing time for the start of the service to the standards which are set for the level of service.

There are two commonly used methods for improving the provision of capacity to follow changes in demand which occur over a daily or weekly cycle:

(a) A staggered shift scheme
(b) Use of part-time people

114

Exhibit 4.1   Numbers of people

	a.m.				p.m.				
	9.00	10.00	11.00	12.00	1.00	2.00	3.00	4.00	5.00
Full time	48	49	36	48	36	48	48	48	39
Part time	8	40	43	46	48	16	16	2	0

As an example of a scheduling scheme using full-time people on an eight hour day and part-time people who work four hours a day, Exhibit 4.1 shows the schedule for people on duty in a cafeteria over a period of a day, allowing for rest periods, training, and other duties.

5.   CONCLUSION

In the management of service operations the aim is to maintain the same level of service at all times. This presents difficulties for the operations manager when there are widely varying demands on the service. The more accurate a forecast that can be made of demand patterns the more there exists the opportunity to arrange the resources of the operation to meet the demand. In the majority of service operations the capacity cannot be changed very greatly in the short term and there will be periods when there is the risk of losing customers because of their unwillingness to wait for the service.

It is important to use the detailed breakdown of the various stages in the service operation and to determine the capacity of each. If bottlenecks in the system can be eliminated it increases the opportunity to deal with peak demands. The provision of extra capacity must be linked to a costing exercise and the best arrangement of the two main capacity management strategies for a particular service operation selected with this in mind.

REFERENCE

Sasser, W.E., Olsen, R.P., and Wyckoff, D.D. (1978). *Management of Service Operations.* Allyn and Bacon, Boston.

Case Study: British Airways

EXCHANGE OF LETTERS

The following exchange of letters illustrate a number of areas of difficulties for those managing service operations. The case is intended for teaching purposes only. It is not meant to illustrate good or bad management practice. The case was compiled by C.G. Armistead: Manchester Polytechnic (material reproduced by permission of British Airways).

The Managing Director
British Airways
West London Terminal
Cromwell Road
London SW7

Dear Sir,
I had a BA ticket (£191) to fly from Warsaw at 13.20 on August 22nd – my ticket had been arranged by the British Council in London and Warsaw.

I arrived as requested one and a half hours before the departure time and joined the end of a long line to the check-in desk. A few people joined the queue after me – although it was now noticable that as time went on some pushed in front.

When the person in front of me arrived at the desk she was told the plane was full and that no one else could be dealt with. Noticeably an American who was originally behind me did make it through and then returned to the desk area and passed some money to someone in the crowd.

Upon enquiry as to what was going to happen I was told by BA assistants that 'It's your fault for arriving late at the check-in', which was patently untrue, and also 'It's your problem for using bad booking agents' – a comment I will duly pass on to the British Council. I would like to point out that BA must have been aware that more tickets than seats had been confirmed, or had already let through passengers without confirmed seats.

I then spoke to Mr. Hopkin and pointed out to him that I had a flight to Morocco booked for August 23rd and that the next plane was 4 days later and that I was being met at Heathrow. Essentially his response was rough.

At all times the BA staff were assertive to the point of rudeness, telling passengers to be quiet and not answering questions. An unsuccessful attempt was made to put us on a flight to Amsterdam and then we were told no-go until the BA flight the following day — totally unsuitable for me as my Air Maroc flight was due to depart from Heathrow at 16.00 hours.

Although I gave a phone number for a telex message which would have prevented my family wasting time and becoming anxious at meeting the flight I should have been on, this was not sent for some hours.

I had just before joining the check-in queue given away my zlotes as they cannot be exported from Poland. There was no offer to look after me by the BA staff until I requested this. It was then suggested that I put my luggage in lost and found and the BA assistant gave me 100 zl to do this. Upon explaining that it cost two times that at Warsaw Station I was given a further 100 zl.

She also made a call and arranged for me to use the LOT hospitality service at the Hotel Fovvar. I explained that I had had nothing since early that morning and that I expected food and certainly a drink on the BA flight — and two meals were then promised. In the event Mr. Hopkin sent a letter to LOT Hospitality asking for only one meal (which could not be taken until the evening) and there was no refreshment — including water — available the whole day.

The BA assistant then told me to buy a bus ticket with what was left of the baggage deposit and take myself to the Hotel Fovvar. This was quite a prospect for me in a completely strange city and with no knowledge of Polish. My request for a taxi was dismissed. In the event the letter sent by Mr. Hopkin arrived before I did (I don't know why I could not have been taken with it) and the bus journey was not only long and hot but absolutely packed. The return journey the next day was equally unnerving.

The BA assistant also arranged for my ticket to be transferred to Swiss Air to Zurich leaving on the morning of the 23rd to change onto a BA flight arriving at Heathrow at 13:30 to connect with my Air Maroc flight. She assured me my seat was confirmed but on being introduced to the Swiss Air Representative he pointed out that my ticked was RQ and that the plane was fully booked — I would have to be on the waiting list.

Throughout the BA staff were not supportive and as the assistants seemed (naturally) harrassed, some training in standard procedures for looking after stranded passengers would be practical and help BA's image. These aspects were put into clear perspective the next day when travelling Swiss Air and found them efficient, calm, reassuring and charming, even when they could not be certain of my flight. Luckily the trip to Zurich worked out.

BA refused my request to telephone London and as I have already mentioned the telex arrived too late to be of benefit. I therefore borrowed money and telephoned from my hotel to make contingency plans with my family in case of my non-arrival on the next day's BA flight as they were also travelling to Morocco and had the tickets. This cost 596 zl, and £10 for my family needed to call me back. I expect these expenses to be met by BA and some other recompense for the unnecessary stress and upset, the lack of refreshment and the sheer inconvenience caused by my attempt to take up my seat on the Monday BA flight from Warsaw to London.

Yours faithfully,

British Airways
8 September 1983

Dear

Thank you for your letter, from which I was concerned to learn of the difficulties you had at Warsaw. There is no doubt we owe you a sincere apology and a full explanation of our policy.

In common with most airlines, we do sometimes deliberately overbook flights. The policy applies on certain routes where we know that a large percentage of passengers are likely to fail to take up their reservations and where there is a tendency for some passengers to make two or more bookings. The whole exercise is closely controlled and is not applied at random to every flight. The overbooking limits for each flight are fixed individually and only after serious consideration of all the factors involved, including the rate of turnover in reservations, the percentage of passengers who fail to turn up for the flights on this route and the type of traffic carried – for example business travellers or holiday makers.

Our action in this respect is part of a conscious effort to reduce the large losses in revenue incurred through passengers who do not turn up for their flights or who make double bookings. The only alternative would be an increase in fares, which we feel would be unacceptable. Furthermore, overbooking does mean that we are often able to accommodate passengers who would otherwise have been told that a flight is full, when our experience clearly shows that seats are likely to become available shortly before departure.

The situation is not ideal and I can assure you that we are not complacent about it. On the contrary we fully realise how upsetting it is for any passenger to be overbooked and we are still trying to find a more satisfactory solution to the problem.

I am concerned that you should have had reason to complain of the attitude of our staff; there is no excuse for discourtesy or unhelpfulness and this has been drawn to the attention of the department head concerned for appropriate action.

Although there is no official compensation applicable to your flight, we would like to make a goodwill payment based on the Civil Aviation Authority approved scheme for flights from the UK. This amounts to £47.75 and in addition we would like to make a goodwill contribution towards the expenses you mention. Therefore, I have pleasure in enclosing our cheque for £70.

Thank you for giving me this opportunity of apology and explanation. I do hope that we shall be able to regain your confidence and goodwill in the near future.

Yours sincerely,

D Karnik
Customer Relations

Case Study: The George Street Medical Centre

Dr. Desmond Bulman was one of five partners at the George Street Health Centre. He had always been concerned as to how well the practice was being managed from a non-medical point of view. None of the partners had any training or experience in management or administration, though they had to manage a large health centre without any outside assistance. In addition to his general worries, he felt that the practice was not facing up to a number of issues, such as the use of a part-time clinical assistant, the recruitment of a new partner, and cash flow problems. To help clarify his thinking he had asked a personal friend, who was a management consultant, to observe and report on the practice.

A. BACKGROUND

Dr. Bulman had joined the practice three years ago. He had previously worked in a small practice in London but had decided to move out because he was unhappy with his predominantly middle class patients. He felt they were overdemanding. For example, for minor complaints, where one would normally expect a patient to visit a surgery, they would demand a home visit. In addition, a small practice was very time consuming and Dr. Bulman felt that he did not have enough spare time to pursue his personal interest in in-hospital clinical work.

The George Street Medical Centre was a group practice of five General Practitioners, located in a new town in the West Midlands. Group practices are practices where a number of general practitioners share physical facilities and sometimes patients. Because of their size they could realize a number of benefits that the traditional one or two doctor practice could not achieve. These benefits were reported to include:

(a) The ability to support full-time nursing staff to do some work that was normally done by doctors
(b) To provide clinics and services such as antenatal clinics and rooms for health visitors
(c) To provide a wide range of specialist skills among the doctors
(d) Ability to support expensive diagnostic machinery such as ECG machines and haemoglobinometers

This case was written by C.A. Voss

119

(e) To generate economies of scale

(f) To develop more efficient and effective patient service

Larger group practices often practised in a medical centre, with the general practitioners forming a practice team and the centre being run by a non-medical practice manager. Most medical centres were built and funded by area health authorities, who leased them and their staff to groups of practitioners. The George Street Medical Centre was an exception in that it was fully owned by the doctors who also funded its operation.

The five doctors (recently expanded from four) shared equally all expenses and revenues associated with the practice. They shared out the various responsibilities between them. The organization was informal, with responsibilities allocated among the doctors, and the head nurse nominally the practice manager (see Exhibit 1).

The practice was located about 300 yards from the main shopping centre and bus station of the town. It was in modern purpose-built premises with a large newly built car park at the rear. The patients were drawn primarily from the prosperous working class population of the town with a small percentage of

Exhibit 1   Allocation of responsibilities

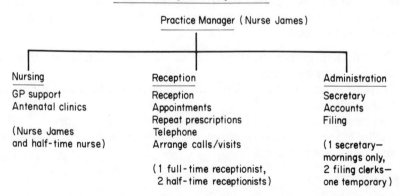

Split of responsibilities — group

Dr. Rose   (age 55) – Financial matters
Dr. James   (age 50) – Legal matters
Dr. Scully (age 40) – New development, work rotas
Dr. Bulman (age 34) – Maintenance
Dr. Allan   (age 32) – Practice personnel

Practice management / organization

Practice Manager (Nurse James)

Nursing	Reception	Administration
GP support	Reception	Secretary
Antenatal clinics	Appointments	Accounts
	Repeat prescriptions	Filing
(Nurse James	Telephone	
and half-time nurse)	Arrange calls/visits	(1 secretary—
		mornings only,
	(1 full-time receptionist,	2 filing clerks—
	2 half-time receptionists)	one temporary)

patients from the surrounding villages. Each doctor had a separate list of patients. Details of the size of lists are shown in Exhibit 2.

B. THE MEDICAL CENTRE OPERATIONS

1. Reception

The inside of the medical centre was bright and cheerful and was more reminiscent of a business foyer than a doctor's waiting room. The reception was opposite the entrance and the consulting rooms were off to one side.

The practice employed one full-time and two part-time receptionists, one for the morning surgery and one for the afternoon surgery. The main tasks of the receptionists were to handle patients who arrive to see the doctor or attend clinics, to handle repeat prescriptions, and to make appointments. The most time-consuming task was handling telephone calls for appointments. These came mainly between 9:00 a.m. and 10:00 a.m.

On arrival, patients were checked off in the appointment book or were allocated a time if they had no appointment. When a doctor was ready for the next patient, he indicated this by a light. The smooth running of the reception

Exhibit 2   Details of the doctors' lists

List size

Month	Doctor					Total
	Rose	James	Scully	Bulman	Allan	
April	3005	2782	3087	2725	1770	13,388
July	2986	2783	3045	2694	2011	13,569
October	2962	2771	2989	2674	2318	13,496
Jan	2945	2740	2960	2655	2700	14,000
April	2950	2788	2956	2731	2712	14,087

Number of patients leaving list

Oct	9	10	11	10	18
Nov	17	26	22	19	53
Dec	7	5	7	16	10
Jan	9	11	10	17	27
Feb	6	13	8	20	40
Mar	1	1	3	9	11
April	8	9	13	6	29
May	15	8	11	25	45
June	12	2	13	12	21
July	23	19	37	29	60

was often upset by peaks, such as telephone calls or a number of patients arriving at once. This was especially true in the early morning. In addition, the receptionists were frequently asked to fetch files for patients who had just arrived, results of smear or pregnancy tests (these were kept in a book in the filing room), or X-ray results from the X-ray files.

2. The Appointment System

The rule of the practice was that all consultations were by appointment; all new patients were clearly informed of this when they registered. A patient wishing to see their doctor phoned up the receptionist, who made an appointment for the patient, usually from the same day to four days' time. The receptionist used an appointments book supplied by a drugs firm, in which she allocated five or ten minute slots throughout the surgery. (She tried to allow for the fact that the average consultation time varied from doctor to doctor). In addition, she would allow a ten minute break for rest or catch-up, twice during the surgery. In making forward appointments she tried to leave some slack for urgent and short notice appointments.

Despite the appointments system, there were always a small proportion of 'take-ups', patients who came in without an appointment. These were fitted into gaps in the schedule or at the end of the surgery. They were not normally turned away. Dr. Bulman estimated that there was a take-up rate of about 5 per cent.

In addition to surgery appointments, the receptionist also arranged home calls to patients who were not able to visit the surgery. The health centre asked patients where possible to phone for a home call before 10:00 a.m. Homes calls were normally done between 11:00 a.m. and 4:00 p.m., though some doctors did a few home calls in the evening. It was normal for such home calls to be done by the patient's own doctor.

Night calls were handled on a rota basis, with all such calls put directly through to the doctor on call.

Details of the number of consultations and calls are given in Exhibit 3.

Appointments systems were not always popular among doctors. A hospital doctor colleague of Dr. Bulman was strongly against them, saying that they were a waste of a doctor's valuable time. He preferred to allow a queue to build up before he arrived to ensure a constant flow of patients. 'It's far more efficient,' he said. Dr. Bulman, on the other hand, felt that appointments could increase efficiency. If a patient had been waiting too long, he felt obliged to chat for a few minutes, whereas if he saw them on time it was 'straight down to business'.

3. Repeat Prescription System

One area that had always taken up much surgery time was the issuing of repeat prescriptions to patients on a course of treatment. To reduce the workload in

Exhibit 3   Details of workload

Sample of workload at surgery

	Dr. Rose	Dr. Scully	Dr. Allen	Dr. Bulman	Dr. James
Friday Aug 8:30 a.m.					
Number of patients	10	16	20	15	14
Time of last appointment	10:10	10:00	10:35	10:10	10:10
Friday Aug 4:00 p.m.					
Number of patients	15	20	13	13	Half-day
Time of last appointment	5:30	5:45	5:15	5:35	off
Friday July 8:30 a.m.					
Number of patients	12	17	23	19	14
Time of last appointment	10:00	10.35	10.55	10:25	10:45
Friday July 4:00 p.m.					
Number of patients	Half-day	17	22	17	Half-day
Time of last appointment	off	5:45	6:00	5:30	off
Monday July 8:30 a.m.					
Number of patients	15	On	23	21	18
Time of last appointment	10:20	holiday	10:50	10:25	10:15
Number of night call-outs April–July	2	7	9	12	10

Day visits (total by all doctors)

Date	Number of visits	Date	Number of visits	Date	Number of visits
Jan 8	27	April 2	26	July 9	13
9	19	3	16	10	10
10	19	4	14	11	10
11	11	5	16	12	5
12	12	6	11	13	8
13	5	7	7	14	9
14	0	8	7	15	6
Feb 5	15	May 7	13	Aug 6	11
6	7	8	11	7	17
7	10	9	10	8	8
8	14	10	12	9	7
9	11	11	8	10	6
10	5	12	10	11	5
11	14	13	10	12	9
Mar 5	26	June 4	12		
6	7	5	7		
7	7	6	8		
8	7	7	6		
9	12	8	8		
10	4	9	5		
11	0	10	8		

this area, the practice had adopted a system of repeat prescription processing, in which much of the work was done by the receptionist. The steps in this process were as follows:

(a) Patient requiring a repeat prescription is issued with a card giving details of this prescription (see Exhibit 4).
(b) Shortly before the existing prescription runs out, the patient posts or brings in his card to the medical centre.
(c) The receptionist writes out the prescription, has it typed, and gives it to the doctor to sign.
(d) Twenty-four hours (or later) after bringing in the card, the patient calls (without appointment) and collects his prescription from the receptionist.

This system, which was being used in a number of practices around the country, had attracted some criticism as it allowed prescriptions to be issued without the doctor seeing the patient.

4. Medical Records

The keeping of medical records for nearly 15,000 patients had always been a major headache. To make matters worse, the NHS had initiated a change in the type and size of medical records. The practice was in the process of changing over to the new A4 files and had employed two temporary filing clerks to work on this.

This change had triggered the practice into reviewing their methods of keeping files, and they had decided to invest in a new, and expensive, carousel filing system. This system was claimed by the manufacturers to have a rapid access time and to minimize the work involved in filing.

5. Telephone

The practice had recently invested in a new PABX exchange. This exchange had the facility of allowing the receptionist to take calls direct and put calls through to any doctor without having to use one receptionist as a switchboard operator. Doctors could in turn dial out direct.

6. Paramedical staff

The surgery made full use of its paramedical staff, one full-time and one part-time nurse, to relieve the load on the doctors.

Most of the doctors, rather than perform routine matters such as dressing and injections, would hand the patient over to the nurse after seeing the patient.

In addition, patients needing treatment for minor accidents, burns, cuts, and dressings, etc., were encouraged to make appointments with the nurse directly and not see their doctor.

Exhibit 4   Repeat prescription card

Health Visitors

are available for consultation at the Medical Centre.
MON - FRI   9.00 a.m. to 11.00 a.m.
Advice on : Family problems
             Children
             The elderly
             Family planning etc.

Clinics

information about Antenatal Clinics, Smear Tests, Vaccination Clinics, can be obtained through reception desk.

MEDICAL CENTRE

Telephone 2507/8/9

EMERGENCY NUMBER 2508

Consultations

by appointment

MON - FRI   8.30 a.m. to 10.30 a.m.
            4.00 p.m. to 6.00 p.m.
SAT   8.30 a.m. to 10.00 a.m.

To make an appointment or to see the practice nurse for treatment of Minor accidents, Burns, Cuts, Dressings or Injection;
Telephone or call at the Centre

THE MEDICAL CENTRE IS OPEN

MON - FRI   8.00 a.m. to 12.00 Noon
            2.00 p.m. to 6.00 p.m.
SAT   8.30 a.m. to 11.00 a.m.
Requests for visits should be made before 10. a.m.

Repeat Prescriptions

Please use this card when requesting a repeat and allow 24 hours. Prescriptions can be ordered by post if a stamped addressed envelope is provided.

Date: Medicine to be repeated

Drs. Signature................................... Date:

The health centre also provided space for health visitors and facilities for midwives, antenatal clinics, and vaccination clinics.

7. Finance

General practitioners were paid a basic salary plus a capitation fee based on the number and type of patients (e.g. if more than 10 per cent were rural patients a higher fee would be paid).[1]

C. ISSUES

1. New Partner/clinical assistant

For a number of months the partners had been discussing the possibility of reducing their workload by recruiting a new partner or bringing in a part-time clinical assistant. Views were very divided on this issue. The partners in favour pointed out that the average number of patients per doctor in the U.K. was 2,200, and the British Medical Association recommended a maximum of 2,500. The others felt that they were coping quite well with their present lists. A new partner would lead to a short-term loss of revenue and a clinical assistant would not be able to benefit all partners equally as he would not have his own list. Dr. Bulman felt that he could cope with up to 2,900 patients, but, at this level, peak loading caused by, for example, a flu epidemic could become severe. He also felt that the older partners were well established financially and could stand a small loss of income better than the younger partners. He also thought that the reason that Dr. Scully favoured a clinical assistant was to enable him to take off on a regular basis one or more mornings a week.

3. Service

Despite the attention being paid to running an efficient practice a number of partners were uncertain as to whether the systems were adequate. For example, despite the recent investment in a new filing system, doctors felt they often had to wait too long for files to arrive, especially in the morning surgery. Similarly, they often had to wait for test results or X-rays. Dr. Bulman felt that part of the problem was that they had no base to compare their performance with.

D. THE CONSULTANT'S REPORT

Dr. Bulman's friend spent two days observing the practice, talking to the doctors and employees and digging out statistics. On the basis of this he prepared a

---

[1] General practitioners were paid by the National Health Service (NHS) a fixed 'salary' plus a capitation fee averaging £3 per patient (higher for older patients and rural patients). This was constant regardless of the amount of consultations.

The NHS reimbursed most of the running costs of the practice and paid 70 per cent of salaries of all staff employed by the practice.

Extra fees could be earned for vaccinations, smear tests, clinics for local employers, etc.

report. This report described his observations and was intended as a basis for discussion with Dr. Bulman from which they should jointly develop recommendations.

Extracts from the report are given in Appendix 1.

Appendix 1

Excerpts from Consultant's Observations

PHILOSOPHY OF THE PRACTICE

There is a very clear, though not explicitly stated and agreed, philosophy of running the practice. The main items are:

(a) *Separate lists*. Each doctor has his own list of patients, rather than sharing the total list between the practice. Every effort is made to ensure that each patient always sees his/her doctor. This is not the most efficient mode of operation — on the sample of surgeries observed. The workload could easily be handled by three doctors, more being needed only at peaks.

(b) *Equal sharing of workload. All work to be shared equally among the* partners.

(c) *Full five day coverage*. All partners to have five morning surgeries and four afternoon surgeries.

(d) *Coordinated timing*. Reception open at 8:00 a.m. and all doctors take first patients at 8:30 a.m.

(e) *Appointments only*. The surgery and clinics to be run on an appointments system.

(f) *No private patients*. No facilities to be provided for private patients in the practice. Individual doctors are free to pursue private activities such as work for companies, as long as this is outside the practice. Private patients seem to be considered more trouble than they are worth, rather than politically or socially undesirable.

GENERAL OBSERVATIONS

Peak Loading

The peak load for reception normally comes between 9:00 and 10:00 a.m. During this period the staff appeared very rushed. In contrast, afternoon surgeries tend to be very leisurely. Monday morning is generally the busiest surgery, with morning surgeries busier in winter than in summer. The following were the average times for each of the main elements involved in appointments.

128

Appointment system
element timing

Activity	Time (approx.)
Make appointment over phone and write in book	30−60 seconds
Collect file or check test report	60−90 seconds
Receive patient in surgery	15 seconds
Send patient into doctor	5 seconds

Observations of a typical peak period are shown at the end of the appendix. The receptionists described their major problems as:

(a) Handling patient changes of address
(b) Doctors asking for files, X-rays, test results during peak periods
(c) Patients not wanting to wait for prescriptions

In contrast with the receptionists, the doctors had little peaking of workload, and all finished their surgeries before 11:00 a.m. and 6:00 p.m. respectively. It is clear that during the period observed (which admittedly was not a peak period medically, there being no epidemics around) that if the doctors shared their lists, the workload could have been handled by only three doctors.

Atmosphere

The doctors and staff all seem to have a high morale. There were some complaints from staff about bossy doctors, requiring everything at once. I ran a simple management grid questionnaire to determine the management style of the doctor and the practice manager. This grid has two axes: one for concern with people, the other for concern with task. Each is measured on a 1 to 9 scale. Thus 9:1 indicates high concern for task, low concern for people − a classic authoritarian style; 1:9 indicates high concern for people, low concern for task − a classic consultative manager; 9:9 indicates a well-rounded approach; and 1:1 indicates general weakness.

The doctors in the sample are in the area of 8:5 to 9:1 (Dr. Bulman was 9:1). The practice manager was 9:9.

Queueing

During the period of observation, the number of patients waiting to see their doctor never exceeded two. The majority of the patients saw their doctor within ten minutes of the appointed time.

About 8 per cent of the patients failed to show up for their appointments.

OBSERVATIONS OF TYPICAL SURGERY RUSH HOUR

8:30 a.m.	First doctors see patients
8:40 a.m.	Four patients waiting
	Receptionist preparing patients' files
8:42 a.m.	Two doctors still chatting in reception
8:55 a.m.	All three phones ring at once
9:00 a.m.	Phone calls coming in for appointments and one call for repeat prescriptions
	Patient arrives with no appointment (fitted in for 9:10)
	Two patients without appointments, for treatment from the nurse
9:05 a.m.	Phone call for doctor
9:08 a.m.	Phone call for doctor
	Patient without appointment (fitted in at 10:00 a.m.)
9:18 a.m.	All three lines busy
9:32 a.m.	Frenchman walks in without appointment
9:35 a.m.	Queue of patients at the desk
	New patient looking for a doctor
	Patient without appointment
9:40 a.m.	Patient rings wanting a home visit, put through to doctor
9:41 a.m.	Queue at desk again
	Patient wanting prescription, but without card, asked to come back later 'I'd like to help you now but there are so many patients'
9:44 a.m.	Rush over

Chapter 5

Operations Control

Colin G. Armistead and C.A. Voss

In service operations, operations control interacts very closely with quality control. It is the activity which is primarily concerned with making sure that the service package is delivered to the customer at the right time and in the right place. Staff performing the role may be called 'operation controllers' but frequently have other job titles. In service operations the term operations control relates to two main areas of activity:

1. The receptionist/despatcher role associated with either allocating customers to spare capacity (hotel reception and airline booking) or scheduling or despatching the service delivery system to the customer (field service and emergency services).
2. A production control role at the interface between the 'front office' and 'back room' activities (repair organizations and some fast food outlets). In some ways this role is analogous to production control in a manufacturing business but the special nature of service operations may impose differences (e.g. speed of response, perishability).

1. THE RECEPTIONIST/DESPATCHER ROLE[1]

Studies of this role in a number of different service organizations have shown that the person or persons who are the despatcher or receptionist carry out several different tasks, as indicated in Figure 5.1. These tasks are carried out in a general sequence starting with the initial contact with the customer or client of the service organization.

1.1 Contact

The receptionist/despatchers are in frequent contact with the customers. In some cases this is by telephone (emergency services and field services) but in others the contact can be face to face (hotel and medical receptionists). This

---

[1] This section is based on the study of a number of different service organizations by Voss (1984).

Figure 5.1 Tasks performed by a receptionist/despatcher in various service organizations. (From Voss, 1984)

Task	Industry				
	Field service	Medical practice	Emergency service	Car hire	Hotel
Contact	x	x	x	x	x
Diagnosis	x	x	x	—	—
Filter	x	x	(x)	—	x
Despatch	x	x	x	x	—
Schedule	x	x	x	(x)	(x)
Selling	(x)	—	—	(x)	(x)
Control information	x	—	—	—	x
Invoicing	x	—	—	—	x

activity is particularly important in maintaining the quality of the service organization in the customers' perception (speed of answering the telephone, pleasantness of response, etc.).

1.2 Diagnosis

In organizations where the service is in response to customer problems (health, emergencies) a certain amount of diagnosis is performed by the receptionist/despatcher. The kinds of benefit which come from this activity are:

(a) To try and determine the exact nature and the cause of the problem.
(b) To determine whether the customer can perform the service without despatching expensive resources (e.g. go to bed and keep warm, turn the switch on, replace a particular part).
(c) To enable the appropriate resources to be despatched (e.g. emergency service).
(d) To ensure the service resource despatched has the correct parts, medicine, etc.
(e) To determine the priority (e.g. medical appointment in a few days or a visit by a doctor that day).

It is interesting to note that the people who perform these kinds of diagnosis are often not formally trained to do so.

1.3 Filter

The filter task is one of the most common activities for those acting as the first contact with the customer for the service organization. It is the task often performed by secretaries, the objective being to deal with the customer initially at the lowest (and thus cheapest) level or to minimize the unnecessary use of expensive resources (e.g. doctor or hotel manager).

1.4 Despatch

In all the examples in Figure 5.1 a major task for the receptionist/despatcher is to receive requests from the customer for the service and to despatch the appropriate resources (a doctor, fire appliance, ambulance, service engineer, etc.). The effectiveness of this operation depends on the information systems which are available to the operations control person. one or both of two sets of information are required:

(a) The availability of the service resources.
(b) The customer's history with the service.

Information systems vary from the use of computer-based systems to planning boards and radio and telephone communication. The structure of the despatch activity may be related to the speed of response that is required (emergency services may have standards which require the service vehicles to be despatched within seconds or minutes). On the other hand, there may be a choice of a number of different levels open to the despatcher (commonly found in field service operations where there may be different response times ranging from hours to days, depending on the nature of the requirement).

Some organizations may have a combination of the two (e.g. the ambulance service with its requirement for emergency work and as a 'taxi' service for patients who are non-emergency).

1.5 Scheduling

If there is no need for an immediate response the despatcher/receptionist may be required to perform a scheduling task. This may be scheduling of customers to match the capacity of the service system (e.g. hotel, airline booking) or the allocation of service resources to customers (e.g. car hire). Generally in service organizations priorities follow a first-come-first-served basis. This may be overridden in some cases where there is freedom on the part of the despatcher and limited resources (e.g. field service where the despatcher builds up a knowledge of the response time required by a specific customer or an ambulance service where an ambulance may be diverted to a more serious case).

1.6 Selling

In many service organizations the receptionist/despatcher has more contact with the customers than the sales force and may be used in a minor selling role to promote further services or to respond to requests to put the customer in contact with the sales force.

1.7 Control Information

The central location of the despatcher/receptionist makes it possible to use them as the means of collecting information that is necessary for further control of the operations. This is found, for example, in emergency services and in field service organizations.

1.8 Invoicing

The preparation of invoices by the receptionist/despatcher is common in services like hotels and some field services. In organizations which have computerized information systems the invoicing is generally isolated from the receptionist tasks.

2. THE PRODUCTION CONTROL ROLE

The 'production' control role found in service operations reflects the control of those operations when the customer does not come into contact with the people who are working on the 'facilitating good' which forms part of the service package. This type of control is more analogous to the manufacturing environment except that in many cases (fast food for example) it is closely linked with a service operation which sets a high level of service for speed of delivery. The operations control in these types of service operations fits with the concept of a 'front office' and 'back room' view of an operation with the operations control being at the interface between the 'front office' (where there is contact with the customer) and the 'back room' (where there is no contact with the customer).

Examples of service operations which have operations control of this type are in those repair services which are not field service operations, restaurants, banks, building societies, and insurance companies (although less so in these last three cases as there may be low contact with customer by letter or telephone by the 'back room' people).

3. INFORMATION SYSTEMS

The fastest changes in operations control in service operations is resulting from the change from manual paper-based information systems to those employing computer-based information technology. This change has already gone a long way in the computer industries and in other service organizations such as travel companies and airlines and emergency services. The information which is required falls into the following categories:

(a) Current status of the service resources
(b) Availability of the resources over time
(c) Response needed to a specific incident or request (often used in emergency and field services)
(d) Information on clients' history or ability to search other records

It may be sufficient to handle this information on a VDU or obtain hard copy from a printer. Some larger organizations have developed message switching of information by way of computer-based systems to replace the slower and lower capacity telex machines.

4. AUTOMATION OF THE OPERATIONS CONTROL FUNCTION

A further consequence of the spread of information technology is to make it increasingly possible for the customer to obtain the services of the service operation directly, without necessarily having any personal contact. Already this has been referred to in the discussion of equipment-based operations in a relatively small way in the banks' use of cash dispensers. Other developments are permitting the automatic diagnosis of faults by a computer and in some cases automatic repair. Home banking allows direct transfer of funds without any personal intervention and ticket booking of airline seats and other services is possible when the customer has direct access to the information on availability of the service. These developments mean a change in the operations control and in the customer's expectation of a particular service organization.

5. MONITORING PERFORMANCE

Service organizations use a range of financial and non-financial operational measures to monitor their performance, which extend outside of those which are covered in the chapter dealing with quality management. A recent study was carried out to determine the measures actually used in organizations for monitoring performance. The results are summarized in Table 5.1. It is perhaps not unexpected to find that most of these relate to the more tangible parts of the service package, reflecting the difficulties if not the unwillingness on the part of

Table 5.1   Actual performance monitors used in service organizations.
(From Morris and Johnston, 1983)

Organization	Performance monitors
Libraries	Book usage, number of issues per branch, stock/issues ratio, issues per capita, customer complaints
Tour operator	Cost per guest, staff/guest ratio, complaints after the event
British Telecom	Traffic analysis, operator response time, operator behaviour, complaints
Banks	Bad debts, number of new accounts, complaints
British Rail	Financial analysis, train/passenger analysis, number of written complaints, special studies (where problems exist or are anticipated, e.g. queueing)
Optician	Number of eye tests, glasses/contact lenses sold, bad debts, financial analysis

service operations managers to face the problem of measuring the intangible service elements.

6. CONCLUSION

Operations control in service operations is important if the service-producing unit is to deliver the service package to the customer as and when it is required or promised. The extent to which this is successfully accomplished will effect the quality control of the service operation and ultimately whether the customer is satisfied. Operation controllers acting in a receptionist/despatch role often perform a wide range of tasks because of their close contact with the customer. Those controlling the interface between front office and back room activities are the main link between those having a high level of contact with the customers and those who have little or no contact.

Examples of issues in operations control can be found in the following cases which follow Chapter 7:

North West Gas – operational control
Operations control for Emergency Services in Greater Manchester
Wickshire Highways Department

REFERENCES

Morris, B., and Johnston, R. (1983). *Perspectives in Service Industries*, Workshop on Service Operations, Manchester Polytechnic.

Voss. C.A. (1984). The service receptionist/despatcher role, *International Journal of Operations and Production Management*, **3**, No. 3.

Chapter 6
Quality Management

Colin G. Armistead

Quality management is concerned with quality assurance, which embraces all activities and functions involved with the attainment of quality including design, specification, and quality control (BSI 1979). This concept of quality is especially important for services because, as recently stated by the Head of Sales at British Airways, 'A service industry is vulnerable at its weakest point – if you go to a restaurant, the food can be magnificent but if the service is lousy the chances are you will never go back again. That's the crux of it.' (Cuthbert, 1983).

Those responsible for managing service operations need to specify and maintain the quality of the total service package, both the physical items and the service elements. It is the control of the service elements so that customers receive the required 'quality' of service whenever and wherever the customer is the recipient of the service package that is the most difficult. The definition of quality rests to a great extent with the expectation of the customers which may have been created by previous experience of the service business, hearsay, advertising, or pricing. The role of marketing is to create an expectation of the service package for the customer. This must be matched by the capability of the operations to deliver the service package in a way that meets the expectation.

1. QUALITY ASSURANCE

Quality assurance is concerned with making sure that quality is designed into the service package and remains as it is produced and given to the customer. The design of service operations has already been covered in Chapter 3. The important factors associated with quality are:

(a) Organization
(b) People
(c) Process
(d) Facilities (including equipment)
(e) Materials

138

Figure 6.1 shows some of the relationships between these factors.

Figure 6.1   Factors in quality assurance of service operations

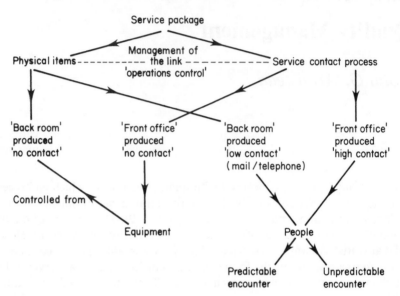

1.1   Organization

The service operation is to give to the customer the service which consists of a mix of physical items and the service elements. The organization of a service operation to deliver the service package to the customer is to some extent a matter of choice, although there are constraints imposed by the nature of the service; e.g. if there is the need to have the customer participating in the production of the service, as happens with travel services, professional services, and live entertainment. The choices will mainly be in the separation of the service package into the production of physical items and the service content and whether these are produced in a 'back room' (non-customer-contact) or 'front office' (customer-contact) environment, as well as the extent to which the service content is given by people or equipment.

1.2   People

People in service operations include (a) non-contact personnel, (b) contact service personnel, (c) customers or clients. Selection and training of contact personnel is especially important in service operations because of the difficulties of the precise definition of quality of the service content (Hostage, 1975). A service operation is reliant to a great extent on the interpersonal skills of the service contact people. The non-contact people may not be directly involved with customers but their activities will have a direct influence on the customers' perception of the service package (often seen in the timing of the service as much as with the quality of physical items). It is important for non-contact people as well as the contact service personnel to be aware of the service philosophy of the business. This may be achieved as part of a training activity and sustained by the use of 'internal marketing' and quality circles or similar activities, all attempting to influence the attitudes of the service operations people.

An aspect of service encounters is the degree of uncertainty which exists about the course the encounter will take. Some encounters will be fairly predictable where the transaction is simple (e.g. buying a ticket or a small purchase). In others there can be a high degree of uncertainty as the transaction between the service personnel and the customer becomes more complex. This can occur in many professional services and would be associated with a customer complaints department. There is the need for the service operations management to try to gauge the predictability of the service encounters and to select and train service contact personnel appropriately.

The customers in the service operation create a resource for which often they have to be 'trained' to perform their part of the service. A customer who is not 'trained' may have a disrupting effect on the operations and influence the quality of the service package for other customers (e.g. not knowing where to go, what to do, what to take, where smoking is permitted, where silence is required, how to seek assistance, and so on). The training of customers depends to a great extent on their willingness to perform part of the service production − something which is influenced by marketing image and pricing. Customers may be trained by the use of service contact personnel as instructors ('pick up your bags and follow me'), the use of written notices, and by other customers who have previous experience of the service.

1.3 The Process

The process is taken to mean the total provision of the service package. If quality is to be designed into it and operationally produced it is necessary to identify clearly the activities which involve the customer directly and those where the customer is not directly needed. Flow-charting of the service operation provides a guide for the different activities and the sequence in which they occur. The establishment of measures of quality performance to cover both physical items and the service contact process can follow, although there is a tendency for service operations to concentrate on measures for the physical items (Morris and Johnston, 1983). The service contact element is the more difficult to manage and it is consequently necessary for service managers to try to reduce the unpredictability of the service encounter and to identify those encounters which have a high degree of unpredictability and to make special provision for dealing with these. The creation of a specialist customer service or information section is one way to deal with unpredictable encounters relating to complaints or the need for assistance.

1.4 Facilities and Equipment

Facilities and equipment must be considered at the stage of setting up the service operation and in its subsequent operation. The choice of equipment will depend on factors relating to the nature of the service organization, which has been discussed earlier in Chapter 2 on design. Where equipment is used as an alternative to people for the provision of the service package, the equipment must be ergonomically designed to ensure ease of use by all users and must be reliable in operation. The facilities of the service operation in the areas where customers have access will have an influence on the customers' perception of the service package and are therefore important in this context, as they also are for the comfort of the people working in the service organization. An increasingly important aspect of equipment in service operations concerns the handling of information and the decreasing costs of information technology, making it available to a very wide range of service organizations. This will undoubtedly lead to a change in the expectation of the level of service by the customers. There are signs that this is already taking place in service organizations like travel agencies, banks, and insurance companies.

1.5 Materials

The specification, procurement, and stocking of materials in service operations depends on the type of service business. In retailing this aspect forms a major area for the operations people in the business, whereas, in a professional service, materials form a very small part of the operations, being restricted to little more than office materials. The main considerations for materials as they influence quality assurance are that they should be specified in a manner which meets the quality requirements of the service package and that they are purchased from suppliers to meet these standards in the quantities ordered at specific delivery times – the whole process being carried out to minimize procurement costs.

2. QUALITY CONTROL IN SERVICES

The particular problem of quality control in service operations can be summarized as:

(a) The subjective nature of the customers' perception of quality leads to:
    (i) Customer assessment of quality can be based on one or a small number of the many features of the service package.
    (ii) The rating of the service by customers will vary by individual.
    (iii) Quality is often judged in relation to price in the absence of more tangible factors.
(b) The presence of the customer in the production of the service package may lead to:

(i) Multiple contacts with different service contact people, resulting in a large number of elements of quality to be controlled.

(ii) Disruption of quality for other customers by a small number of untrained or unruly customers.

(iii) Difficulty in measurement.

(iv) Difficulty of correcting mistakes (rectification).

(c) The intangibility of the service encounter in the service package makes it difficult to set rigid standards (which may of themselves be undesirable from a consideration of the individuality of the perception of the service).

(d) The use of agents or subcontractors who are removed from the direct control of the service organization can make control difficult.

3. QUALITY CONTROL PROCEDURE

Any quality control system follows a number of basic steps:

(a) Define the stages in the service operation.

(b) Specification of:
  (i) Variables which can be measured.
  (ii) Attributes which permit classification against a standard or on a scale as 'good' or 'bad' with respect to:
    People
    Service process
    Facilities
    Physical items

(c) Set limits for the measurements.

(d) Measure and assess against standards.

(e) Provide corrective action if necessary.

3.1 Defining the Stages in the Service Operation

This may be carried out by creating a flow chart for the operation (see Chapter 2 on the design of service operations).

3.2 Specification of the Service Package and the subsequent Quality Control

This must link the customers' needs and the service package as expressed through advertising and the capabilities of the service-producing unit to deliver the service package. This is important as both of these aspects are brought together in the customers' perception of the service package when it is received (Figure 6.2).

Consideration of specification must relate to the price, to the customer of the service, and the cost of producing the service package. The relationship between price and service level is not well defined and the resolution for a particular service organization lies both with the marketing and the operations sides of the service business.

Figure 6.2 Service quality framework.
(Adapted from Sasser, Olsen, and Wyckoff, 1978)

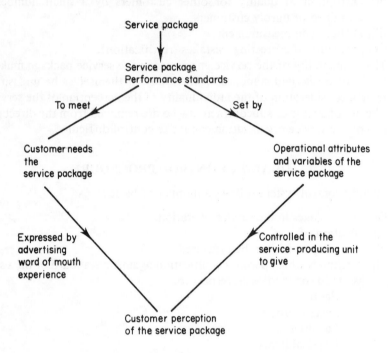

The expectation and perception of a consumer will be influenced by the price of the service. A customer for a high-priced package holiday to a tropical island may feel dissatisfied with a poor-quality hotel, whereas the passenger travelling on a cheap 'bucket-shop' ticket has little expectation of comfort and is concerned only with safe arrival at the destination. The matching of service level and price is obviously one of the main concerns of the process of marketing services. The important consideration is to keep a match between the service level and quality and that achievable from the service-producing unit.

The specification of the service package can best be considered in two parts, relating to the *physical items* and the *service intangible elements*.

3.2.1 The Physical Items

Physical items can be defined in terms of variables such as size and weight or of attributes such as taste or sound. Physical items are associated both with items which are directly part of what is bought by the customer and those which form other parts of the service environment (e.g. seating and decorations). It is generally easier to specify for the physical items in the service package.

3.2.2   The Service Elements

The service elements of the service package are more difficult to specify and to define because of the intangible nature and subjective assessment. We can split the service elements into service attributes (soft measures) and service variables (hard measures). Although good service may easily be recognized (at least within one cultural group) it is not so easy to identify precisely the factors or the reasons. Consequently, much of the specification for the service content of the service package is in terms of attributes rather than variables. Some service attributes and variables are:

Service attributes

(a) Advice/diagnosis, which are part of any service encounter.
(b) Attitudes relating to the behaviour of the service contract people to the customers (friendly, helpful, rude, officious).
(c) Security relating to the customer or things belonging to the customer.
(d) Accessibility, which may be in terms of geography (i.e. the customer is close to the service operation or the ease of reaching it by transport).
(e) Environment of the service encounter (cleanliness, decoration, level of sound/lighting).
(f) Consistency of the service from one encounter to another.
(g) Breadth of the service package relating to the number of complementary services which are offered (station car parking, food on a train, swimming pool in a hotel).
(h) Timing (psychological) relating to the perceived time waiting for the service and for the service to be performed.
(i) Control of the service encounter by the customer. This may relate to the degree of choice offered to the customer.

Service variables

(a) Timing (actual) of the time to respond to a call for the service and for the service to be performed.
(b) Availability of the service in periods of time.

A specific example of 'hard' and 'soft' measures is given in Chapter 7 on field service.

The details of both parts of the service package may be recorded in written specifications. The physical items may have specifications much as would be found in a manufacturing operation. The service aspects, on the other hand, are more likely to be specified by a procedure to be followed by the service personnel. In many cases a service business will choose to inform customers of the procedures, at least in outline if not in detail. They may form part of the advertising literature used by a company, as, for example, some car rental organizations.

Some organizations, in attempting to produce a consistent service encounter, produce detailed procedures for the encounters. The degree to which this is desirable or possible depends to some extent on the predictability of the service encounter with the customer. Thus selling tickets is likely to be more predictable than dealing with complaints about the travel service.

3.3 Measurement and Assessment

The ease or difficulty of making measurements and assessments of the variables and attributes associated with a particular service package in part mirror the problems encountered in setting the specifications. However, there are other constraints:

(a) The presence of the customer/client makes the 'front office' measurement more difficult than the 'back room' measurement.
(b) The service encounter is more difficult to measure than the physical items in the service package because of its intangible nature.
(c) Measurement often needs to be made away from the service operation centre. This is the case for field services and transport operations.

The ease of making measurements of the service package vary considerably according to whether they are associated with the physical items or the service encounter and whether they are made in the 'front office' or the 'back room' (see Figure 6.3).

Figure 6.3   Ease of measurement of quality and the measurer

* Telephone: Mail Contact

	'Front office'	'Back room'
Service encounter	High contact Difficulty: High Measurer: Customer Service person	Low contact * Difficulty: Medium Measurer: Customer Service person
Physical items	Difficulty: Medium Measurer: Customer Service person	Difficulty: Low Measurer: Service person

3.3.1 Physical Items

Physical items fall into a number of different categories:

(a) Physical items bought from a supplier, when the service operation will often rely on the measurement and quality control of the original manufacturer or supplier with occasional subjective checks.
(b) Physical items made by the service operation predominantly involve food or equipment being repaired. While it is possible to employ manufacturing quality control methods of sampling and control charts, in all but large service operations measurement takes the form of subjective estimates and checks that set procedures have been adhered to.
(c) Physical items which are part of the service environment are usually assessed by subjective estimates against standards and checks for procedures being followed (e.g. cleaning).
(d) Physical items which are part of the customer are a special case where measurements must take place with the customer's participation, although the customer or client may not be party to knowing how a measurement is being made or assessed (this is particularly true for medical services).

3.3.2 The Service Encounter

The quality of the service encounter is difficult to measure, as for the most part it relies on a subjective assessment by both the service person and the customer, and these may not correspond. If the service encounter is highly proceduralized, an inspection of the records or the use of a checklist may be used to ensure that all parts of the procedure have been carried out. Service operations employ both random inspection and more continuous inspection and supervision.

The measurement of the quality of the service package can be carried out and reported both by those who are part of the service operation and from outside:

(a) *Within the service operation*
    (i) Inspection and recording by service personnel using log books and other records or by following a procedural checklist for checking and inspecting (particularly common in repair operations)
    (ii) Continuous assessment of the service personnel and other aspects of the service package by supervisors
    (iii) Routine or spot inspections by supervisors
    (iv) Use of visiting inspectors who may pose as customers (sometimes called 'mystery shoppers')

(b) *Outside the service operation*
    (i) Measurement and reporting by customers through:
        (1) Immediate verbal and non-verbal feedback to the service contact personnel
        (2) Complaints, either verbal or written, to the service operations management

(3) Customer surveys asked for by the service organization
(ii) Measurements by consumer associations who may or may not report to the service organization directly

3.4 Corrective Action in the Quality Control Process

In the areas of the service where the customer participates it is very difficult to make good any shortfall in standards without the customer being aware of them. This is not the case in those areas where the customer does not participate directly, although in some service operations (notably catering) there is a constraint of limited time for making good any faults.

If the customer must participate in the correction of errors, the manner in which a service organization deals with this event becomes of itself a further indication to the customer of the quality of the service. The service operations manager has to rely heavily on the skill of the service personnel for this process, which may be developed through training. Some service organizations choose to have separate people to make good any mistakes; such people may be employed at a higher level in the service organization to increase the customers' perception of status.

As correction is often difficult because of the participation of the customer (even if a fault is detected with the problems associated with measurement), service operations managers must often take actions such as paying compensation or offering alternative service at some time in the future. As the effect of this policy on the perception of the customer is difficult to establish, most service operations must try to pursue pro-active policies to prevent or minimize the occurrence of faults in the service quality. These are all the actions associated with quality assurance.

4. AN EXAMPLE OF QUALITY CONTROL IN A SERVICE ORGANIZATION

The varied nature of the quality control process in a service operation is illustrated in the following example.

Education Service – A Department in a Polytechnic

It is difficult to establish a single customer for the education service; it could be considered to be the student, a future employer, parents, or society at large. It is not surprising that a number of different elements are employed in the quality control process shown below.

(a) *Quality of the institution*
  (i) The Council for National Academic Awards (CNAA) makes a five-yearly review.

(ii) Her Majesty's Inspectorate makes recommendations to the Department of Education and Science as the result of inspections.

(b) *Quality of the awards*
   (i) External examiners (vetting of staff and staff activities).
   (ii) External examinations (where the courses are for external bodies).

(c) *Quality of the course*
   Course management teams are responsible for day-to-day quality and for reports to the validating body for the awards (CNAA).

(d) *Quality of teaching*
   The only formal control relates to the number of hours a member of staff teaches, and infrequent HMI assessments. Informally, year tutors' reports of student interviews and student replies to any questionnaires may be seen as attempts at quality measures.

(e) *Quality of intake of students*
   The use of past examination results is common, although there is much debate as to whether they are a good guide to the 'quality' of students for courses. Thus polytechnics frequently use interviews and other tests as a further indication of quality.

The quality of the system in the end may well rest in the perception of the students, who for the most part wish to enhance their career expectations, and the perception of employers, who wish to enhance the operation of their organizations.

5. CONCLUSION

Quality management and quality assurance in service operations is particularly difficult. The quality control process alone is hindered by the special constraints of having the customers or clients participating in the production of the service at some point and the intangible and subjective nature of the service encounter with the customer. The setting of standards for the service and communicating them to the customer present problems for the service operations manager. If there is a greater customer expectation of the quality of the service package than the perception at the time of consumption there is the likelihood of dissatisfaction.

The difficulties of setting standards for the service encounter are further exacerbated by difficulties in measurement and correction of faults without the customer being aware of the shortcomings. Satisfaction for the customer and success for the service operations management only result from a close attention to all aspects of the quality assurance of the service package; in achieving this objective, training, supervision, and organizational commitment to maintaining quality standards are all important. Example of issues in quality management can be found in the North West Gas field quality control and Wimpy (B) cases which follow Chapter 7.

148

REFERENCES

British Standards Institute (1979). *British Standard 4778*, British Standards Institute, London.

Cuthbert, G. (1983). How British Airways is climbing out of its corporate turbulence, *Achievement*, June **1983**.

Hostage, G.M. (1975). Quality control in service businesses, *Harvard Business Review*, July–August **1975**.

Morris, B., and Johnston, R. (1983). *Perspectives on Process in Service Industries*, workshop on Service Operations, Manchester Polytechnic.

Sasser, W.E., Olsen, R.P., and Wyckoff, D.D. (1978). *Management of Service Operations*, Allyn and Bacon, Boston.

Chapter 7

Field Service Management

C.A. Voss

Field service is the function concerned with the servicing and maintainance, by the manufacturer or supplier, of products (usually owned by customers, hence often called 'after-sales service') used away from the manufacturer's or supplier's site. It is of particular interest as it is usually a function within a larger organization that does not consider itself part of a service industry. It is effectively a service organization within a manufacturing industry. Because of this its role is frequently misunderstood.

1. THE CHANGING ROLE OF FIELD SERVICE

The traditional view of field service is that it is an internal function whose responsibility is to provide adequate service at minimum cost. If we view field service as a service business in the fullest sense we can envisage four new roles for field service: competitiveness, profit, sales support, and user base support. Let us examine these in turn.

1.1 Competitiveness

The basic hypothesis for using service in a competitive role is that in many industries buyers will buy from company X because their after-sales service is better than company Y.

There are a number of areas where we might expect this to occur:

(a) Where products are becoming more homogeneous. In these markets service differentiation can provide a serious competitive strength and an attractive alternative to price competition.
(b) Where good service provides real value to the customer. In particular, where the cost of down time to the customer is high, strength of service will be important.
(c) Where life cycle costs or costs of ownership are important. In many products the impact of new technology has been to reduce the cost of the product but to increase the cost of servicing it. In such cases customers will pay much more attention to the cost of service as part of its total life cycle costs.

(d) Where systems rather than products are sold. In these cases a major role of service is to prevent the customer becoming dissatisfied with the system, so as to keep him/her locked into the original supplier and to prevent switching to other suppliers. In particular, this allows suppliers to guard against 'leapfrogging'. Leapfrogging occurs when a competitor introduces a technically superior product and there is a delay before the company can catch up or leapfrog itself. During this delay, service-based competition is an effective way to keep customers locked into the company's products in the short term.

Over time these factors are making customers more service aware and more sophisticated in their purchasing. In response to this, service-based competition is developing in many markets.

1.2 Profit

The second major role of service is profit. In many product areas new technology and international competition has led to increasing pressure on product costs and on margins. The product homogeneity mentioned in the previous section often leaves little alternative. On the other hand, if service can be differentiated, it can lead to the opportunity of charging a premium price for good service. Secondly, the intensity of competition in field service is not as great as in products (even though in most industries, if service or spares prices are too high, competitive forces will work to bring in third party suppliers of service and spares). This emphasizes the profit opportunities.

As products move towards a pattern where cost of ownership is important, pricing becomes an important cross-functional consideration. Product/service pricing must be considered as a package to maximize total profit of the company, not just product profit.

The final consideration in the consideration of the profit potential is the cost structure of field service. Field service is:

(a) Labour intensive
(b) Travel intensive

In most high technology firms, it is probably the most labour-intensive part of the company's operations. This provides considerable leverage for good management. Labour and travel intensity provide those able to manage these areas well and achieve high productivity with the opportunity to provide the same level of service as their competitors at lower cost and thus increasing profitability.

1.3 Sales Support

In most organizations where field service is an important part of their activities, an examination will show that the number of calls made by the field service organization is orders of magnitude greater than those made by the sales force. For example, the British Gas Corporation makes an estimated 14 million service calls a year and virtually no sales calls. There are clear opportunities for utilizing these service calls to increase sales.

These opportunities are reinforced by a number of trends. In many markets there is an increasing rate of product change requiring more frequent customer contact. Field selling, on the other hand, is labour and travel intensive and becoming much more expensive relative to product costs. If field service calls are 'free', how can we best use them? Experience in a number of companies has indicated that getting the field service force to sell is not usually successful. The selling task is very different from the servicing task (although many field service forces sell spares). In addition, in many organizations the service person does not meet the person making the buying decision.

Service people can, however, be used to support sales. This can take a number of forms. The service person can be used to gather intelligence about the customer's needs, so that a salesperson can be briefed. One step further is to train the service person in the application of other products. (Contrary to expectations, service people often know little about applications.) The service person can then generate customer interest in other products as well as generating sales leads.

A number of companies support this strategy with incentives for sales leads based on eventual sales made. In one office machinery company, 27 per cent of sales resulted from leads from the service force.

Involving service in the selling function raises some interesting organizational issues. The field service force deals only with the 'user base', the existing customers of the organization, whereas the sales force sells to non-users as well as users. An examination will reveal that there are significantly different tasks in selling to new customers than in selling to existing customers. This leads to the concept of user base organization. A user base organization will have, under the same management, the field service operation and a sales force selling to existing users, a separate organization being responsible for selling to new customers.

1.4 User Base Support

Having bought a product, a user may need a considerable degree of support. Support includes providing suitable documentation, training of the user, supply of consumables, help with applications, etc. (In some organizations where the use of consumables is high, suppliers sometimes offer free service and support if enough consumables are purchased.) Recognizing that customers require support throughout the life cycle of the product can often change the way in which the service delivery system is designed and service sold. For example, rather than selling after-sales service in the form of a service contract, a support agreement can be sold.

A support agreement will include in a single contract all the elements of service *and* support that the customer will require over the life cycle of use. Often this will build into the contract many things that would normally be given away free.

2. FIELD SERVICE PERFORMANCE

Field service performance can conveniently be divided into three parts: 'hard' performance, 'soft' performance, and cost.

2.1 Hard Performance

The customer using a machine wants to have his machine running for the maximum amount of time and down as little as possible. The percentage of planned time that the machine is running can be called the availability. There are a number of elements that go into availability. Firstly there is the reliability of the machine. The more reliable the machine, the higher the availability. A simple measure of reliability of a machine is the mean time between failure (MTBF).

There are a number of determinants of MTBF. The first is the design of the machine. The quality of the design and the trade-offs made in design can play a major part in determining the MTBF. For example, it is possible to design 'redundancy' so that if one part of the system breaks down, through duplicates or alternatives, the total system will still function. The second determinant is the quality of manufacturing. Many of the sources of breakdown can arise from faults in manufacturing. The final determinant of the MTBF is the quality of the maintenance and repair. For example, a good service representative will not just repair a fault, but will fix the cause of the fault and take steps to prevent future faults occurring.

The second element of availability is response time: the time between the machine going down and the arrival of the service representative. Breakdowns are in effect random events and queuing theory, described later in the book, tells us that to get a faster response time, we must put in more resources. The higher the level of resources, the greater the response time and the lower the percentage of utilization of those resources. Determining the appropriate balance between resource level and response time is one of the main policy decisions in field service.

There are many other factors that affect the response time and the cost of meeting it. These include the siting of service offices and service representatives (e.g. an on-site service representative can give very fast response), the management information system supporting despatching, the communications systems, and the diagnostic systems (e.g. a good diagnostic system can enable a service representative to be despatched before breakdown occurs).

The final element of the MTBF is repair time. A fast repair time is a function of the availability of spare parts and the efficiency with which the repair process is designed and performed. Experience has indicated that customers tend to associate fast response time, rather than fast repair time, with good service.

2.2 Soft Performance

In addition to the hard elements of performance, a customer's *perception* of the service level can be strongly influenced by the soft elements.

These cover every element of the contact between the customer and service process. Examples include:

(a) The attitudes and appearance of the service representative
(b) The quality of the service documentation and training
(c) Proper cleaning up after repair
(d) Perceived completeness of repair
(e) Perceived efficiency of the company and service representative

It is very easy for a service representative to create a bad service image, for example, through blaming the customer, the product, the service organization, or the company for problems with the product. Proper selection and training is an essential element of delivering high levels of soft service.

For a given level of hard service, good soft service can often substantially increase the customer perception of service, both hard service and overall (and vice versa). It is often more cost effective to increase the soft service level than to increase the response time.

2.3 Cost

The 'value' of service to a customer is a combination of the level of service and its cost. We have already discussed one major determinant of cost, the response time—resource trade-off. There are other important elements of cost related to the labour and travel intensity of service. There are a number of areas of action which can reduce the number of service calls and travel, or make them more efficient and effective. These include:

2.3.1 Despatching and routing

The training and skills of the despatchers and the quality of the information available can lead to better routing of service representatives and hence less travel time.

2.3.2 Diagnosis

A substantial proportion of service calls are either spurious or can be repaired by the customer. If these can be detected before a service representative is despatched, substantial cost savings can be made. Customer training, machine diagnostics, and phone diagnosis by the despatcher can all contribute. In addition, good diagnosis can result in the appropriate resources being despatched.

Diagnosis is an important factor in determining the nature and competitiveness of service. The easier it is for customers to diagnose, the more likely they are to shop around for the cheapest source of repair and the more likely it is that companies specializing in pure service will develop.

2.3.3 Customer involvement

Customer involvement can reduce costs. The most significant impact on costs can be made by the customer bringing the item to be serviced to the supplier, instead of a service representative being sent out. In addition, getting the customer to do maintenance and repair can reduce service costs. The impact on revenue and profit will depend on the contractural basis under which service is performed. If it is done under service contract, then the profit impact of customer involvement will be great. If service revenue is derived on a per item basis, cost savings will be accompanied by some revenue loss.

2.3.4 MTBF reduction

The MTBF is the main determinant of both cost and down time. Reduction in failure rate can lead to major cost savings. The two major routes into this are product design and improved servicing. Both benefit by the availability of appropriate management information systems (MIS).

3. OTHER ISSUES IN FIELD SERVICE

3.1 Profit or Cost Centre

Most service organizations are businesses in their own right. Field service organizations, on the other hand, are generally part of a large organization selling goods and providing service. There are good arguments for and against letting field service be a business or a profit centre. The main argument against revolves around business or profit centre managers setting their own prices. Short-term profit maximization may result in high price levels. In some circumstances these may result in loss of product sales. If service prices are set 'from above', the service manager is implicitly reduced to a cost centre manager. It can be argued that profit centres are managed more effectively and with more entrepreneurship than cost centres. If prices are set outside the service organization, then a more appropriate form of organization may be the 'performance centre', where the organization develops specific quantified performance targets for the field service organization.

3.2 Coping with Adverse Situations

Much of the service task is routine and can be easily programmed. However, a certain proportion will involve adverse and unexpected situations, such as an irate customer's unexpected problems, etc. An analysis of adverse situations (or 'war' stories from service representatives) will usually indicate that many particular adverse situations occur frequently. Responses can be determined and proceduralized. If a service situation involves a significant level of unexpected, and hence difficult to programme, adverse situations, then the response may be to recruit people who have the education and/or ability to 'think on their feet' and respond appropriately.

3.3 Management Information Systems (MIS)

Field service is information intensive and MIS (computerized or not) have a major part in system design and operation. The main systems required are:

(a) *Repair feedback to engineering.* The feedback of data and breakdowns. These data can be used for product and process improvements, and cost estimating.
(b) *Service person records.* Similar to the above but by a service person rather than a machine. The data can be used primarily for measuring a service person's performance.
(c) *Despatching support.* A despatching data base requires data on customers, their location, machinery and service history, the service representatives, the status of outstanding repairs.

In addition there will be appropriate cost accounting systems and inventory management systems.

3.4 Logistics and Materials

A major consideration in field service management is the development and movement of spares. Good management of logistics can have a major impact on cost through minimizing capital stock, profit through the ability to sell spare parts, and customer satisfaction through spare part availability.

The concepts of materials management will be covered in Chapter 9. In the field service context, particular attention should be paid to the chain of stocks. A big decision is in how to deploy spares between central warehouses, local stores, and parts in the service representative's van and parts on site. The availability of good MIS and good transportation can generally allow lower stock levels either through centralization to minimize duplication of stock or using decentralized stores effectively through cross-shopping.

4. CONCLUSION

Field service, although mainly part of a manufacturing or supply business, is an important service operation. Through its locus in manufacturing or supply, it has particular problems concerning the way it is organized. The following cases include examples drawn from field service in different contexts (North West Gas and Computer Technology Ltd.). These cases illustrate both the particular issues of field service as well as more general areas such as operation control.

ACKNOWLEDGEMENT

This chapter draws on work by Roddy Nicol. This contribution is gratefully acknowledged.

Case Study: North West Gas

FIELD SERVICE

Ronald Flynn is a District Service Officer responsible for one of the service depots of North West Gas. He has four supervisors working for him who look after a total of twelve service engineers and four apprentices (approximately one engineer for 1,000 consumers). Ronald reports to the District Service Manager who is also responsible for the activities of the Customer Service Section and the radio control serving more than 100,000 consumers.

The work carried out by the service engineers comes via three routes from the consumer: telephone calls, written requests, and orders from showrooms. A number of the service engineers are allocated to control from the radio room (the number varies according to the time of the year, with more being needed in the winter months).

The service depot manager and the supervisors work in close collaboration with the customer service section and the radio control. The supervisors prepare statements of the manpower availability which are sent to a programmer in the customer service department and the radio room (additional copies also go to wages, security, and other supervisors). The programmer receives the statements of manpower availability (Exhibit 1) fourteen days in advance and prepares jobs for each service engineer by the day. This work is usually of a servicing or installation nature, although it may include jobs which have arisen from a prior visit to a consumer from an engineer. The lists of jobs are sent to the appropriate supervisor for allocation to the engineers.

The service engineers who are allocated to the radio control room receive instructions of jobs via the radio which is installed in the service van. The work may be of an emergency leak of gas or it may involve service and maintenance jobs depending on the demand for high priority emergency work. Most of these jobs originate from direct calls to the telephone switchboard.

The scheduling of service engineers follows a five day week with cover given on Saturday by two to three engineers and on Sunday by one engineer. One service engineer is on call overnight (Exhibit 2).

This case was prepared by Colin G. Armistead. The information and the exhibits are included by permission of North West Gas.

Exhibit 1 Manpower Availability

NORTH WEST GAS

STOCKPORT SERVICE DEPARTMENT

BRAMHALL DEPOT

MANPOWER AVAILABILITY

SERVICE SUPERVISOR – M HART

STANDARD MINUTES (SMV's)

WEEK COMMENCING

CHESHIRE AREA

NAME	DESIGNATION	CALL SIGN	FLEET NO.	KIT	SUN	MON	TUES	WED	THUR	FRI	SAT	REMARKS
A Dove	SERV. TECH.	26	1756	18F	//////	8.15/445	8.15/445	//////	8.15/445	8.15/445	8.15/445	RADIO
F Herd	SERV. ENG.	25	3675	18F	//////	8.15/445	8.15/445	8.15/445	8.15/445	8.15/445	//////	RADIO
G Roy	" "				//////	C/HEATING					//////	C/HEATING
L Rix	" "	20	1875	18F	//////	8.15/445	8.15/445	8.15/445	8.15/445	8.15/445	//////	RADIO
E Angle	" "		142	18E	//////	400	400	400	400	400	//////	SERVICING
T Smith	" "		3370			400	400	400	400	400	//////	FITTING/SERVICING
F Rogers	" "		3618		//////	400	400	H	H	H	//////	S/R SERVICING
T Jakes	" "		3220		//////	H	H	400	400	400	//////	S/R SERVICING
C Flynne	" "		916?		//////	H		C/HEATING			//////	
F Wright	" "				//////	400	400	400	400	400	//////	SERVICING
H Long	" "				//////	400	H	400	400	400	//////	SERVICING
S Jones	" "				//////	H	C/HEATING	C/HEATING			//////	
G Barr	" "				//////	400	400	H	400	400	//////	
	" "											
	" "											
K Farmer	3rd YR.APP.				//////		ASSISTING				//////	
	2nd " "											

Exhibit 2   Weekly Standby Rota

NORTH WEST GAS			STOCKPORT		DEPOT					Week 3 CHESHIRE AREA		
WEEKLY STANDBY ROTA					WEEK COMMENCING							
NAME	SUN	MON	TUE	WED	THUR	FRI	SAT	FLEET NO.	CALL SIGN	KIT	VAC	MATE
T SMITH	8.15 to 7	11.15 to 10	11.15 to 10	11.30 to 10					32			
C FLYNNE		8.15 to 4.45	8.15 to 4.45	8.15 to 4.45	8.15 to 4.45	8.15 to 4.45			05			
G BARR		8.15 to 4.45	8.15 to 4.45		8.15 to 4.45	8.15 to 4.45	8.15 to 4.45		02			
H LONG		8.15 to 4.45	8.15 to 4.45	8.15 to 4.45	8.15 to 4.45	8.15 to 4.45			03			
R JONES		10.15 to 7	10.15 to 7	10.15 to 7	10.15 to 7	10.15 to 7						
T PARKS		8.15 to 4.45	8.15 to 4.45	8.15 to 4.45	8.15 to 4.45	8.15 to 4.45			12			
F ROGERS				8.15 to 7	11.30 to 10	11.15 to 10	11.15 to 10		25			
G ROY		8.15 to 4.45	8.15 to 4.45	8.15 to 4.45	8.15 to 4.45	8.15 to 4.45			04			
F WRIGHT		8.15 to 4.45	8.15 to 4.45	8.15 to 4.45	8.15 to 4.45	8.15 to 4.45			32			
M SHORT		10.15 to 7	8.15 to 4.45		8.15 to 4.45	8.15 to 4.45	8.15 to 4.45		30			
T JAKES		8.15 to 4.45	8.15 to 4.45	8.15 to 4.45 j	8.15 to 4.45	8.15 to 4.45						
F HERD		8.15 to 4.45	8.15 to 4.45	8.15 to 4.45	8.15 to 4.45	8.15 to 4.45						
		8.15 to 4.45	8.15 to 4.45	8.15 to 4.45	8.15 to 4.45	8.15 to 4.45						
		8.15 to 4.45	8.15 to 4.45	8.15 to 4.45	8.15 to 4.45	8.15 to 4.45						
		8.15 to 4.45	8.15 to 4.45	8.15 to 4.45	8.15 to 4.45	8.15 to 4.45						
		8.15 to 4.45	8.15 to 4.45	8.15 to 4.45	8.15 to 4.45	8.15 to 4.45						
		8.15 to 4.45	8.15 to 4.45	8.15 to 4.45	8.15 to 4.45	8.15 to 4.45						
		8.15 to 4.45	8.15 to 4.45	8.15 to 4.45	8.15 to 4.45	8.15 to 4.45						

AMENDMENTS   G BARR COVERED BY M SHORT MON/TUE

Each service engineer is allocated a service van which is equipped with special tools and a number of spares. The range of spares and tools in a van depend on the type of work being undertaken: either servicing or installation. The actual range of spares in a van is predetermined from the actual and forecast populations of the different applicances in the area. If an engineer is unable to complete a job because of lack of spares he has details of price and location of these on micro fiche in each van. The spares may be immediately available from the Depot stores or have to be obtained from the Central stores near Bolton. The service engineer completes the documentation to obtain the spares and returns this to the Depot. Also before leaving in cases where spares have to be obtained, the service engineer gives the customer a promise that the job will be completed within four days (not including Saturday or Sunday).

Some spares are 'one-time buys' consisting of obsolete spares and decorative fixings which have to be ordered specially from an outside supplier. Ronald says that these spares cause the main problems in maintaining a high level of customer service.

Ronald is concerned with the service standards of the depot and there is a competition organized within North West Gas which measures the performance of the different Depots from questionnaires sent to customers. Training is given to service engineers of the importance of the way in which work is carried out in a consumer's home. Standards Officers will make spot checks on the work being carried out by an engineer.

FIELD EMERGENCY SERVICE OPERATIONS CONTROL

Dorothy Gainsborough is the Customer Service Officer and Derek Brown a District Service Officer (Radio) in the Service Department of a District of North West Gas. The responsibility for the control of the emergency service operations rests with them and they work with three service depots run by District Service Officers who are responsible for the service engineers. Dorothy and Derek report to the District Service Manager who looks after the interests of over 100,000 consumers.

Dorothy's customer service section includes (a) a telephone bureau to receive calls from the public; (b) units which prepare work for those service engineers in the depots who are not controlled via the radio, and also order parts, bill customers, and deal with the organization of service contracts for central heating.

Work arrives at the Service Department via a number of routes:

1. Consumers calls through the telephone bureau
2. Instructions from showrooms (usually about new appliances)
3. Maintenance contracts (details are stored on a computer)

When calls are received by the telephone operators the operator makes an assessment of the priority of the call and fills in the appropriate record card (Exhibit 3).

Exhibit 3　Record Card

APP MADE FOR	PATCH	ADDRESS
TEL No.		MR MRS MISS

KEY ADDRESS

ACCOUNT ADDRESS

EXP. CODE	CUSTOMER'S ORDER NO.

BREAKDOWN ☐　SERVICE ☐　INSTALLATION ☐　J.V. _____

Description _____

C.H. ☐　Cooker ☐　Fire ☐　Water heater ☐　Meter ☐　Other ☐

Appliance Location _____

ON CONTRACT	THREE STAR ☐　TWO STAR ☐　ONE STAR ☐
FREE?	GUARANTEE _____
	CALLBACK　MONTH AND YEAR INSTALLED　A.O.F. NUMBER
	DATE OF LAST VISIT
	OTHER _____

OTHER INFORMATION

RECEIVED BY	TIME	DATE
ISSUED BY	TIME	DATE
ISSUED TO		J.V. No.

NORTH WEST GAS

P3 CONTROL CARD HQ752

Priority 1 (yellow)	Escapes of gas classed as controlled and uncontrolled
Priority 2 (white)	Breakdown of essential applicances like fires and cookers
Priority 3 (pink)	Maintenance and non-essential appliance breakdowns

Exhibit 3 (cont)

BE THERE BEFORE	PATCH	ADDRESS

TEL NO. | MR / MRS / MISS

KEY ADDRESS

ACCOUNT ADDRESS

EXP. CODE

WHERE IS THE ESCAPE? _____

OUTSIDE ☐

Is the exact location of escape known? YES ☐
Has the meter been turned off? YES ☐ → NO
Has this stopped gas leaking? YES ☐

CONTROLLED ☐ UNCONTROLLED ☐

WHEN was the escape first noticed? _____

WHO reported it? customer ☐ neighbour ☐ other ☐

Are neighbours affected? YES ☐ NO ☐

Are elderly or infirm people involved? YES ☐ NO ☐

Have you advised the customer to turn off at the meter, to put out naked lights, to ventilate the room, not to use electrics and that IMMEDIATE ACCESS IS REQUIRED? YES ☐ NO ☐

| OTHER EMERGENCY | fire ☐ fumes ☐ low pressure ☐ no gas ☐ |
| | explosion ☐ sootfall ☐ excess pressure ☐ coinfast ☐ |

OTHER INFORMATION

RECEIVED BY	TIME	DATE
ISSUED BY	TIME	DATE
ISSUED TO	J.V.	

P1 CONTROL CARD HQ 750

NORTH WEST GAS

Exhibit 3 (cont)

CONTROL
REFERENCE
NUMBER _____

REPORTED TO
DISTRIBUTION AT _____ A.M.   DISTRIBUTION   A.M.
P.M.   ARRIVED AT _____ P.M.

FIRST VISIT

Is the job complete?   YES ☐   A.M.
           NO ☐   Time of Arrival?   P.M.

Part ordered ☐   ORIGINAL
House closed ☐   J.V. No.
Further work ☐
Other _____

Follow up
J.V. No.

SECOND VISIT

ISSUED BY	TIME	DATE
ISSUED TO		J.V. No.

Is the job complete?   YES ☐   A.M.
           Time of Arrival?   P.M.
           NO ☐

Part ordered ☐
House closed ☐
Further work ☐
Other _____

THIRD VISIT — INFORM D.S.O. (RADIO)

ISSUED BY	TIME	DATE
ISSUED TO		J.V. No.

Is the job complete?   YES ☐   A.M.
           Time of Arrival?   P.M.
           NO ☐

Part ordered ☐
House closed ☐
Further work ☐
Other _____

Exhibit 4   Forecasting Sheet

NORTH WEST GAS   RETURN OF JOBS RECEIVED   DATE <u>28 6 83</u>
HIGH PEAK   AND OF JOBS FORECAST

P1 REC'D	FORECAST TILL 5PM AT 10 11 12 1 2 3 4 AM AM AM PM PM PM PM	P2 REC'D	FORECAST TILL 5PM AT 10 11 12 1 2 3 4 AM AM AM PM PM PM PM		P3 FOR TODAY
XXX	10 5 3 2 1 1	XXX	6 3 3 2 1 1	///	XXX
XXX	20 10 6 4 3 2 1	XXX	12 6 4 3 3 2 1	///	XXX
XXX	30 15 9 6 4 2 1	XXX	17 9 6 5 4 3 1	///	XXX
XXX	(40) 20 12 8 5 3 1	XXX	23 12 8 6 5 3 1	///	XXX
XXX	50 (24) 15 10 7 4 2	XXX	29 15 10 8 6 4 2	///	XXX
XXX	60 29 18 12 8 5 2	XXX	(35) 18 12 10 8 5 2	///	XXX
XXX	70 34 (21)(14) 9 6 2	XXX	41 21 14 11 9 6 2	///	X//
XXX	80 39 24 16 11 6 3	XXX	47 24 16 13 10 7 3	///	///
XXX	90 44 27 18 (12) 7 3	XXX	52 27 18 15 12 8 3	///	///
XXX	100 49 30 20 13 8 3	XXX	58 (30) 20 16 13 8 3	///	///
XXX	110 54 33 22 15 (9)(4)	XXX	64 33 (22)(18) 14 9 4	///	///
///	121 59 36 24 16 10 4	XXX	70 36 24 19 15 10 4	///	///
///	131 64 39 26 18 10 4	XXX	76 39 26 21 (17) 11 4	///	///
///	141 69 42 28 19 11 5	XXX	82 42 28 23 18 (12) 5	///	7//
///	151 73 45 30 20 12 5	XXX	87 45 30 24 19 13 (5)	///	///
///	161 78 48 32 22 13 5	XX/	93 48 22 26 21 14 5	///	///
///	171 83 51 34 23 14 6	///	99 51 34 27 22 14 6	///	///
///	88 54 36 24 14 6	///	105 54 36 29 23 15 6	///	///
///	93 57 38 26 16 6	///	111 57 38 31 24 16 6	///	///
///	98 60 40 27 16 7	///	116 60 40 33 26 17 7	///	///
/////	106 65 43 29 17 7	/////	65 43 35 28 18 7	/////	/////
/////	114 70 47 31 19 8	/////	70 47 38 30 20 8	/////	/////
/////	122 75 50 34 20 8	/////	75 50 40 32 21 8	/////	/////
/////	131 80 53 36 21 9	/////	80 53 43 34 23 9	/////	/////
/////	139 85 57 38 23 9	/////	85 57 46 36 24 9	/////	/////
/////	90 60 40 24 10	/////	90 60 48 39 25 10	/////	/////
/////	95 63 43 25 11	/////	95 63 51 41 27 11	/////	/////
/////	100 67 45 27 11	/////	100 67 54 43 28 11	/////	/////
/////	105 70 47 28 12	/////	105 70 57 45 30 12	/////	/////
/////	110 73 49 29 12	/////	110 73 59 47 31 12	/////	/////
/////	77 53 31 13	/////	77 62 49 32 13	/////	/////
/////	80 54 32 13	/////	80 65 51 34 13	/////	/////
/////	83 56 33 14	/////	83 67 54 35 14	/////	/////
/////	87 58 35 14	/////	87 70 56 37 14	/////	/////
/////	90 61 36 15	/////	90 73 58 38 15	/////	/////
/////	63 37 16	/////	75 60 39 16	/////	/////
/////	65 39 16	/////	78 62 41 16	/////	/////
/////	67 40 17	/////	64 42 17	/////	/////
/////	70 41 17	/////	66 44 17	/////	/////
/////	43 18	/////	69 45 18	/////	/////
/////	44 18	/////	47 18	/////	
/////	45 19	/////	48 19	/////	
/////	47 19	/////	49 19	/////	
/////	48 20	/////	20	/////	
/////	21	/////	21	/////	
/////	21	/////	21	/////	
/////	22	/////	22	/////	

At the time of the call the operator checks the general availability for priority 1 and priority 2 from a board set in front of the operators (the board is updated by the radio room people). Also at the time of the call the operator may give advice to the customer ('turn off at the mains') or in non-urgent cases give details of the various services offered by North West Gas (e.g. service contracts).

The cards from the telephone operators are placed on a conveyor which passes into the Radio Room which is managed by Derek. Here the cards are handled by an 'allocator' who sits next to the radio operator. The allocator checks the assessment of the priority and decides which service engineer should be given the work. In the case of priority 1 work there are standard response times of one hour for uncontrolled leaks and two hours for controlled leaks and so the allocator will select engineers who are close to the incident. The lower priority work is programmed after the priority 1 and priority 2 jobs.

The allocator has a guide to the level of expected work from a forecast sheet (Exhibit 4) and the number of men available (each expected to complete on average ten jobs in one day on emergency work). For example, by 10 a.m. the forecast division of work is forty priority 1, thirty-five priority 2, and twenty-five priority 3 for ten men working. The allocator places the cards in racks against the different service engineers and the radio operator instructs the engineers of the work to be carried out and receives information from them (e.g. further assistance, order spares). The racks (or boards) for the next day are set up with lower priority work. The units in the customer service section have a programmer who prepares work for service engineers who are not given their work via the radio. This work relates to fitting of new appliances, central heating maintenance contracts, and the fitting of parts which were not available at the time of a first visit by an engineer. The programmer deals with the maintenance contracts.

FIELD SERVICE QUALITY CONTROL

Fred Winterbottom is a Standards Officer with North West Gas in the Cheshire Area and is attached to a section in the Head Office although he works from one of the District Offices. There are a large number of standards which the Board applies to keep to a given level of service (e.g. Exhibit 5).

Fred and his assistant are responsible for monitoring the work of the customer service department, the service depots, and the radio control room. Much of what they do is concerned with making spot checks of work being carried out in a consumer's home. They will visit and check that the work has been carried out to the set standards and that the customer is satisfied with the performance of the engineer. If faults are found they are reported to various levels of service management on a duplicate form (Exhibit 6) which also states the actions required.

There is an awareness among the service management of the importance of maintaining standards for the service level, and the Standards Officers, while

Exhibit 5   Service Standards

 Customer Contact

1.1.   Telephone Contacts

1.1.1.   Published Telephone Numbers:

a) All Post Office telephone directories will contain a display advertisement of customer contact numbers.

b) Cross reference will direct the customer to the "GAS" display. For example, in the Yellow Pages section, in alphabetical section "G" and regional letter section.

i) GAS - For Service and Enquiries see opposite/following page(s).

ii) "BRITISH GAS CORPORATION" - see "GAS"

iii) "SCOTTISH GAS" - see "GAS"

Telephone numbers which are not specifically for customer use should be omitted from the "GAS" section and display.

1.1.2.   Levels of Service:

a) Customers will not be expected to pay more than the cost of a local call to contact the Region by telephone. However, Regions may publish an alternative, non-local number in support of a Freefone number, where used.

b) Advertised contact numbers should not change for "out of hours". Even if the reception location has to change it should be effected by switching to ensure that, as far as the customer is concerned, the same number applies at all times.

c) Customers should normally receive at least a one-in-twenty five grade of service when calling British Gas.

d) Where Regions use a "Gas-Escape-Only" facility, it must be installed with a separately published number which gives priority on the answering position to escape calls.

e) Having been connected to British Gas and received the ringing tone, customers should not have to wait more than 30 seconds to be answered.

f) Customer Service calls should ring out on a bureau or answering position and not be routed via a switchboard unless the call is to be dealt with there, i.e. in very small units. (The customer should not be kept waiting for more than 15 seconds after being transferred from the initial point of contact.)

1.2.   Other Contact Facilities

1.2.1.   Showroom and Office Addresses.

A list of showrooms and local office addresses may be printed in the appropriate telephone directories on the "GAS" display page.

1.2.2.   Competence of Reception Staff:

Any customer contacting British Gas for service or enquiries, whether in person (e.g. in a showroom) or by telephone, should only be dealt with by an adequately trained person.

1.2.3.   Advice on Reporting Gas Escapes:

a) Meter Notices
All gas meters will have the standard notice concerning gas escapes as defined in the Gas Safety Regulations, 1972.

b) Gas Accounts, etc.
Accounts will include the standard notice advising customers to contact their local office in the event of suspecting an escape of gas and will direct them to the telephone directory display under "G" -"GAS".

c) Showrooms and Offices
All Gas Showrooms and Offices where appropriate will display a notice visible from the street giving instructions to customers about reporting emergency situations. These notices should include the appropriate telephone number for the locality.

d) Public Utilities, Official Bodies, etc.
Arrangements should be made to give direct exchange line numbers to the Police and Fire Service by which they can contact Customer Service in the event of difficulty in making contact by normal published numbers. These arrangements should be regularly tested and annually confirmed.

 Appointments and notification of planned date of visit

2.1.   Generally an appointment should be agreed with the customer for all visits for customer service work, including regular servicing, surveying and calls by supervisors. Where this is not appropriate, customers will be notified of the planned date of visit.

2.2.   Generally an appointment should be agreed with the customer for all deliveries of appliances, materials and spare parts requiring access. Where this is not appropriate, customers will be notified of the planned date of visit.

2.3.   The starting date for all work should be on an AM/PM basis where requested.

 Speed of service

3.1.   General Note

The work delays mentioned here are expressed in working days and are not fixed lead-times. In the case of Gas Escapes and other Emergency work they represent a *minimum standard*: in all other cases they represent the target standard that Regions should be able to offer the customer. The best Customer Service would enable the receptionist to say ". . . when would it be convenient to call" and to be able to comply within the speed of service standards.

See also Section 4.2. for Speed of Supply -Appliance Spare Parts.

3.2.   Gas Escapes and Other Emergency Work

Resources must be provided to enable Regions to attend reported gas escapes or similar hazardous situations as follows:—

a) to visit all uncontrolled escapes within 60 minutes;

b) to visit all controlled escapes within 2 hours.

3.3.   Escape Follow-up

If there is only time for "make-safe" at the first escape visit, follow-up work will be carried out at least to the standards that apply to the appropriate type of work to restore the service, e.g. depending on whether the service provided is impaired or failed.

Exhibit 5 (cont)

3.4. On-demand Breakdown

3.4.1. Contract Customers:

In the case of central heating customers with a regular servicing agreement, Regions should be able to provide same day attention on all calls received up to 19.30 hours.

3.4.2. Non-Contract Customers:

In the event of the total breakdown of an essential appliance (i.e. a major appliance for which the customer has no reasonable alternative) or a central heating appliance not on regular servicing, Regions should be able to attend on the same working day, provided the request is made before noon.

Where the appliance is still providing a service, though impaired, Regions should be able to attend in 2 working days, or later if requested by the customer.

3.5. On-demand Servicing

When a customer requests servicing, as opposed to asking for a repair, Regions should be able to offer a service for all appliances in 5 working days, or later if requested by the customer.

3.6. Appliance Fixing

Regions will maintain special fixing priorities for "no means of cooking", "no heat", etc.

Fixing of cookers, fires and refrigerators, when available from stock both to point and with additional supplies should be able to be done in 5 working days, or later if requested by the customer.

Other appliances with a longer constructional element (e.g. multi-points, circulators, wall heaters, etc.) should be able to be done in 10 working days, or later if requested by the customer.

For central heating the standard will be to start within 5 weeks of receiving a firm order, or later if requested by the customer and to complete the work within 5 days except on larger installations.

3.7. Inspection for Servicing Contracts

When a customer asks to join a servicing scheme for which an inspection is necessary, the inspection should be carried out in five working days or later if requested by the customer. Any subsequent rectification work should be able to be started in 5 or in 10 working days, depending on the complexity of the job.

◉ Appliance Spare Parts

For non current appliances, parts will be made available within the 3, 10 and 15 year rules agreed with the S.B.G.I., subject to agreements with the S.B.G.I. being honoured by all concerned. These standards apply to the following categories:—

a) All former British Gas/Gas Council Approved Appliances

b) Current Sales Listed Appliances

c) Appliances accepted for Regular Servicing.

In the case of BSI/QAC safety approved appliances not Sales Listed by BGC, Regions will endeavour to obtain spare parts at the specific request of the customer. Spare parts will not be obtained for any other appliances.

4.1. Appliance Spare Parts Availability

Regions should establish stock lines of appliance spare parts. As a minimum these must include:

a) any lines which move 6 or more times per annum, except where such demands are known to be transitory.

b) any lines likely to be needed to support comprehensive, regular servicing schemes.

c) "short list" and/or other selected parts for newly introduced stock-list appliances for which a demand of 6 or more per annum is anticipated.

Lists of stock parts should be published from time to time. Stock parts should normally be available off the shelf.

4.2. Speed of Supply

In this section "D" is defined as the day the requirement for a spare part is established. Any subsequent action including a follow-up call should be agreed with the customer. If this is not practical customers should be kept informed of developments.

a) Category One Spare Parts
These are defined as:-

i) Essential spare parts (i.e. parts required as the result of a total breakdown of an essential appliance);

ii) Short-list and/or other selected parts for appliances under warranty.

Regions should establish stocking arrangements and procedures that will enable:-
70% of Category 1 spare parts to be fitted on D or D + 1
90% of Category 1 spare parts to be fitted by D + 3.

If the part required is a non-stock item, the order should be given to the stores not later than the working day after the Service Engineer's visit and the order should be placed the same day.

b) Category Two Spare Parts

These are defined as: Non-essential spare parts and decorative parts. Regions should establish administrative arrangements and procedures that will enable non-essential stocked spare parts and decorative parts to be fitted by D + 10.

If the part required is a non-stock item, the order should be given to stores not later than the working day after the Service Engineer's visit and the order should be placed not later than the following working day.

c) Spare Parts Not Available

When a part is not in stock or is not on the standard list of parts and has to be ordered the customer will be informed and, where possible, given an estimate of the likely delay.

Exhibit 6   Service Inspection Report Form

MR/MRS/MISS		APPLIANCE	JOB No. _____
JOB ADDRESS_____		TYPE	A.O.F. ☐ E.S.V. ☐ I.O.F. ☐ M.J.V. ☐ 4 pt SERV. ☐ CNTR. MAINT. ☐
		MAKE	
		MODEL	
			SERVICE DISTRICT
REPORT_____			
			SERVICE UNIT
			Tradesman or Contractor
ACTION REQUIRED_____			SUPERVISOR
			WHEN REMEDIAL WORK HAS BEEN COMPLETED THIS FORM MUST BE RETURNED WITH JOB VOUCHER TO SERVICE STANDARDS DEPT.
Materials Required	Qty	Materials Required	Qty
SIGNED:- STANDARDS INSPECTOR	DATE:		DISTRICT SERVICE OFFICERS COPY

not being welcomed by the service engineers, are more than tolerated and action reports of faults are usually acted on.

Some indication of the breadth of the work carried out by Fred is a non-exhaustive list of areas which are covered in inspections:

(a) Work of the customer service section units in progressing jobs, ordering parts, and handling telephone calls from consumers
(b) Work of the service engineers including payment of bonuses
(c) Store movements
(d) Assembly of applicances
(e) Testing of the competence of apprentices
(f) Compilation of service performance records for depots

Exhibit 6 (cont)   Bonus Adjustment Form

BONUS ADJUSTMENT

NORTH WEST GAS

HQ 824

Area

District

Customers Name _____

Address _____

_____

Fitter/Estimator

Fitter

Maintenance Man

Payroll No.

Faulty Work

_____
_____
_____
_____
_____
_____

DEDUCT	S.M.V.	S.Ms	Job Constant	S.Ms	Total	S.Ms

Originated by   Date   /   /

Deducted by   Bonus Clerk Date   /   /

Case Study: Operations Control for Emergency Services in Greater Manchester

INTRODUCTION

Greater Manchester is a Metropolitan County in the North West of England. It covers an area of about 500 square miles stretching from the Pennine Hills to the Lancashire plain. The County includes densely populated urban areas and less populated rural countryside. The total population is about 2.7 million. The County includes the city of Manchester and a number of surrounding large towns; there are large petrochemical and other industrial complexes and an international airport within the boundaries.

The case presents the operations control arrangements for the emergency services of Police, Fire, and Ambulance. At the time the case was written these services were in various stages of implementing computer systems to assist them in the operations control activity. The case is not intended to be used to decide which is the best system, but rather to illustrate how services which operate in similar areas to preserve lives and property have evolved different systems which take account of their special needs and duties.

I am grateful for the assistance given to me in the preparation of the case by the Greater Manchester Police, the Greater Manchester Fire Service, and the Manchester Metropolitan Ambulance Service, and for their permission to use the material in the case.

AMBULANCE SERVICE

Introduction

The Greater Manchester Ambulance Service is divided into three Divisions, 'A', 'B', and 'C'. The three Divisions have their own control and the three are linked by private telephone lines. Resources may be transferred between Divisions for emergencies but not for other work. The case describes the divisional control which covers the City centre as part of its area. The control was not computer assisted at the time the case was prepared but plans were being made for the introduction of a computer system.

This case has been prepared by Colin G. Armistead.

Activities

The work of the ambulance service is split into four types for the Division:

(a) *Emergency cases* (approximately 3,600 to 4,000 cases/month) are those which require immediate attention (traffic accident, maternity cases, household and industrial accidents). The target times for dealing with emergency cases are:
> *Activation* (i.e. time from receipt of the call until vehicle moving to the incident), 3 minutes
> *Response time* (i.e. time from receipt of the call to arrival at the incident), 7 to 14 minutes

(b) *Urgent cases* (approximately 1,000 to 1,500 cases/month) are those which require action within one to two hours with the facility to amend (e.g. the transfer of a patient from one hospital to another). The distinction between emergency and urgent cases is not always clear-cut and although there is guidance from the DHSS a great reliance is placed on the experience of the control personnel.

(c) *Special planned cases* (approximately 1,700 to 2,000 cases/month) are those cases where a patient has to be at a hospital at a specific time (e.g. for treatments using barium meals or radioactive isotopes).

(d) *Planned cases* (approximately 25,000 to 30,000 cases/month) include general outpatient cases, day cases where a patient is going for a minor operation on the same day, and rehabilitation cases.

Operations Control

The operations control is divided into three main areas:

(a) A planning section which prepares a Journey Schedule Sheet for each ambulance crew including day care and planned cases. Gaps are left to accommodate emergency and urgent cases as they arise.

(b) A Control Room staffed by Control Room Assistants who receive calls into the operations control.

(c) An Operations Room staffed by Controllers who maintain radio contact with the ambulance crews. There are two radio channels during the day and one for the night. During the day the resources they control are about forty ambulances and thirty-five dual-purpose vehicles (used mainly for the planned services activities) and at night about fifteen vehicles. There are also about ten vehicles on standby at the ambulance stations in the Division.

Activation of Ambulances

The processing of calls from outside and the activation of ambulances or dual-purpose vehicles is a two-stage activity. Calls are received by Control Room

Assistants (CRAs) and the messages are passed to the Controllers in an adjacent but separate operations room.

Calls arrive on:

(a) Emergency lines – British Telecom '999'
(b) Direct lines to the airport
(c) Direct lines to the Police and Fire Services
(d) Direct lines to the other ambulance divisional controls
(e) Lines to Ambulance Liaison Officers at the major hospitals
(f) Lines for general calls (used for planned cases)

Emergency calls

The CRA takes the call from the British Telecom operator: in most cases the BT operator will say 'I have a call from . . .' and give a telephone number; in others the caller comes direct to the CRA (about 20 per cent of 999 calls). The CRA asks the caller for details of what has happened, where, how many people are involved. (At this point the CRA may stop the caller if it is clearly not an emergency: e.g. people using the 999 line to try to alter an appointment for a hospital.)

If the incident happened some time ago (e.g. a fall in the last twenty-four hours) the CRA may advise the caller that the operations people may not send an ambulance immediately but the CRA continues to take details on the emergency line.

The CRA records the details on a pink form: time of the call/date/caller's name/telephone number/location of the incident/nature of the incident. All 999 line calls are also recorded on tape. The CRA puts the pink form onto a conveyor which carries it into the operations room, although if the case is clearly a matter of life and death the CRA takes the form directly.

The CRA attempts to obtain additional information from the caller which may help the ambulance crew. This is written on a message form and passed on to the operations room. Sometimes the caller may become abusive during questioning and the CRA may pass the call to the Control Room Supervisor or the appropriate Shift Superintendent. The CRA may give the caller advice like not to move the patient.

Operations Room

In the operations room there are two controllers and a superintendent for each radio channel. The controllers are in radio contact with the vehicles. The pink emergency form is taken by the controllers or superintendent and a decision made whether to continue to treat the request as an emergency or to downgrade it to an urgent case (examples might be a tight plaster making toes turn blue or an accident which happened twenty-four hours ago); approximately 10 per cent of calls are downgraded in this way.

The controllers take the pink form and look at their Journey Schedule Sheets, called 'running sheets', to see where vehicles are located and contact the nearest vehicle. This may be a vehicle which is on duty or it may be on standby at an ambulance station. The controller contacts the crew by radio (if the ambulance is away from a station), by direct line to an ambulance station, or by a general call to 'any vehicle in the area'.

At the same time the superintendent decides whether to inform other services like Fire and Police.

At the same time the controller continues to update information on the pink form: 'Time passed to vehicle', 'Method of contact', 'Location of vehicle', 'Call sign of the vehicle', 'Time of arrival at the incident', 'Time of departure from the incident', 'Time of arrival at the hospital'.

The ambulance crews make the decision as to which hospital to take a patient. At times when they are not dealing with emergencies the controllers continue to schedule work to the ambulance crews, updating the 'running sheets' and adding other jobs which were not available when the sheet was originally compiled in the Planning Section, and filling times which were left to cover emergency work if these are not needed.

The pink emergency forms are checked once every twenty-four hours to establish that the target times for the activation and response times are being met.

POLICE SERVICE

Introduction

The Greater Manchester Police Force is divided into 14 Divisions and thirty-two SubDivisions. There is a single Force Control Room and separate Divisional Control Rooms. Resources may be transferred between Divisions. At the time the case was written GMP were in the middle of a programme stretching over several years to introduce computer-assisted policing. The case describes the activities of the Force Control and a Divisional Control.

The Force Control

The Force Control accepts all of the 999 calls from British Telecom and controls directly the traffic and motorway patrols and relays requests for assistance to the Divisional Control Rooms. The level of calls is 1,000 to 1,500 per day (although this may rise in severe weather conditions to about 2,000).

The Force Control receives calls from a number of sources on emergency lines:

(a) British Telecom 999 lines
(b) Direct lines from the airport
(c) Direct lines from the Fire and Ambulance Services

(d) Direct lines from high-risk places like the Prison, the Bank of England, and the North West Regional Water Authority

(e) Alarm companies either by automatic dialling of '999' or by a call from the alarm company in response to an alarm sounding in their control

The calls are taken by an operator who takes details from the caller and records on a message pad: time/date/name of caller/telephone number/address/nature of the incident. (A tape recording is made of all calls.) The operator decides on the response which may be:

(a) To refer the caller to a police station

(b) Pass the request for assistance to the appropriate Divisional Control for response some time in the future (e.g. a burglary which has been committed some time ago so there is little chance of catching the criminals near the scene of the crime)

(c) Pass the request to the Divisional Control for immediate response (e.g. a burglary where the criminals have been disturbed by someone who has made a report to the Police)

(d) Despatch a car to back up the divisional response to the action resulting from (c)

(e) Despatch a car or cars without alerting the Division

The choice is at the discretion of the operator to make the most appropriate response. There are no target times for response, only that it should be as quick as possible (response times are measured). Also there is no way of judging which of the incoming '999' calls is the most important and should be given the highest priority.

The operator may advise the caller on what to do (e.g. 'don't touch anything or tidy up' after a burglary) or seek further information about the incident (e.g. the description of people who were committing a crime). The operator is able to give this information to a Division and/or a traffic car crew.

Despatch of a patrol car to an incident is assisted by an up-date computer system which shows the status of all the cars (over 300 in the Force) and the availability of each car and the manning level. The traffic cars are regarded as the Force's most immediate response to any incident. The operator maintains radio contact with the cars and may answer requests for information from the officers in the cars. It is not always possible to give sensitive information over the radio because of the lack of security. Such information is transmitted to the car's base station by teleprinter or telephone line for collection by the crew. Information may be taken from the Police National Computer at Hendon via a separate terminal in the Force Control Room (vehicle owners, stolen vehicles, missing persons).

A separate section in the Force Control looks after the policing of the motorways in the Greater Manchester Area. There is a radio control to the motorway traffic police and calls from the motorway telephone are taken in the section. There are links with the Automobile Association to give assistance to motorists who have broken down.

The motorway control section also controls the traffic signs on those sections of the motorway which is fitted with them. The operators have a model of the motorway system on the wall with lights to indicate the operation of various signs.

Divisional Control

The Divisional Control maintains a contact with the Force Control by direct telephone lines and by teleprinter. The Divisional Control looks after the police officers on the beats and the cars and vans used by the Division.

Calls come to the Divisional Control from the Force Control and from telephone calls direct to the Division. The contact to the police officers is through personal radios and radios in the cars and vans. When a call is received the operator takes details on an incident form in the same manner as in the Force Control. The aim is to have a complete record of the incident in terms of the time to respond, the nature of the incident, and the action taken. Copies of the incident form are kept as records and they are also used in compiling statistics.

The Divisional Control also have a terminal to access the Police National Computer which allows a rapid check on vehicles (a process which previously could take several days using manual systems).

The Control have a duty board which shows the officers who are on duty at any particular time with the individual officer's call sign.

FIRE SERVICE

Introduction

Greater Manchester Fire Service has forty-one Fire Stations divided into five Divisions with sixty-eight pumping appliances and about thirty-four special appliances ranging from hydraulic platforms to a decontamination unit. There are some 2,000 full-time officers and firefighters. All the Divisions are controlled from a single purpose-built Control Room which became operational at the end of the 1970s with a computer-assisted mobilization system and the virtual elimination of manual recording.

Mobilization Activity

Targets

The targets for mobilization are for a turnout from a fire station within one minute from receipt of the call. Arrival at the incident within an 'A' risk area is two applicances within five minutes and one appliance in eight minutes and one appliance within five minutes and one appliance within eight minutes for a 'B' risk area.

Attendance times are further reduced for incidents in areas with a lower risk categorization.

Calls

About 55,000 calls are received by the Fire Service each year; of these approximately 60 per cent are fire incidents, 20 per cent are false alarms, and the remainder are requests for special services, e.g. persons trapped in lifts, flooded premises, etc.

Calls are received into the Control Room via a number of routes:

(a) British Telecom '999' lines
(b) Direct lines from high-risk premises (airport, hospitals, chemical factories, etc.)
(c) Direct lines from the Police and Ambulance Service Control Rooms

Each emergency call to the Control Room is taken by one of the mobilizing operators and monitored by another. The operator is alerted by a flashing light on a console and the call is normally taken within thirty seconds. The procedure adopted by the operator is as follows:

(a) Type details of the telephone number of the caller, the address of the incident, and details of the incident on to the Visual Display Unit (VDU).
(b) When the computer accepts the address, it displays on the VDU:
   (i)   The map reference of the incident
   (ii) The Division in which the incident is located
   (iii) The predetermined attendance for the address
   (iv) The time of the call
   (v) A unique serial number of the call
   (vi) Position in the Control Room where the call is taken
   (vii)First attendance resource display showing the nearest seventeen pumping appliances and three special appliances for the incident

Mobilizing

So long as the computer does not inform the operator that it is a repeat call for an incident already being attended the operator commences mobilization.

The operator checks the first attendance resource display and mobilizes the nearest available appliances. The selected appliances are mobilized by keying in their call signs and the fire station is alerted by the sounding of an alarm in the station and the teleprinting of messages for the appliances attending giving details of the incident. (The firefighters take this with them in the vehicle.) If the call is not acknowledged by the fire station an alert is received on the operator's VDU screen in the Control Room. The operator then checks to ensure the appliances have responded to the incident. This is done by referring to the large special display map which shows all the fire stations and lights for each appliance which indicates their state of availability.

The operator will at the same time contact other public services who may be required at the incident, like the Police and the Ambulance Service, and mobilize the necessary fire officer(s) to attend the incident.

The operator maintains a 'status' radio contact with the appliances and fire officers as they proceed to the incident. At the incident both appliances and officers are in radio contact with the operator and they may request additional resources or information (e.g. on chemical hazards). The operator obtains information of this type directly onto the VDU from the computer.

The operator continues to update the log of the incident in the computer until the incident is closed.

The senior control officer in the Control Room is able to monitor all calls and also have access to a printed record of all calls.

A typical mobilization would be:

(a) A house fire: two appliances with an officer
(b) A house fire where persons are known to be trapped: three appliances and a senior officer

Large-scale fires

The first problem is that with large fires a large number of people report the fire and may not be exactly sure where it is as large fires can be seen from a distance. The large number of calls tend to block the telephone lines and make it necessary to check that all callers are reporting the same fire. If this cannot be verified with the caller then appliances are mobilized to check. As the appliances are mobilized from the various stations the operators mobilize standby appliances into those stations to maintain cover at each station. If, exceptionally, the resources of GMFS are not adequate to cope with the scale of the incident, resources may be requested from Fire Brigades in the surrounding areas on a prearranged basis.

Case Study: Computer Technology Limited (A)

In August 1982, Andrew Knight, the newly appointed Customer Services Manager, was considering the challenge of improving what the company felt was an excellent customer services operation. The company felt that it provided high levels of service to its customers in a number of dimensions and that this was a major asset in marketing its products. In the 1981 Datapro Research Corporation 'British User Rating of Computer Systems' CTL had ranked first (out of twenty-eight minicomputer companies) in 'overall statisfaction' and reliability of mainframe. (The full results are shown in Exhibit 1.)

BACKGROUND

Computer Technology Limited (CTL) was founded in 1966 when a group of talented computer design engineers got together to produce one of the world's first 16-bit minicomputers.

All in all, 25 per cent of CTL's product line changed from year to year, but because this was an evolving rather than a dramatic process it was difficult to follow in detail. Software was upgraded bit by bit and the odd extra circuits were added to the hardware to provide additional features.

CTL had recently started to act as a hardware distributor by marketing Convergent Technology's hardware to software houses (CT was a microcomputer manufacturer). With computer hardware rapidly getting physically smaller, microcomputers were starting to compete with the smaller minicomputer applications. At the same time, CTL's minicomputers were starting to compete with the smaller mainframe machines. The deal with Convergent Technology was a strategic move to give CTL continuing business from the smaller end of the market which it would have otherwise lost.

Although the only British minicomputer manufacturer, CTL found that it was competing with about eighty companies in the same business. It regarded IBM, ICL, Hewlett Packard, Data General, Digital Equipment Company,

This case has been researched and written by Mark Law under the direction of Chris Voss, London Business School. It is not meant to illustrate good or bad management practice. Some figures and names have been disguised.

Exhibit 1   CTL's Ranking in the Datapro 1981 British User Survey (1980 figures in brackets) on minicomputers and small business systems

	CTL Rank out of 28 (36) companies		Series 8000 Rank out of 54 models
Overall satisfaction	1st	(12)	3rd
Reliability of mainframe	1st	(22)	3rd
Ease of program conversion	2nd	(14)	3rd
Maintenance effectiveness	2nd	(23)	5th
System response times	3rd	(19)	5th
Early deliveries	4th	(—)	7th
Easy system expansion	5th	(25)	10th
Productivity aids	6th	(3)	7th
Ease of programming	7th	(27)	14th
Operating system	7th	(28)	20th
Compilers	7th	(4)	14th
Troubleshooting	8th	(28)	19th
Education	8th	(9)	18th
Applications S/W	9th	(29)	25th
Documentation	22nd	(21)	47th

Note
Datapro Survey with 5,000 questionnaires to a random selection of *Computer Weekly* readers resulted in 645 user responses on 840 Mini and SBC systems in 1981.

Burroughs, Honeywell, Wang, Tandem, and Systime as it main competitors. They felt that CTL's machines were technically second to none and were well backed up by its service operations, but because of the sheer number of competitors, they found it difficult to get the message across to potential customers.

Cash flows from the minicomputer business came from two main sources:

(a) The new system revenues from the hardware and software
(b) The on-going revenues which were made up by the maintenance contract and system upgrades, both hardware and software

Roger Fulton, the Marketing Support Manager, estimated that a typical customer paid £100,000 front end cost for a minicomputer system that lasted between five and ten years. The maintenance contract cost £12,000 p.a. Finally, the customer generally required his system to be upgraded as he realized further application of benefit. This could cost him a further £100,000 over the next three years and on average £10,000 p.a. thereafter.

Roger felt that CTL regarded its main strengths in the business as the high quality and efficiency of its Customer Services Division. He felt its main weaknesses were:

(a) Potential customers had a low awareness of CTL's products and services.
(b) The company had difficulty in getting shortlisted for tendering with so many other competitors in the business.

THE CUSTOMER SERVICES DIVISION

The Customer Services Division (CSD) was responsible for the installation and maintenance of CTL's computer systems along with organizing all the backup facilities they required. There were 250 systems in the field under service contracts, of which 130 were Modular One systems and the remaining 120 were PM80 systems. This proportion was changing all the time as the older systems were being phased out.

The division was run as a profit centre and carried out the pre-installation planning, installation, and after-sales support in the field. In practice, much of their work consisted of attending to customers' calls when they had problems. Although mainly a UK company, CTL had several systems installed in France, Holland, and Switzerland, along with the trained staff to maintain them.

Exhibit 2   The Customer Services Division

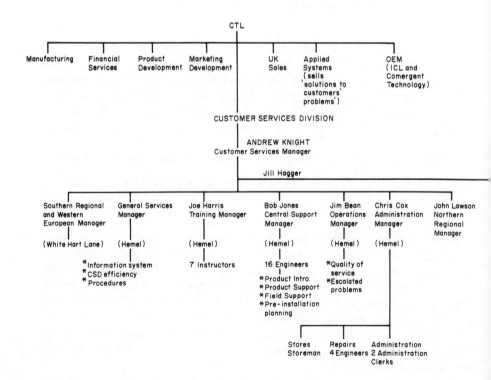

The total revenues and costs of the division over the previous several years were:

Date	Total revenues, £m	Total direct costs, £m
1982/3	2.87	2.32
1981/2	2.19	1.96
1980/1	1.97	1.76

The division had eighty-four field service engineers and forty-one support staff and technicians operating from fifteen sales and service area locations throughout the United Kingdom (Exhibit 2). These area offices were run from and were backed up by the two regional offices in Manchester and London.

Selling Service

Normally CTL sold customers one of its regular maintenance contract plans (Exhibit 3). These specified the response times to customer calls, the amount of planned maintenance, and the availability (serviceability) of the machines.

Andrew Knight tried to insist that customers got the service they paid for — no more, no less. This prevented them trading down in the expectation that their level of service would not change. He expressed this service policy during the various meetings he held with his managers.

Normally several companies were invited to tender for installing a new system. The hardware and software maintenance part of the tender was prepared by the salesman in consultation with the Central Support Manager. The maintenance contract was prepared by the General Services Manager. All

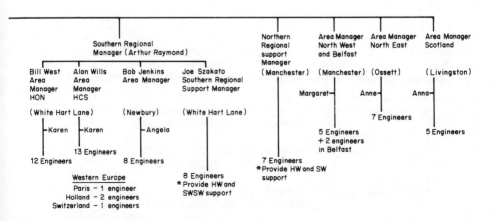

Exhibit 3   Service plans

Service plans currently in operation

PLAN 1	Dedicated site engineers, and spares holding
PLAN 2	Weekly PM* visits; availability target 92 per cent
PLAN 2a	Four-weekly PM visits; availability target 95 per cent
PLAN 3	Lowest level offered. Quarterly PM visits; lowest priority of response to fault calls (same day service)
COMMERCIAL PLAN	All attempts at two hour response. PM at agreed times/intervals up to one week; extra on-call service on request

Service plans for future systems

| COMMERCIAL PLAN | All attempts at two hour response. PM at agreed times/intervals up to one week; extra on-call service on request |
| BASIC PLAN | Quarterly PM visits. All efforts to respond to fault calls within twenty-four hours; additional on-call service on request |

* PM = planned maintenance

sales included maintenance contracts. Renewable one year maintenance contracts were normal, but in some cases were negotiated for up to seven years. Customers were given a choice of service levels; obviously the more comprehensive the service cover, the more expensive it was. Maintenance contracts were worded so that the company was not obliged to maintain obsolete equipment.

Quotes often needed to be structured to meet the potential customer's capital budgeting system. For example, many managers found it easier to get approval for capital projects rather than the on-going spending required for maintenance contracts. This clearly affected the sort of tender that could be approved.

Exhibit 4   System down Escalation procedure

These procedures will apply to those customers who have a commercial contract.

(a) *Escalation levels*
1.   Regional Support Manager and Area Manager produce plan
                    Arbitrator – Regional Manager
2.   *Regional Manager*
     Regional Manager and Operations Manager produce plan
                    Arbitrator – CSD Manager
3.   *CSD Manager*
     CSD Manager and necessary managers produce plan
                    Arbitrator – Managing Director

(b) *Automatic escalation by time*

Elapsed hours	Critical site	Non-critical site
0	Level 1	
1		
2		
3	Level 2	
4		Level 1
5	Level 3	
6		Level 2
7		
8		Level 3

(c) *Real time default escalation*

1645	Level 2
0900	Level 3

(d) *Overnight working*
Work will continue during the night on those faults reported by commercial customers prior to 1600.

(e) *Critical Sites*
Sites are designated critical when either their current downtime or number of system incidents reaches a level where further occurrences are likely to cause a breach of contractual commitment. In figures this becomes 2½ per cent downtime or greater and one system incident or more during a four week period (assuming a 40 hours week, 2½ per cent equals 4 hours). Downtime on commercial sites must therefore always be available in the area office on a rolling four week basis.

(f) *Interface to customers*
Irrespective of the level that escalation has reached, the interface to the customer will remain with the Area Manager.

(g) *Status information*
Status will be issued at 0915 to JJ, RAF, and Sales Manager and will consist of the following:

1. Any commercial contract that reported a fault prior to 1300 the previous day
2. Any system fault that has been outstanding more than eight working hours
3. Any critical site that has a problem which is likely to take cumulative downtime or incidents beyond contractual commitment
4. Political problems as decided by Regional Managers

(h) *Variations*
Where contracts stipulate conditions different to 95 per cent availability, and no more than two system incidents per rolling four week period or the contract includes liquidated damages, it will be necessary to devise definitions of criticality and escalation levels bearing in mind the need for the escalation level to be at level 3 no later than the point at which we have run out of time.

This will be the responsibility of the Regional Manager and must be approved by the CSD Manager.

Service Organization

Andrew Knight estimated the total number of service engineers and technicians needed in the field and their deployment using the rule of thumb of one service engineer or technician for every £50,000 of service revenue (varying slightly depending on an area's geography). (See Exhibit 2.)

Area offices, although sometimes in the same buillding, had their own staff of technicians and service engineers. They also had access to a stock of spares as well as a range of test equipment for modules and printed circuit boards. Faulty printed circuit boards were sent back to the factory in Hemel Hempstead. The area offices also had an operational backup computer which could be exchanged with a customer's if the latter broke down.

Procedures

One of the key elements in CTL's service performance was the use of its 'Escalation' procedure, whose objective was to achieve minimum customer downtime at the lowest possible cost to itself. When a fault occurred the service engineer tried to fix it for the first three hours. If he did not succeed he had to call the Area Manager at base and the service 'Escalated' to the next level when the regional people came on site. If they did not succeed the product development people were called in along with a Systems Designer. The final level in theory ended up with the arrival of the Managing Director. The Escalation procedure is described more fully in Exhibit 4.

Although in practice the current customer call procedure worked fairly smoothly, the Customer Services Division occasionally had problems if the customer directly called Bob Finch, CTL's Managing Director. When the routine was broken like this, with Bob calling up the various experts and not going through channels, all the normal paper work was bypassed, making it difficult to find out what was happening at the time, and, after the event, what had happened.

Interface with other functions

Andrew felt that it was vital that the Customer Services Division was in intimate contact with product developments that were taking place. Each step in the development of new systems had important consequences on future servicing costs. As the company's income came from both supplying the system and selling maintenance service contracts, corners cut on the initial cost could have made it very expensive to service. The Central Support Manager was personally responsible for this function. Andrew had the power to veto any project he considered to be uncommercially maintainable.

CTL also faced the problem of the blurred division between the maintenance and sales support functions that the Customer Services Division carried out. In the maintenance function the Division acted as a 'Mr. Fix-It'. The sales support function of the Division was more of a sales task, where the customer's hand was held if there were any problems when the system was being installed.

MANAGEMENT INFORMATION, REPORTING, AND CONTROL SYSTEMS

Each area produced a four weekly period report. This summarized both technical problems and the income received during the period.

These reports went to the Regional Manager who analysed his areas' performances. These reports were then passed on to Jim Bean, the Operations Manager, who summarized them, giving him a complete picture of the company's service performance from both financial and quality measures. Andrew summarized the information and presented it at the end of the month to the Managing Director.

Equipment performance was monitored by area, region, and customer. Service response, repair times, and fault frequencies were recorded for each item of equipment. Mean Time Between Failure and Mean Time to Repair were periodically evaluated in a 'Spread Report' to detect variances in performance. These details of in-service reliability were then fed back to the Quality, Design, and Manufacturing Departments, for use in upgrading the reliability of present and future products. They were also used to make sure that bought-in peripherals were performing up to standard.

In addition Jim Bean prepared a Daily Status Report (Exhibit 5). This kept top management posted on current escalated problems and any other serious situations.

From time to time, top management would take the initiative and run a survey on the customers to evaluate all aspects of CTL's products. This survey was not regularly done and in the view of some managers resulted in disturbing the customers. A customer could not really be expected to say nothing was wrong when confronted by a senior CTL manager. The smallest faults were brought up which resulted in middle management being harassed and the customer being increasingly aware of small but inevitable imperfections in his system.

HARDWARE RELIABILITY AND FIELD SERVICE PERFORMANCE

CTL's products were very reliable. Before any system was assembled, key components were 'burnt-in' to provoke premature failures which might otherwise have occurred on site. The same was done for bought-in peripherals. In recent years there had been a 50 per cent increase in system reliability. Typical hardware reliability figures are shown in Exhibit 6.

In period 6, 1982, the Home Counties North area's average response time for all customer calls was 2.18 hours and its average repair time was 2.07 hours. In many cases the system did not completely break down, so that the downtime was the time the service engineer switched the machine off to repair it. For the above period the average downtime per call was 0.75 hours for all calls.

Exhibit 5   Sample Daily Status Report

<table>
<tr><td>Escalation levels</td><td align="right">6th July, 1982
Issued by J. Bean</td></tr>
<tr><td>1.   Area Manager</td><td align="right">CSD Operations Manager</td></tr>
<tr><td>2.   Regional/Operations Manager</td><td></td></tr>
<tr><td>3.   CSD Manager</td><td></td></tr>
</table>

Systems Down Situations

SITE AND AREA: HRM Ltd   ESCALATION LEVEL: 2

DATE FAULT REPORTED 1.7.82   AGREED FIX DATE: P4W2

DATE ESCALATED TO PRESENT LEVEL: 1.7.82

PROBLEM: Parity error on MMD disc, cannot be recovered except at OTL

EFFECT ON CUSTOMER: SYSTEM DOWN!

ACTION: Disc removed from site on FRIDAY 2.7.82.
           Disc will be fixed at OTL on MON 5.7.82. and returned to site same day.

DISC RE-INSTALLED-CLEARED FROM STATUS.

SITE AND AREA: J. Belkington Ltd.   ESCALATION LEVEL: 2

DATE REPORTED: 10.6.82.   AGREED FIX DATE: P4W4

DATE ESCALATED TO PRESENT LEVEL: 10.6.82

PROBLEM: Last byte of header causing problems

ACTION: Central Support investigating tape from customer.
           Additional information from customer is being investigated at Hemel by
           Central Supprt.

SITE AND AREA: CSD SPARES   ESCALATION LEVEL: 2

DATE REPORTED: JUNE 82   AGREED FIX DATE: NOT KNOWN

DATE ESCALATED TO PRESENT LEVEL: 1.7.82

PROBLEM: 4 out of 5 300Mb discs held as spares are unservicable all due to the
           same PCB having the same fault.

EFFECT ON CUSTOMER: No customer affected now, but the next fault will create
           problems.

ACTION: Central Support investigating

POLITICAL SITUATIONS

SITE AND AREA: HMGI   ESCALATION LEVEL: 2

DATE FAULT REPORTED: 26.5.82   AGREED FIX DATE: P4

DATE ESCALATED TO PRESENT LEVEL: 26.5.82

PROBLEM: Faults in peripheral microcode as follows:
           1. INVERSE VIDEO ON VDUs
           2. PRINTER CORRUPTION WHEN USING 2 PRINTERS

EFFECT ON CUSTOMER: NOT KNOWN

ACTION: 1. New issue of microcode being tested at WHL.
2. Loaned hardware fitted to Design System.
   Problem being progressed.

New Issue of microcode tested at WHL successfully will be issued with printer fix when it is available.
Printed fix tested at WHL on Friday 25.6.82, awaiting results.
Customer has experienced INVERSE VIDEO on THURSDAY 1.7.82.

Exhibit 6   Equipment reliability: Mean time between failure*

CTL-produced hardware:

Central processing unit	16,000 hours
Bus controller	40,000 hours
Disc controller	25,000 hours
Communications card	40,000 hours
Peripheral controller card	57,000 hours
Power supplies	100,000 hours
Memory	25,000 hours

Bought-in peripherals:

Visual display units	6,000 hours
Magnetic tape units	2,500 hours
Exchangeable disc drive units	4,000 hours
Fixed disc drive units	8,000 hours
Printers	2,000 hours

* These are mean figures; the actual distribution of failures was very skewed for certain components. Some would fail in a short period of time, while others seemed to go on for ever. There were also occasional problems with batches of faulty semiconductors, resulting in high failure rates until they were all replaced.

NEW APPROACHES

Three different approaches to field service were being experimented with: 'self-diagnosis', 'resilient computers', and 'remote diagnostics'.

'Self-diagnosis' techniques were already being used but could be extended and made more sophisticated. In their then current form the customer ran a 'Test' programme before calling CTL with a fault. The results of this could be used to help decide what was wrong and what sort of repair would be necessary. On arrival at the site the service engineer ran a set of more sophisticated programmes to pin down the fault further. These techniques concentrated on CTL-made hardware, rather than peripheral problems, though the latter were a greater source of failure.

A 'resilient' system was one that had redundant components in it, e.g. an extra processing unit. When one of these failed the computer automatically switched over to the other. It then told the operator that something was amiss, but not to worry because it would be fixed next time routine maintenance was carried out.

'Remote diagnostics' involved line connection between field sites and one central service centre. If a customer's machine broke down, he phoned the site and put the computer on line. Service experts at the centre extracted information over the line and diagnosed what was wrong – software or hardware. In many cases software faults could be fixed over the phone, otherwise a service engineer would be sent along. These systems could also work by a central diagnostic computer connecting automatically with each computer in the field at regular intervals to get a status report on each. Many problems could then be recognized and cured before the customer even noticed them.

Although one of their competitors, DEC, had installed such a system (at reputedly vast expense) to enable them to perform remote hardware diagnosis, CTL were yet to be convinced that this was necessary.

One future problem faced by the company was how to keep its service operations tangible to the customer and yet still justify a profitable maintenance contract if their system hardly ever needed maintenance. Many customers only felt that they were getting their money's worth if they saw service engineers regularly doing something.

THE MANAGING DIRECTOR'S VIEW

Bob Finch, the Managing Director, had stated publicly that CTL's overall objective was 'Profitable Customer Satisfaction'. He felt that the Customer Service Division's objective should be the same.

Service and the Market Place

Bob Finch felt that good customer service was vitally important. Their customers were drawn from second and third time users, many of whom had had bad experiences with previous suppliers. He felt that many customers had specifically switched to CTL for better service. The changing nature of the market place also led to increasing importance of customer service. He felt that with more and more suppliers, hardware and software was increasingly becoming similar and that service would be more of a discriminator. In addition CTL typically kept its customers for over ten years, and in the long term customer service was particularly important. He stated that the availability of different service plans were a 'tremendous sales aid' to his salesmen.

Measuring Service Performance

When asked how he judged the performance of CSD Bob Finch replied that he had three methods. The first was the monthly report that he received from

CSD. He felt that this gave useful information though he treated the figures with care as they could be 'fiddled underneath'. His second method was 'keeping his nose in the market place'. 'I always know when customer service is bad. I have usually met at least one person (usually a senior executive) in each client. They phone me if anything goes wrong.' He only recalled having received four such calls in the previous year. In addition he found that managers from other functions came to him if there were problems such as poor service affecting sales.

Finally he received the daily status report. 'I therefore know if a machine is unrepaired at the end of the day and I know of any "political" problems. I want to know about any problems before I get phoned by a customer.'

Issues facing CSO

Bob Finch was concerned that the profitability of CTL, in particular CSD, was going to be squeezed in the future. Many customers were beginning to make a more thorough analysis of their computing costs. In particular, the government had introduced 'cost of ownership' approaches in evaluating computing procurement. This was putting considerable pressure on service pricing. Bob was worried about service productivity. There were about fifty direct (not on customer site) service engineers answering 300 customer fault calls per month. Even allowing for preventive maintenance, training, and travel, this seemed to him to be a poor ratio. Part of this was due to deliberate policy maintaining a reserve of maintenance engineers to cope with the expected expansion of ITL and NTL.

Bob was concerned about how much change could or should be accomplished with the present service group culture. The CSD was mature and stable and it was difficult to introduce change. For example, in April 1980 he had stated that it was the company's policy to exchange ten skilled service engineers for ten technicians by April 1982. He felt that it had taken six months for CSD to get to grips with the policy and they had not fully implemented it.

Case Study: Computer Technology Limited (B)

The customer service division of Computer Technology Limited was responsible for maintenance and service of customer's computers in the field. The division was divided into a number of areas.

'There's no substitute for local knowledge', said Bill West, the Area Manager. 'We cover the area from North London to the borders of East Anglia.' A large map with coloured pins sticking out of it emphasized his point. After London, Cambridge had the most pins, the rest of them being fairly evenly dispersed. Red pins signified Modular One systems, blue pins PM80s, and the green pins were where the Service Engineers lived.

Bill told the casewriter, when he was about half-way through counting them, that there were forty-eight sites altogether, thirty-five of them having PM80s while the remaining thirteen were Modular One systems. He also said that there were six service engineers and three technicians employed within the area.

FIELD OPERATIONS

Telephone Reception and Base Administration

The base in White Hart Lane, North London, had most of the features of the company's service operations. On one site there were two area offices, Home Counties North and South, together serving the East Anglia area. There was also the London Region Office which provided administrative and technical backup, mainly software.

Anne, the telephone receptionist, was the nerve centre of the whole operation there. She ran the administration of the base and was the customer's initial contact with the company.

Anne handled hardware faults and software enquiries while passing complaints and queries on to the Area Manager concerned with them. She dealt

This case has been researched and written by Mark Law under the direction of Chris Voss, London Business School. It is not meant to illustrate good or bad management practice. Some figures and names have been disguised.

with any miscellaneous calls by passing them on to the person she thought best
suited to deal with them.

When a customer called to report a fault, she logged the call on the service
request log (Exhibit 1) and then looked at the notice board to see which engineer
was available. She then radiopaged him. He phoned her back to find out which
customer had called and roughly what sort of fault had been reported. He then
'phoned the customer to find out exactly what had gone wrong and asked him
to do some tests on the computer. From 5 to 10 per cent of the time the problem
was solved over the 'phone, but more normally he had to visit the customer with
the spare parts he thought necessary. On arrival at the customer he called Anne;
who then entered the time on the service request log.

When he had fixed the fault he called her back to clear the log. He then filled
out a field visit report, a copy of which he left on site in the machine log book.
The other copies of this were then brought back to Bill who passed them on to
Jim Bean, the Operations Manager, who would put them in his product records
to work out the MTBF, investigate any recurring problems, and provide feedback to CTL's peripheral suppliers.

Normally each engineer was assigned eight specific customers. He then built
up a working relationship with them. In spite of this, full records had to be kept
on each site so that if another engineer had to fix a fault there, he knew exactly
what had happened to that computer system. Service engineers worked from
home and tended to cover the area nearby. This enabled them to get on site
quickly. If parts were required a service technician brought them along.

The Home Counties North area office had between 80 and 100 hardware
faults calls per four week period, with an annual service contract income of
£½million p.a. One of its service engineers was permanently on site in Hemel
Hempstead where CTL had four computers in operations, three in design, one
in sales, as well as about 130 VDUs and numerous printers.

Over the five periods from 10th February 1982 to 22nd July 1982 there were
466 calls which were distributed as follows:

Fault calls per day	Total number of days during the 5 periods with this number of calls per day
0	5
1	8
2	18
3	22
4	16
5	17
6	13
7	13
8	6

Exhibit 1 Service Request Log

AREA CODE __66__   PERIOD __4__

SERVICE REQUEST LOG

FAULT NO.	SITE NAME	PLAN	FAULT DESCRIPTION	CALL RECEIVED DATE	CALL RECEIVED TIME	ASSIGNED TO	ARRIVED ON SITE DATE	ARRIVED ON SITE TIME	COMPLETED DATE	COMPLETED TIME	NO. OF Visits	NO. OF Reports	SUPPORT Req'd	SUPPORT Logged	SUPPORT Final Report		RESPONSE TIME	REPAIR TIME	DOWN TIME	SPARES WAIT TIME
4/1	BLC	C	Floppy drive, 2 files not copying properly	28/6/82	9.3	Chris	28/6/82	9.5	28/6/82	10.0	1	1				PM	0.2	0.5	–	–
4/2	BLC Wishts	C	VDU s/spare – no response	28/6/82	9.3	Chis	28/6/82	11.0	28/6/82	12.2	1	1				PM	2.7	0.2	–	\
4/3	System B	1	Unable to access dual drives	28/6/82	9.3	Nigel	28/6/82	10	29/6/82	13.0	2	2				PM	–	8.5	11.2	–
4/4	AMV	C	Printer hammer	28/6/82	9.0	Steve	28/6/82	9.5	29/6/82	12.5	1	1				PM	0.5	3.0	–	\
5/5	Asat	3	Floppy disc drive	28/9/82	12.5	Nigel	28/6/82	15.0	7/7/82	11.5	2	2				UM	5.2	0.5	–	\
4/6	Cambridge 1	2a	Consl producing spurious characters	28/6/82	11.5	Don	29/6/82	12.0	29/6/82	12.0	2	1				PM UM	UK	1.0	–	\
4/7	BLC	C	TT Nigrinins	28/6/82	12.8	Chris	28/6/82	13.5	30/6/82	14.0	2	2				PM UM	4.0	4.0	–	–
4/8	Smyths	3	System error cant set system up	28/6/82	16.5	Tom	28/6/82	17.0	30/6/82	11.0	3	3				#M UM (System c)	5.0	4.5	1.05	–
4/9	System A	1	Tape punch rn jammed	28/6/82	9.8	Nigel	29/6/82	12.0	29/6/82	13.0	1	1				PM	2.2	3.5	–	\
4/10	BLC 82	C	VDU.	29/6/82	10.3	Chris	29/6/82	2.0	7/7/82	10.2	2	2				PM	2.7	0.4	–	12.0
4/11	BLC 82	C	VDU dd 29 Screen wavy	28/6/82	14.5	Chris	29/6/82	16.5	29/6/82	15.0	1	1				PM UK	UK	5.0	–	–
4/	S.Allan	3	Hammer fault	28/6/82	9.0	Steve	30/6/82	9.1	30/6/82	10.1	1	1				PM	10.1	0.1	5.0	0

Exhibit 1 shows the hardware fault service request log filled in for the busiest day during that period.

The Area Manager's job

Bill West, the Home Counties North Area Manager, found that his work was split up as follows:

(a) He sorted out any engineer/technician scheduling problems. These usually arose from the non-routine nature of computer faults, combined with scarce resources, such as the necessity of getting yet another part from Hemel Hempstead. He also controlled the movements of the technicians as they ferried equipment from base to base.
(b) He kept track of any 'Escalated' problems (see the CTL(A) case study).
(c) He supervised the installation of some of the new systems in his area, ironing out any problems that arose.
(d) He sorted out any maintenance contract queries and the occasional complaints that got passed his way by Anne. Any item that could not be handled by Bill was referred to Arthur Raymond, the Southern Regional Manager.

Bill was responsible for ensuring that the customers' contracted service levels were adhered to. He pointed out that although he agreed in theory with maintaining the differing service levels for each customer contract, in practice it was very difficult to administer. He said that he could delay the response so that the engineers arrived only when the contract stated. However, he would then be left with the problem of covering himself, if, at the end of a delay period, several top priority fault calls came into the office at once. This situation could leave him a couple of engineers short and result in an unhappy customer, who may be prepared to take legal action.

The final part of Bill's job was to visit customers and keep an eye on their systems. He knew when an old system needed replacing, and he reminded a customer one year in advance to make sure it was being allowed for in their next budget.

The Service Engineer's Job

Ray, a service engineer, was on standby in White Hart Lane when the case writer visited. He said that he did not like waiting around much, but it was necessary to ensure that customers were covered at all times. He also said that he was on call during the night once every six weeks.

He commented that CTL was a good company to work for. It had good 'self-diagnosis' software, and the people got on well. He said that his experience of the competition, when working for them before joining CTL, was that there service was not so good. He also sadly mentioned the massive growth of their competitor Wang, and how he had turned down a job offer to work for them when they had been a small outfit, in the mid-1970s.

He said that when he was not fixing faults he was visiting customers, checking their machines over, and that he sometimes picked up faults before they were spotted (Exhibit 2 shows a typical maintenance schedule).

Even though the planned maintenance visits were contractually set, Brian said that they preferred to visit each site once per month and do the maintenance in smaller, more manageable chunks. When back at base a service engineer spent his time fixing minor faults in a small workshop or answering simple enquiries that Anne sent in his direction. Exhibit 3 is Bill's summary, breaking down the time spent by the engineers in his area.

Exhibit 2   Schedule of maintenance to be performed at ACT Chesham by CTL engineers

MONTHLY: 8046   Clean air filter
Check operation of fans
Clean floppy disc drive head
Check floppy disc drivebelt

AD disc   Clean heads on all disc drives
Clean primary air filter
On ONE drive only:
Check drive motor and brake belts
Check power supplies
Clean shroud and spindle
Clean and lubricate lock shaft
Clean carriage rail and bearing
Check spindle ground spring

The above items to be performed on a different drive each period giving an effective frequency of once every three periods.

Line printers:
Check condition of drive belt
Hoover out paper dust
Replace any faulty lamps
Check condition of paper out and ribbon reverse switches
Clean barrel of LP1 one period, LP2 the following period, and neither the third period, effectively cleaning each barrel once every three periods.

VDUs   Remove cases and clean screen and inside of four VDUs each period. Rotate VDUs cleaned so that effectively each VDU is cleaned every three periods.

ANNUALLY: Check 8046 power supply settings
Replace AD disc absolute filters
Wash out AD disc primary filters
Check AD disc index to burst and CE alignment
Check printers for character alignment and print quality using E4LPAT
Check printer power supplies

Exhibit 3   Area Manager's summary sheet

Departmental Strength   10
Possible prime hours   1500

Contract activities	Period (1982)					
	5	7	9	13	Total	Total
1. Travel	14.4	16.0	15.4	16.1	15.2	53.5
2. On site	38.9	36.2	40.9	40.5	38.3	
Installation and related + travel	7.0	6.6	8.8	7.2	7.3	7.3
Training + travel	13.3	2.7	0	8.5	5.5	
Repairs – Local in office	3.9	7.8	13.1	9.1	8.4	39.2
Holidays/sickness	9.4	16.5	6.9	10.0	10.3	
Unallocated, doing nothing	13.1	16.6	14.1	17.6	15.0	
Overtime	5.8	5.5	9.4	6.1	6.7	6.7

All figures are percentages.

Case Study: Wimpy International (B)

In February 1980, Ian Petrie, Managing Director of Wimpy International, was faced with the dilemma of what to do with one of his more profitable franchisees whose four stores were failing to meet Wimpy's standards of quality. Ian Petrie had taken over as Managing Director in 1977, shortly after Wimpy was acquired by United Biscuits. Soon after his arrival it had become evident that improving the quality of the 500 franchised table service restaurants was one of his major tasks.

Quality problems were almost entirely in the older table service restaurants. The new McDonalds style counter service restaurants had been designed and were managed to meet very high levels of quality.

OPERATIONAL CONTROL AT WIMPY

At the time of the UB takeover the Operations Director was responsible for operational control of the Wimpy franchised restaurants. Reporting to the Operations Director was an Operations Manager who in turn controlled six District Managers. Each district had one to three franchise negotiators and four to five catering advisors. As part of their responsibilties the catering advisors carried out store audits and checked standards. A store audit report of a problem restaurant is shown in Exhibit 1. Part of the catering advisor's job was to ensure that the franchisee was using supplies bought from Wimpy International and not 'alien' hamburgers or other supplies.[1] When aliens were identified, franchisees were given a formal warning that their franchise agreement could be terminated. The franchisee invariably returned to buying Wimpy supplies, but many reverted to using aliens after a short period.

Ian Petrie had not been happy with the effectiveness of the operational control at Wimpy. Many of the franchised restaurants were being run at very low standards and the existing organization had had little effect. He therefore

---

This case was written by C. Pollard and C. Voss, London Business School. It is intended for teaching purposes only. Some names and figures may have been disguised.

Copyright material is reproduced by permission of Wimpy International Ltd.

[1] This was a vital task as Wimpy's franchise revenue came from a mark-up on supplies rather than a franchise fee or percentage of sales.

Exhibit 1 Sample pre-1980 store audit report

DATE 14.1.75
TIME AND DURATION
OF VISIT 3.50 – 5.45
CATERING ADVISER: R: JOHNSON   DATE OF LAST VISIT ...

GENERAL APPEARANCE AND CONDITION OF PREMISES
The Bar was clean and tidy, although in two or three areas the orange wallpaper has been torn and was hanging off the wall. It would be a simple matter for the manager to paste these pieces back onto the wall. there are a number of tiles missing from the downstairs potato preparation area, above the sink. These should be replaced as soon as possible.

CONSUMABLES
Wimpy products are being stored and presented correctly.

EQUIPMENT
Although the ventilation is working, the fact that no filter is used above the deep fat fryer means that the entire system is suffering, and will become blocked up with grease and dirt thereby becoming a fire hazard. I would recommend that the system be thoroughly cleaned and a filter used above the fryers.

STAFF AND SERVICE
Staff were all wearing protective clothing. The Chef was not wearing the required hat. The Bar was quiet during my visit so the service was the required standard.

SUMMARY (including recommendations and points requiring immediate attention)
Still concerned about the fact that a cat is still kept on the premises. Not only is this contravening the Health Act, but the smell downstairs is becoming quite overpowering. I would suggest that the animal is removed and the cellar and stores fumigated.

decided to separate operations and franchising sales and appointed John Servent to the new post of UK Operations Director. The organization of this department is shown in Exhibit 2. Each district had four or five Operations Supervisors.[2] The Senior Operations Supervisor would be responsible for the new counter service outlets in his district and the remaining supervisors would be responsible for the twenty to twenty-five table service outlets. The task of the operations supervisor included:

(a) Carrying out store audits and checking standards
(b) Arranging local promotions
(c) Training the franchisee, the manager, and staff (see Exhibit 6)
(d) Coordinating locally any national promotional activity, etc.
(e) Helping sort out any problems, e.g. legal, food cost, etc.
(f) Checking the quality of the products supplied to the franchisee

[2] These had formerly been catering advisers.

Exhibit 2   Wimpy International operations organization (United Kingdom only)

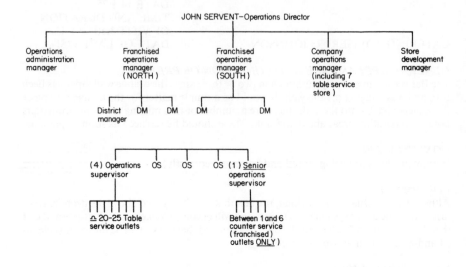

THE STORE AUDIT

Each store was audited bi-monthly, though outlets scoring badly were audited monthly. The Operations Supervisor recorded his observations on a store audit form (see Exhibit 3). The Operations Supervisor tried to ensure that any problems were rectified. One copy of the audit was given to the franchisee, a second was retained by the Operations Supervisor, the third copy went to the District Manager and then to headquarters. If a franchisee scored below 70 per cent on three consecutive audits, Wimpy's policy was to close the outlet or withdraw the franchise. Above 80 per cent on two occasions entitled the franchisee and his staff to wear the Wimpy tie, and above 90 per cent on two occasions entitled them to the full Wimpy uniform. This was a new policy and had yet to be tested in practice.

THE FRANCHISE AGREEMENT

Table service restaurant franchise agreements were for five years, and could be terminated by either side (with six months notice) at the *end* of the five years. The implicit understanding was that after five years the franchise would be renewed unless there had been problems. About fifty franchises changed hands each year. Provided that Wimpy approved the new franchisee and that the franchisee agreed to any renewals required by Wimpy, there were no obstructions to franchises changing hands. In these cases the new franchisee had to sign a new five year agreement and make a payment of £100 + VAT to Wimpy.

Exhibit 3 Wimpy International Limited – store audit

WIMPY INTERNATIONAL LIMITED — STORE AUDIT   № 000651

WIMPY
The Home of the Hamburger

FRANCHISEE ....

STORE ADDRESS ....

....

Date of Visit .... Time from .... to ....

Territory No. .... Period No. ....

Previous Audit No................ Period No. .... Date ....

MINIMUM ACCEPTABLE SCORE 70%

| | CLEANLINESS | | CUSTOMER | PRODUCT | TOTAL | | LEVEL OF | Tick as |
	EXTERNAL	INTERNAL	SERVICE	QUALITY	%		BUSINESS	appropriate
MAX SCORE	10	20	30	40	100		QUIET	
THIS AUDIT							AVERAGE	
LAST AUDIT							BUSY	

CLEANLINESS (EXTERNAL)	Max. Score	Actual Score	Where points are deducted a comment must be made prefixed with the appropriate section letter. † Actioned on site. COMMENTS/ACTION
A. Neighbourhood Free of all litter immediately outside and Wimpy litter 50 metres either side.	2		
*B. Fascia and Projecting Sign Clean, in good repair, illuminated as appropriate.	2		
C. Windows, Doors and Frames Clean and in good repair.	2		
D. Painted Surfaces, Tiling and Walls Clean and in good repair.	2		
*E. Menu Displays, Posters, Notices and Signs Clean, in good repair, illuminated as appropriate, no unauthorised signs.	2		
SECTION TOTAL	10		

Score Guide: 1 point deducted for any item which is not as specified. Any item which is dirty scores no points for the specific area.

CLEANLINESS (INTERNAL)			
*A. Customer Area Entrance, floors, seats, tables, wastebins, lighting, walls, mirrors, ceiling and vent grills—clean and in good repair. Background music (not radio) reasonably audible and store temperature appropriate. Plants in good condition. Red fire extinguishers full and correctly sited.	5		
B. Menu Displays and Promotional Material Clean, in good repair, illuminated as appropriate. No unauthorised signs or handwritten additions.	2		
*C. Production and Kitchen areas Counters, floors, walls, lighting, ceiling, air vents, wastebins, equipment, cables and sockets—clean and in good repair. Blue/Black fire extinguishers full and correctly sited. Fire blanket correctly sited.	4		
D. Public/Staff Toilets Clean and in good repair with hot and cold running water, soap, hand dryer or towel dispensers. Well ventilated and correctly signed. Nail brush in staff toilet.	3		
*E. Office, Store and Staff Room Clean and in good repair. Tidy and well organised and correct notices displayed. Stock secure, good rotation and perishables clear of floor.	2		
F. Extraction and Ventilation Filters and louvres clean and in good repair. Store free of all smells.	2		
•G. Service Areas/Wash Up/Yard Clean and tidy, fire exits free, fully lit and signposted. Fire extinguisher full and correctly sited.	2		
SECTION TOTAL	20		

Score Guide: 1 point deducted for any item which is not as specified. Any item which is dirty scores no points for the specific area.

CUSTOMER SERVICE	Max. Score	Actual Score	Where points are deducted a comment must be made prefixed with the appropriate section letter. † Actioned on site. COMMENTS/ACTION
A. Staff Pleasant greeting and smile, accurate order taking and money transaction, positive/suggestive selling, correct order assembly/presentation, helpful, alert and friendly to all customers. Effective use of seating.	10		
B. Service Speed (1) Counter Service—time taken by customer from entering store to reaching cashier: 0-2½ mins—4 pts. Over 2½ mins—Nil pts. Average time to complete transaction: 0-1 min—8 pts. 1-2 mins—6 pts. Over 2 mins —Nil pts.	4 8		
(2) Table Service—time taken to have order taken: 0-5 mins—4 pts. Over 5 mins—Nil pts. Average time to receive meal: 0-5 mins—8 pts. 5-10 mins—4 pts. Over 10 mins— Nil pts.	4 8		
C. Staff and Management Appearance Staff wearing clean and smart Wimpy uniforms (including hat for ladies). Griddle staff wearing clean whites and hat. Good standard of personal appearance including well kept hair, nails and suitable footwear. Management presenting a smart overall appearance. No smoking on duty.	6		
*D. Cutlery, Crockery, Serviettes, Straw Dispensers, Menus, Ashtrays and Condiments (where applicable) Clean, adequately stocked and positioned ready for use. Branded materials in use where available.	2		
SECTION TOTAL	30		

Score Guide: 2 points deducted for any item which is not as specified (except for service speed score, where scale applies).

PRODUCT QUALITY

	Max. Score	Actual Score
(ITEMS A-F). Correct preparation, cooking, make-up, portions and presentation/branded packaging—as per the Operations Manual. Holding times correct (Counter Service).		
*A. Hamburgers, Fish, Chicken and Grills	12	
*B. Chips	8	
*C. Cold Drinks	6	
*D. Shakes	4	
E. Ice Cream Items (Desserts)	2	
F. Hot Drinks	6	
G. Other Items Correct preparation, portions, presentation and served in clean containers.	2	
SECTION TOTAL	40	

Score Guide: 2 points deducted for any item not as specified as per check list or not prepared using products specifically recommended by Wimpy International. Where any product is improperly cooked/undercooked no score should be given for that item.

PRODUCT CODES IN STOCK								
	Hamburger	Fish	Bender	Chicken	Quarter-pounder	Baconburger	Bun	Seeded Bun
CODES								
DATES								

No 000651

MANAGEMENT/OPERATIONAL CONTROL: This should include the ability and awareness of the management on duty. Also include comment on management/staff/customer relationships.	DATE ACTION REQUIRED BY:

EQUIPMENT:
This should highlight problems with equipment, recommendations for cleaning rota and extra equipment (if either are required) etc.

TRAINING:
This should include comment on training carried out by the Manager/Supervisor. e.g. Have all staff seen the slide tape training films, operations manual etc.?

BUSINESS DEVELOPMENT PLAN:
This should include positive recommendations to increase sales and/or profits.

* REFER TO STORE AUDIT BRIEF

AUDIT COMPLETED BY:

NAME IN CAPITALS ....

POSITION ....

SIGNED ....

REVIEWED WITH:

NAME IN CAPITALS ....

POSITION ....

SIGNED ....

ADDITIONAL COMMENTS:

COPIES SENT TO: WHITE: ....   YELLOW: ....   PINK: ....

WIMPY INTERNATIONAL LIMITED, 214 Chiswick High Road, London W4 1PD. 01-994 6454. Registered in London under Number 812856.

There were a number of occurrences where Wimpy could (at least in theory) terminate a franchise. These were if the franchisee:

(a) Died or ceased to become the registered franchisee
(b) Failed to purchase a minimum number of hamburger patties a year (50,000) (Wimpy had never terminated because of this)
(c) Was in default of payment
(d) Was in breach of agreement
(e) Failed to meet standards (see Exhibit 4)
(f) A five year term had expired

There was no specific clause detailing the use of alien supplies as a reason for termination. How Wimpy dealt with a breach of agreement can be illustrated by the change from onions to relish. Some years ago Wimpy had decided to replace fried onions in hamburgers with relish. Many customers still wanted fried onions and for some years franchisees continued to fry onions. In 1980 John Servant set out to implement this policy properly. Twenty franchisees resisted and were threatened with termination. Ten franchisees still resisted and Wimpy gave twenty-eight days notice. One franchisee still refused to change and had his contract terminated.

JAMES HEATHER

The problems of implementing operational control were typified by the Heather franchise. James Heather owned four Wimpy restaurants in one of the major provincial cities. These restaurants were in prime sites and were used by out of town as well as local customers. These restaurants had always had a reputation for poor quality. (A 1975 store report is shown in Exhibit 1.) On the new store audits his restaurants were getting extremely low scores and many letters of complaint had been received (see Exhibit 5).

One of the factors hindering the solution of this problem was that the Heather franchises were extremely profitable (both to Heather and to Wimpy). One restaurant was grossing over £10,000 per week. Despite pressure, threats, and meetings with Ian Petrie and his predecessor, Heather refused to do anything about quality. 'As long as £500 goes into my bank account every week, I'm happy', he told Ian Petrie at one meeting. Petrie felt that there had been a number of reasons why Wimpy had not terminated Heather's franchise. They included:

(a) He had enough capital to revitalize the business if he wanted to.
(b) He had enough money to fight in court any termination of his franchise agreement.
(c) The store audit and documentation had never been tested in court (the old documents were felt to be legally weak).
(d) Heather had at some stage in the past expressed an interest in selling some of his restaurants and Wimpy had waited, hoping that he would.

Exhibit 4   Extracts from table service franchise agreement

5. STANDARDS AND UNIFORMITY OF OPERATION

The Franchisee agrees that the Franchisor's special standardised design and decor of buildings, uniformity of menu, equipment and layout, and adherence to the Manuals are essential to the image of a Wimpy. In recognition of the mutual benefits accruing from maintaining uniformity of appearance, service, products and marketing procedures, it is mutually covenanted and agreed:

A. **Buildings and Premises** Except as specifically authorised by the Franchisor, the Franchisee shall not alter the appearance of the exterior or interior of the Premises. The Franchisee will maintain the Premises and will promptly make all repairs and alterations to the Wimpy and to the Premises as may reasonably be determined by the Franchisor to be necessary.

B. **Signs** The Franchisee agrees to display and maintain the Franchisor's names, trade marks, and advertising and promotional material including posters, at the Premises, in the manner authorised by the Franchisor. The Franchisee shall not place additional signs, posters or trade marks on the Premises other than those authorised by the Franchisor.

C. **Equipment** The Franchisee agrees to obtain through the Franchisor and other approved sources by purchase or lease, machinery, equipment, furnishings and signs (hereinafter collectively called "Equipment"). The list of Equipment which must be used by the Franchisee in the operation of his business is set out in the Manuals. The Franchisee agrees to maintain such Equipment in excellent working condition. As items of Equipment become obsolete or require to be replaced, the Franchisee will replace such items with either the same or substantially the same Equipment as is being installed in Wimpy at the time replacement becomes necessary. All Equipment used in the Franchisee's Wimpy, shall meet the Franchisor's specifications.

D. **Vending Machines** No coin or token operated machines are to be installed in Wimpy unless authorised by the Franchisor.

E. **Menu and Service** The Franchisee agrees to serve the Menu Items specified in the Manuals to follow all specifications and formulae of the Franchisor, to sell no other food or drink item or any other merchanidse of any kind without the prior written approval of the Franchisor. The Franchisee agrees that all food and drink items will be served in containers approved by the Franchisor bearing accurate reproductions of the Franchisor's trade marks. The Franchisor will establish approved sources of supply of Menu Items and other food and drink items and properly imprinted containers, and such items shall be purchased by the Franchisee through the Franchisor or such approved sources of supply.

The Franchisee agrees that it will operate its Wimpy in accordance with the standards, specifications and procedures set out in the Manuals. The Franchisee agrees further that changes in such standards, specifications and procedures may become necessary from time to time and agrees to accept such modifications, revisions and additions to the Manuals which the Franchisor in good faith and the exercise of its commercial judgement believes to be necessary. The Franchisee agrees not to deviate from the standards of cleanliness and sanitation as set by the Franchisor.

The Franchisee shall remain open for business daily during such hours as are agreed between the Franchisor and the Franchisee.

F. **Alternative Supplies** Where the Franchisee identifies a supplier of any item as an alternative to the Franchisor or its nominated supplier, the Franchisee agrees to obtain the written consent of the Franchisor before the use of such an alternative supplier in order to preserve the standards of quality, appearance, size, portion and taste as set out in the Manuals. The Franchisor shall require that samples from such alternative suppliers be delivered to the Franchisor and/or a designated independent testing laboratory for testing prior to approval and use. The costs of such testing to be shared equally between

Exhibit 4 (contd.)

the Franchisor and Franchisee.

In the event that the Franchisor and/or its nominated suppliers for any item, are unable or unwilling to supply such item(s), the Franchisee may obtain those item(s), but no others, from alternative suppliers for as long as the Franchisor and/or its nominated supplier shall be unable or unwilling so to supply.

G. **Right of Entry and Inspection** The Franchisor or its authorised agent and representative shall have the right to enter and inspect the premises and examine and test and remove food products, supplies and equipment for the purpose of ascertaining that the Franchisee is operating the Wimpy in accordance with the terms of this Agreement and the Manuals. Inspection shall be conducted during normal business hours. The Franchisor shall notify the Franchisee of any deficiencies detected during inspection and the Franchisee shall forthwith correct any such deficiencies. Upon notification by the Franchisor that any equipment, food, supplies or imprinted containers do not meet the specifications, standards and requirements of the Franchisor, the Franchisee shall desist and refrain from the further use thereof.

10. DEFAULT: TERMINATION

A. **Default** The occurrence of any of the following events shall constitute good cause for the Franchisor, at its option and without prejudice to any other rights or remedies provided for hereunder or by law or equity, to terminate this Agreement forthwith by notice in writing to the Franchisee except as provided below.

1. If the Franchisee is adjudicated bankrupt, has a receiving order made against him, calls a meeting of or makes any arrangement or composition with his creditors or has an attachment execution or distraint issued against or levied upon him or his effects, or (where the Franchisee is a partnership) any of the foregoing being done by or to the property of any of the partners of the Franchisee or the partnership being dissolved or (where the Franchisee is a body corporate) being unable to pay its debts within the meaning of Section 223 of the Companies Act 1948 or having a Receiver or Manager appointed of any part of its undertaking or assets or uncalled capital, or an order being made or a resolution being passed for winding up or liquidation of the Franchisee except where any such event is only for the purpose of amalgamation or reconstruction.

2. If the Franchisee defaults in the payment of any monies due to the Franchisor as a results of the operation of this Agreement.

3. If the Franchisee fails to maintain the standards as set forth in this Agreement, as may be supplemented by the Manuals.

4. If the Franchisee ceases to do business at the Premises or defaults under any lease or sublease or loses his right to the possession of the Premises.

5. If the Franchisee for any reason ceases to be entitled to remain registered as a registered user of any of the Trade Marks.

6. The Franchisee or any Manager being convicted during the term of this Agreement of any offence relating to the sale of alcoholic liquor or the use abuse sale purchase or possession of drugs or narcotics or theft or fraud, or where the Franchisee is a partner in a firm, or a body corporate any person being so convicted who was, at the time of such conviction a partner in such firm or a director of such body corporate, or where the Franchisee carries out or knowingly permits to be carried out any activity on the Premises which would bring the Wimpy into bad repute.

7. If the Franchisee prepares, stores, advertises, or sells products other than Menu Items or ceases to carry out the preparation, storing, advertising and selling of Menu Items and any other products supplied by or with the authority of the Franchisor.

8. The Franchisee commits any other breach of any of his obligations hereunder and the Franchisee fails to remedy any such breach within thirty (30) days following the receipt of written notice from the Franchisor to remedy the same.

Exhibit 5   Customer letters concerning the Heather franchise

Dear Sir,

I met my sister and relations from Leicester last week and we popped in the Wimpy outside the station. We soon popped out again, the smell outside and inside was disgusting, the staff were smelly, and greasy clothes, what an advertisment!! I'm surprised no-one has complained before, and the person behind the counter was having a smoke on the sly, I just gave him a withering look, and he couldn't care less, the smell is revolting, and it needs reporting to Health Inspector which I intend to do, the entrance floor is filthy, no wonder McDonald's are flourishing. Some of your staff and shops could take a few lessons.

Yours disgusted

and embarassed for my visitors. God! knows what it is like back in the kitchens.

J. Smyths

Dear Sir,

I am writing to complain about the conditions at one of your Wimpy Bars in the High Road.

I took my children for some lunch to the above Restaurant and found the floor looked as though it could have done with a good wash.

I waited for 15 minutes to be served, the table was cluttered with dirty plates, it was cleared when our food was brought to us.

I asked for tea, when I received it, well I was not sure if I maybe had a combination of both tea and coffee mixed together, but it was awful. Also, since when have you served dried milk powder instead of milk with tea.

I cleaned our table with the paper napkins before we all started to eat.

Oh for McDonalds, where everything is so clean, floors, tables, etc.

Wimpy seems to have gone down the drain lately, what a shame as my family used to enjoy eating at Wimpy Bars, but we do like an eating place to be clean, plus tables to be cleared before we eat. Oh for Cleaner Wimpy Bars.

From

Jones (Mrs.)

Ian Petrie considered that the time for waiting was over and more positive action was needed.

QUALITY CONTROL DEPARTMENT

The Quality Control Department was concerned primarily with the quality of items purchased by the franchisee, particularly meat. Prior to 1976 Wimpy's practice was to specify the product quality, then to randomly test items and to investigate franchisee complaints. This practice could cause many problems, particularly if a substandard batch of meat was discovered. It was often impossible to find all of the batch. In 1976 the policy was changed to that of requiring the supplier to carry out quality tests specified by Wimpy prior to release of the meat. Initially this met with supplier resistance. Suppliers tended to be sales oriented and found this new concept strange. They now had to do the work and did not like rejecting marginally below-specification products.

Exhibit 6   Extracts from table service Procedure Manuals

14

EXTRACTS FROM TABLE SERVICE PROCEDURE MANUALS

WIMPY

Ensure that griddle is sufficiently hot. Separate steak from stack and place on R/hand side of griddle with paper uppermost. Peel off paper and deposit in waste bin. When more steaks are added, maintain neat rows.

Using spatula pick up ½oz. onion and place on steak, using the outside of tongs as a guide.

After approx 1 minute, juices will appear on the surface of steak. It is then sealed. Using spatula, lift steak.

Turn over to L/hand side of griddle. Onions will now be under steak.

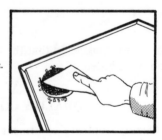

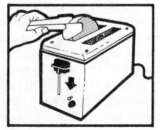

Load bun into toaster and depress lever.

15

Scrape debris from the griddle into the gulley.

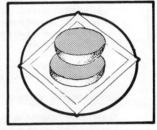

When bun pops up, using tongs, remove the two toasted halves of Wimpy bun from toaster. Place base half with toasted side uppermost on the centre of servietted plate. Then place the top half with the toasted half uppermost upon the base half.

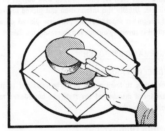

Pick up the cooked steak and move it across to the servietted plate.

At the same time, using the tongs in the left hand, lift the top half of the Wimpy bun.

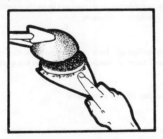

Place the top half of the Wimpy bun into position on top of the steak.

Lower the steak, together with the top of the Wimpy bun onto the base half of the Wimpy bun and withdraw the spatula.

NEVER, EVER SQUEEZE A WIMPY STEAK. This will not speed the cooking and will only help to make the meat dry and unpalatable. IT IS MOST IMPORTANT that the griddle plate is sufficiently hot. The number 3 setting on the griddle simmerstat is normally appropriate.

16

TRAINING

It is the responsibility of Management to ensure that all staff are properly trained in their respective duties.

It obviously takes time to train staff, and Managers are usually very busy people, but it pays to make the time to train. An untrained member of your staff can cause you to lose more time correcting his or her mistakes than it would to train that person properly in the first place; it also saves you, your staff and your customers aggravation.

A new member of staff, on arrival, should be made to feel welcome, and should be shown how YOU want him or her to perform their duties. They should be made aware of hygiene and safety factors.

WHY SYSTEMATIC TRAINING?

TRADITIONAL TRAINING METHODS
Traditionally staff were left to their own devices to gain any information they needed, from any source available. Usually this information was picked up from the more senior members of the staff, but bad and dangerous aspects of the job were picked up at the same time as any good points. This method resulted in lowering output and increasing the danger of accidents.

SYSTEMATIC APPROACH

REDUCED LEARNING TIME
Time taken to learn a job, or to be retrained to the speed and quality of performance of the most experienced member of the staff can be reduced to as much as one half of the time taken under the traditional method.

LABOUR TURNOVER –
Labour turnover can be quite drastically cut by the introduction of systematic training, especially in the case of initial training. The new member of the staff realises that interest is being shown in his development and this creates an atmosphere conductive to learning and under these conditions the new staff member settles in more quickly and is more likely to remain.

QUALITY
Staff learning by watching and imitating without any form of instruction quite often pick up wrong methods as well as correct ones, and form habits of performance resulting in bad quality, the habits themselves become hard to break.

Systematic training can help in reducing wastage through poor quality.

ACCIDENTS
Correct working methods are usually safe methods. Staff learn from others by imitation and may imitate incorrect and unsafe methods directly; frustration at their inability to produce the quality and quantity required or the resultant poor morale may induce staff to take unsafe short-cuts or work carelessly.

Systematic training can reduce accidents and save costly insurance claims.

METHODS AND TIME
Where methods have been carefully studied and laid down, they are often not correctly followed when training is not systematically given. Machine time is frequently under-utilised by operatives not efficiently taught their jobs (i.e. a poorly trained chef will not get the full capacity from the griddle).

17

SUPERVISORY TIME

Supervisors are frequently over-burdened where staff have not been systematically trained. They have to make up quantities or quality by correcting faulty work themselves or pressing staff to do work again.

Systematic training relieves supervisors to carry out their proper supervisory duties and may sometimes reduce the amount of supervision needed.

All these points can be related to the operation of a successful Wimpy Bar.

REDUCED LEARNING TIME

The quicker you get your new staff trained or your existing staff re-trained the quicker your Bar will be back to full staff efficiency.

LABOUR TURNOVER

The turnover of labour has long been a main point of frustration to Wimpy Bar owners, anything to lessen this turnover must be an advantage. Good training and good staff relations will do this.

QUALITY

Proper training can produce high quality food presentation, service and customer relations, which will all add up to greater profits.

ACCIDENTS

The reduction of accidents is important. A bad accident will upset and un-nerve the remainder of the staff for quite some time, thus the efficiency of your Bar will further be reduced.

METHODS AND TIME

Where a job method has been worked out, tested and found to be satisfactory, it should be taught and practised. Take advantage of other peoples knowledge and work.

SUPERVISORS

A great deal of worry and work can be taken off your management if the staff have been correctly trained.

ALWAYS LOOK FOR A TRAINING NEED

A training need is the difference between how a job SHOULD be done and how it IS being done.

210

A FEW HINTS ON HOW TO INSTRUCT

STEP 1 – PREPARE

(a) Put the trainee at ease.
(b) State what the job will be.
(c) Check the trainee's existing knowledge.
(d) Try to create an interest in the trainee to learn.
(e) When demonstrating, make sure the trainee is in a position where he or she can see everything that you do.

STEP 2 – PRESENT

(a) Tell, show, illustrate as appropriate, one stage at a time.
(b) Stress important points.
(c) Instruct clearly, completely and patiently.
(d) Give information at a suitable pace.

STEP 3 – TRY-OUT

(a) Have the trainee do the job or explain the subject.
(b) Correct errors as they occur.
(c) Check that the trainee understands the important points as the job is being done again.
(d) Continue until you are satisfied the trainee can perform the task correctly.

STEP 4 – PUT TO WORK

(a) Indicate personal responsibilites.
(b) Name somebody who can help the trainee if you are not around.
(c) Always encourage questions.
(d) Make a later check to ensure that the trainee has fully settled down.

KEEP A TRAINING RECORD (Example overleaf)

19

HYGIENE

This is intended to be a guide to enable you to achieve and maintain the highest standard of hygiene and cleanliness. Good hygiene doesn't cost a great deal — Poor hygiene can be VERY expensive. Expensive in two ways.

(1)   AT LAW

If the Food Hygiene Regulations are broken the penalties are (for each offence)

A fine not exceeding £100 or 3 months prison.
OR
Both a fine and prison.
For each day after conviction an offence continues a fine of £5 may be imposed!

DANGER POINTS

(2)   IN BUSINESS

The clean bar is always a busy bar. Good hygiene practised by staff will make customers want to come in again.

Bad hygiene will drive customers away and, if a court case follows, the bad publicity would do tremendous harm to your business and to the good name of WIMPY on which we all depend.

Those are the reasons WHY. Now let's look at the standards laid down by law, those Wimpy International would like to see in every Wimpy Bar and how simple it can be to reach those standards.

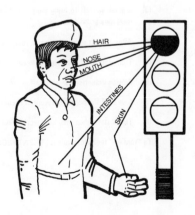

DO NOT

(1) Shout and bawl in the bar. It gives a bad impression to the customers and makes the staff nervous and self conscious.

(2) Reprimand staff in front of customers or in front of other members of the staff. When someone is reprimanded in front of another they will react in an aggressive way in an attempt to "save face". This could lead to a slanging match in public or the person walking off the job. It is best to wait until a quiet time and take the person to one side and quietly explain what they have done wrong and how to correct their mistake.

(3) Bully staff – lead them by example. The ideal situation would be for the staff genuinely to want to please.

(4) Have favourites.

(5) Take staff for granted, like a piece of furniture.

(6) Be sarcastic. It can be very irritating to many people.

(7) Over work a willing horse. The horse will not be willing for ever and you will lose a valuable member of your staff.

DO

(1) Treat staff fairly. All staff to be treated the same.

(2) Be consistent in your attitude.

(3) Encourage staff to bring their complaints to you. It is bad for people to slowly boil over true or imaginary grievances.

(4) Allocate staff duties (be fair in your allocation).

(5) Train your staff properly and keep training records.

(6) Provide induction for new staff.

(7) Give staff the occasional word of encouragement.

(8) Thank staff when they have worked well.

To "sum up" the golden rule is "TREAT PEOPLE AS YOU WOULD LIKE TO BE TREATED".

Wimpy controlled the process at two levels. Firstly, there were two Quality Control Managers who monitored the suppliers' production sites visiting them as appropriate, usually every three weeks. Secondly, all suppliers were required to submit samples for approval once a week.

The work of the Quality Control Department had been considerably eased by a rationalization in the number of suppliers. The Quality Control Department also conducted random audits of products at restaurants to ensure that they were fresh and being stored properly.

Case Study: Wickshire Highways Department

'The situation is getting worse,' said John Hattersley, the Assistant Chief Engineer (ACE). 'The only certain thing is our yearly budget figure. We never know how much work we are going to get or how labour or capital intensive it might be.'

John Hattersley has been the ACE in the Northern Division of the Highways, Maintenance, and Construction Department, a Direct Labour Organization (DLO), with Wickshire County Council for just over two years.

> The work we do in this Division is maintenance, construction, resurfacing of all the Highways, vehicular crossings, safety maintenance, white lines and traffic management, and we are responsible for street lighting. Some of the work is rechargeable; when the Gas Board, for example, have been digging holes in the road, we would come along afterwards and patch-up the surface and send them the bill for it.
>
> Our work comes from two sources. Our central planning department issue us with anything from minor works to major constructions of new roads, and under Section 41 of the Highways Act we are charged with the task of maintaining all the highways in our area. Although they call themselves the planning department they never seem able to tell us well in advance what work is coming up, even with the large schemes; when we know what the job will be, they won't tell us when it might start. The whole thing is made even more difficult by the fact that more and more work has got to go out to tender, so when we finally know of a job we cannot be sure that we will get the tender.

Central Government introduced legislation in the form of the Local Government (Planning and Land) Act, 1980, which came into force on 1st April 1981. The intention of the Act is that the local authority DLO should be treated as closely as possible as an outside contractor to the authority. To achieve this regulations were issued governing all the allocation and tendering procedures to be adopted for works of maintenance and construction. Those that most affect Wickshire are:

(a) Separate accounts must be kept for the DLO.
(b) Using current cost accounting methods, the DLO must achieve a 5 per cent return on its capital employed. (The figure of 5 per cent may vary from time to time as directed by the Secretary of State.)

(c) If the DLO fails to achieve the required rate of return for three consecutive years, the Secretary of State has the power to close it down.

(d) From April 1st 1982 all Highway works costing more than £100,000 were subject to competitive tendering from at least three other persons in addition to the DLO. This limit was reduced to £50,000 on 1st October 1982. Further to this, with effect from October, the Local Government (Direct Labour Organization) (Competition) Regulations 1983 states that 30 per cent by value of Highway work below the threshold of £50,000 should also be made subject to competitive tender.

John continues:

We are also being squeezed by the cuts in local government expenditure. This year spending on capital equipment has dropped to 40 per cent of the 1975—76 level, and even that year was below the peak of the early 1970s. We feel that we have been taking more than our fair share of these cuts. To make matters worse, if you consider the state of the construction industry as a whole, you will understand that the shift in the balance of new work done against maintenance work means that there is a growing interest in maintenance work by the private sector. Overall the economic environment has lead to keener competition. We just can't afford to waste or underutilize our resources. We have to put out realistic tenders that are not only competitive but ensure us enough of the right sort of work and an adequate return on capital. That's the problem, we have never had to do this sort of thing before. All our work used to be assured; now anything could happen.

I have been doing some calculations. I reckon that we will have to win somewhere between 72 and 85 per cent of an increasing amount of tender work and this will represent about 40 per cent of our total workload. You can see that the effect of the Act and the Regulations have serious implications for arriving at an assured workload for the DLO. This in turn has a serious consequence in terms of the ability to meet the County Council's policy on employment.

The Council's policy on employment is essentially that there will be no redundancies, and limited replacement of people who leave. At present there is a workforce of fifty in the Division. John readily admits that it is not easy trying to keep all the men fully and usefully employed:

When this years budget, about £2m, was allocated to us, virtually all the schemes for the coming year were of unknown type or design. Yet it is the Division's function to control, plan, and schedule the annual programme of work based on that budget allocation. There is no agreed method within the four regional divisions; each unit has their own way. I think most of us have been using the backs of cigarette packets! So far we have got by, we have even been turning in some impressive returns on capital, but I don't think it can last.

Expenditure breakdown 1982/83

	£
Motorway and trunk road work	2,193,600
Rechargeable jobs	3,564,600
Highway improvement schemes	7,220,600
Highway maintenance	8,789,200
	21,768,000

Return on capital 1982/83

	£
Income	21,975,000
Expenditure	21,768,000
Surplus for the year	207,000
Surplus after adjustments	185,000
Capital employed in DLO 1982/83	
Depots, buildings	768,000
Stocks	572,000
Transport	379,000
	1,719,000
Rate of return on capital	10.8%

Chapter 8

Queueing Systems Design and Management

Colin G. Armistead and C.A. Voss

As service systems cannot buffer the variability of demand through the use of stocks, queues are an integral part of service systems. Queueing systems include not just those where a physical queue form, but those where customers are waiting for service to arrive (i.e. a car breakdown service) and those where calls are infrequent but high service availability and responsiveness are required (i.e. fire services). Good design of queueing systems can lead both to increased customer satisfaction and improved use of resources. This chapter describes some of the basics of queueing theory and practice.

1. QUEUE BEHAVIOUR

The fundamentals of the behaviour of queues can be illustrated by consideration of a simple example. Let us take a service process with a given processing rate and people arriving at a given arrival rate. If the processing rate (say six customers per hour) was exactly matched by the arrival rate (one customer every ten minutes), what would be the capacity utilization and would we expect a queue? At first sight it would seem that the capacity utilization would be 100 per cent and there would be no queue. Let us look more closely at the possible behaviour of the process and the customers. Firstly, it is quite likely that even if customers arrive at an average *rate* of one every ten minutes, they will not arrive at exactly ten minute intervals. If a customer arrives early he or she will have to queue until the previous customer has been processed. If late, the process will have to wait, causing a loss of utilization. In addition, all the following customers will have to wait because of the delay introduced by the late customer. Clearly the greater the variability of the arrival time, the greater will be the average queue and the lower will be the utilization.

Similarly, if the customers arrive at exactly ten minute intervals but the process time varies from customer to customer, a short process time will cause loss of capacity utilization, while a longer than average processing time will cause a queue to form.

It is thus clear that if we wish to reduce queueing in a system where there is variability of arrival and/or processing rate, the average processing rate must exceed the average arrival rate. The greater the variability, the greater the ratio of processing to arrival rate must be to achieve a given queue length. It is also clear that, when there is variability of arrival and/or processing rates, to achieve high levels of process utilization we must have a queue. The higher the variability, the greater the queue we must accept to allow a given utilization rate.

The above is a non-mathematical description of simple queueing theory (called waiting line theory in the United States). It is possible to take a more analytic approach.

2. ANALYTIC MODELS

If arrivals are random, analytical models can be used for analysis. It is necessary to determine the probability distribution time between arrivals. It can be shown mathematically that if the probability distribution of the interarrival times is exponential, calling units arrive according to the so-called Poisson process. Poisson arrivals are very common in queueing systems; they generally exist in situations where the number of arrivals is independent of how many arrivals have occurred in previous time intervals. Given Poisson arrival patterns, it is possible to calculate mathematically relationships between queue length, arrival rates, process rates, and utilization. A second analytic method applicable to queueing is simulation. These analytic methods are outlined in Appendix 1.

2.1 The Serving Structure

Queues and the service stages may be arranged in a number of different ways as shown in Figure 8.1 according to the number of separate queueing channels and the number of serving stages in the total service operation:

(a) *Single channel and single stage* is the simplest type of queue and serving structure. It may be seen in queues waiting to be served in a small shop with one server or in a bus queue.

(b) *Single channel and multiple stage* occurs where a customer goes through a number of different stages to complete the service process. This occurs for passengers travelling on trains, boats, and planes and in many service organizations where it is necessary to visit several departments in the organization. Government and Local Authority organizations frequently exhibit this structure.

(c) *Parallel single channel and single or multiple stage* is again very common in service operations such as banks, railway ticket offices, fast food restaurants. If the serving times vary the different queue channels will move at different rates exacerbating any problems of queue switching.

(d) *Multiple channel and single stage* is a way of reducing the real or perceived

Figure 8.1   The serving structure

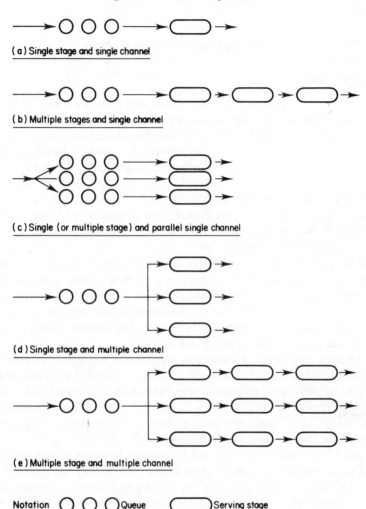

(a) Single stage and single channel

(b) Multiple stages and single channel

(c) Single (or multiple stage) and parallel single channel

(d) Single stage and multiple channel

(e) Multiple stage and multiple channel

Notation   ◯ ◯ ◯ Queue   ⬭ Serving stage

problems of the previous structure (c) and has been adopted by banks, post offices, and other service organizations. Customers form a single queue and go to individual servers as they become free. Some problems can arise with customers who wish to be served each time by the same server.

(e) *Multiple channel and multiple stage* is similar to (d) except that a number of stages are involved in the service. Such a structure is common in a hospital clinic where all start at a reception desk and subsequently take different routes.

Where multiple stages are part of the overall service operation the position is further complicated by the formation of queues between the different stages.

This makes the analysis of these complex queueing and serving structures very difficult.

3. QUEUEING SYSTEMS DESIGN

3.1 Queue Length

The mathematics of queueing theory indicates that there is a trade-off between cost and queue length. For a given level of demand, to achieve higher levels of server utilization, we must have lower levels of server capacity which results in longer queues. It is relatively simple to quantify this trade-off either by calculation, simulation, or observation in the field. It is again easy to quantify the cost implications of various levels of utilization, but costing the impact on customers is difficult. For example, what is the benefit to the business of reducing queue length? What is the cost in short-term lost sales and longer-term loss of goodwill of lengthening queues? For a public sector operation, what is a satisfactory length of queue?

Such questions can be approached in a number of ways. Firstly, a company can refer to its competition. This provides a baseline against which to match queue levels or to decide to gain competitive advantage by bettering them. Market research can provide data on customer perceptions and attitudes to queue lengths. Field observation and experiments can be used. Finally, absolute standards can be set and used as a baseline.

The reasons for setting a particular queue length are that it influences customer behaviour. It follows that the customer perception of queue length is important. An interesting question is whether a short slow queue and service is perceived as preferable to a long fast queue and service if both give identical times in the system. If customers equate length with time, then this has important considerations for queue system design.

Customers' attitudes to waiting will be partly a function of their perceived value of time. Waiting may imply wasted time on behalf of the customer.

It is usually assumed that queues are essentially undesirable to customers and should be minimized. However, in some cases, a queue will encourage more people to join, and lack of a queue where one is expected may turn people away who think that 'there must be something wrong with the service if no-one is queueing'. In some cases the queue can be made part of the service. Buskers play to queues outside theatres, a popular restaurant serves appetisers to people waiting for seats thus making the queue far more acceptable. In other cases, customer dissatisfaction with queues can be minimized. For example, in a newly built office block, there were many complaints about long waits for lifts. The owners of the building called in an operations management team who studied the demand pattern in order to ascertain whether some scheme might be designed to reduce waiting time, such as certain lifts being express only at various times of the day, having non-stop service to particular floors, or perhaps increasing the speed of the lifts. After considerable study, they came to the conclusion that the only viable alternative for providing better service was to add two more lifts. This represented a considerable cost and the owners of the building were eager to find some alternative solution. They called in a psychologist who knew nothing of queueing problems. After several days of wandering about the building and listening to conversations, he proposed a solution: install full-length mirrors in the lift waiting areas. His proposal was implemented and the complaints stopped; people spent their time looking in the mirrors checking hairdos and ties − they did not mind waiting.

A customer's attitude to waiting will also be shaped by perception of fairness and whether the queue is under control. If customers perceive that they are being treated unfairly, e.g. through other customers arriving later and being served first, they may become annoyed and this annoyance can affect their perception of subsequent services. If, in addition, the customer perceives that this is caused by inefficiency, such as lost reservations or late arrival of the server, then matters become worse. Many organizations will try to set expectations of waiting time that are slightly worse than will usually occur so that customers will be 'pleasantly surprised'.

3.2 Reservation Systems

An alternative approach to achieving high utilization and high service is to find a method of reducing demand variability. A reservation or appointment system does this. As the amount of demand variability is substantially reduced for an expected level of waiting time or people waiting, an increased utilization of the facilities can be realized.

For the customer we are substituting a possibly longer wait for service for a much shorter wait at the point that the service is delivered and/or greater certainty that it will be delivered.

3.3 Queue Structure and Design

The issues associated with design of queues can be illustrated by looking at the very common case of a single service being provided by multiple channels, e.g. fast food restaurants, ticket offices, banks, etc. The simplest form of structure is to have multiple queues, i.e. a different queue at each serving point.

The disadvantage of multiple queues in a busy facility is that customers often will shift queues if several previous services have been of short duration, or if those customers currently in other queues appear to require a short service time. Although the overall characteristics of the facility and the expected waiting time of each customer remains the same, the variability within a customer's waiting time will increase if customers are not equally skilled in the art of switching lines. When this inequality exists, the effect is the same as if special priorities are given to a particular class of customer. This problem occurs particularly when the variability of service time is high. The response to this problem is to form a single queue from which, as a server becomes available, the next customer in the queue is assigned to that server. This structure requires good control of the line to maintain order and a good system to direct customers to available servers. In some instances, assigning numbers to customers in order of their arrival is used.

The disadvantage of a single queue is that in high volume facilities the queue length can become very long. Even if the customer waiting time is the same or less, customers may perceive the wait as being longer, and customers may be deterred from joining the queue.

A different approach to variability in service time is queue structuring. 'Personal cheques only' in a bank and a fast checkout lane for shoppers with six items or less in a supermarket are examples. Such queues are formed of a specific class of customer with similar characteristics. Queue structuring can reduce the variability of service time to individual customers, provide selected groups of customers with faster service, and allow specialization of the delivery system. On the negative side, it can result in lower utilization of the service facility, which can lead to customer perceptions of poor management and unfairness. For example, a customer in a long queue may see a staffed channel, providing a different service, which is empty.

There are, of course, more complex queueing situations; e.g. multiple services and sequential services served by a single queue. The admission of patients in a hospital follows this pattern as a specific sequence of steps is usually followed: initial contact at the admissions desk, filling out forms, making identification tags, taking the patient to the ward, etc. Since several servers are usually available for this procedure, more than one patient at a time may be processed. Analytically, the more complex queue configurations are most easily examined by simulation, testing various decision rules and capacities.

3.4 Queue Discipline

A queue discipline is a priority rule, or set of rules, for determining the order of service to customers in a queue. The rules selected can have a strong impact on the system's overall performance and the customer's perception of service.

Queueing systems usually operate with a first-come-first-served rule, even when it is inefficient, because people believe it to be fairer than other systems. Queue disciplines can be divided into two categories – preemptive priority and non-preemptive priority. Preemptive priority disciplines allow customers that arrive at the queueing system to replace customers already receiving service. For example, consider a surgery when only one doctor is on duty. Obviously, if at the time a critically ill patient arrives while that doctor is treating a patient whose condition is not critical, the patient who was being served will be preempted because a patient with a higher priority has arrived at the system. Non-preemptive priority simply causes the customers in the queue to be arranged so that when a service facility becomes available the customer with the highest priority receives service first. There is no displacement of customers in service. It is also possible for a queueing system to have no formal queue discipline, in which case the server selects calling units at random. One often finds random selection in pubs, for example.

There are a wide range of priority rules such as reservations first, emergencies first, highest-profit customer first, first class passengers first, best customers first, longest waiting time, and soonest promised date. Each rule has attractive features as well as shortcomings. Whatever system is chosen, the customer's perception of fairness will strongly influence customer attitude to queueing.

4. QUEUEING THEORY AND FIELD DELIVERY OF SERVICE

An interesting example of the way in which different criteria call for quite different system performance levels can be seen by viewing a fire station or a breakdown service in a queueing context. Fires and breakdowns may be regarded as arrivals and the servicing as required times for extinguishing fires or repairing machines. A major criterion or objective is directly related to the expected waiting time. It is unacceptable to have someone call up and report a burning house and have to reply that there are two other houses ahead of his. In terms of the queue discipline, one might expect that first come, first served would be the rule. However, if the fire service was putting out a fire in a family home and the local hospital suddenly caught fire, it would seem appropriate to shift resources to the hospital even if it meant permitting the home to burn to the ground.

If we studied work patterns in a fire station, we might find that firemen played poker 80 per cent of the time. If we concluded that the fire station needed fewer firemen, we may be incorrect. In a queueing context, we must accept a fire operation with a low utilization, firemen being unoccupied for most of the time, so that they will be available when an 'arrival' occurs.

In considering queueing cost trade-offs, we must look at incremental costs. If a task can be identified that field service engineers can do in their idle time, which can be immediately dropped when a breakdown occurs, that task has zero incremental cost. Another example of low incremental cost can be seen in a hamburger restaurant. If there is a surge in demand so that short-term capacity is insufficient to prevent major queueing, the manager will leave his job and will speed up the process, often by taking orders from queuers. The incremental cost of moving the manager into the operation is very low in the short term, though would be high in the longer term.

5. QUEUE MANAGEMENT

It should already be clear that the evaluation of queues can be complex and difficult for the service operations manager to reduce or eliminate queueing (i.e. waiting in line) or other waiting for the service. This might imply that queues are always undesirable, but this may not always be the case.

Remembering that many aspects of service operations relate to the customer's expectation of the service and perception of what happens during interactions with the service organization, the presence or absence of queues may in some instances be taken by the customer to indicate a 'good' service organization and service package (restaurants, theatres, sporting events) rather than in other cases where the customer perceives queues to indicate 'bad service' (common in travel offices and post offices and banks).

What, then, can a service operations manager do to manage the aspects relating to queues and waiting? The starting point before deciding on the methods to be used in a particular circumstance is to consider the queue from the standpoint of the customer. In the customer's view a number of factors may to a greater of lesser extent be important:

(a) It is *reasonable to expect to wait* for a particular service at a particular time. So queueing may be accepted at peak times but not at other times.

(b) The *waiting time* spent waiting *must seem reasonable and acceptable*.

(c) *Priority for serving must seem fair.* This may be a cultural acceptance of the first-come-first-served queue discipline or other acknowledged priority system or a priority established by the strongest or the swiftest of the waiting customers (as seen at bus stops in many parts of the world when a bus arrives).

(d) There must be a *low degree of uncertainty* of the length of time a customer will have to wait at a particular time which is associated with the extent to which the *customer feels in control* of what is happening.

(e) The *conditions* in which the customer has to wait. Apart from the more obvious aspects relating to comfort there is the factor of personal space which may be reduced in a crowded queueing area to an extent that customers feel uncomfortable and may even leave the queue.

The service operations person needs to consider these views of the customer when deciding how best to manage a particular queueing system. In making a choice there are a number of different possibilities:

(a) *Distract the customer* so that they are less aware of the actual waiting time. This may be done in a variety of ways. Some of the more common are:
   (i) Give the customer something to do, like filling in forms.
   (ii) Provide entertainment (buskers for a theatre or cinema queue, or magazines in a waiting room).
   (iii) Provide comfortable waiting conditions – seats, heating, light, space for queues to form, toilets.
   (iv) Provide refreshment (which the customer may or may not pay for directly, e.g. bars in a restaurant, coffee in hairdressers).
   (v) Start the service process, for instance by taking orders for food before sitting at a table in a restaurant.
   (vi) Split the waiting times, for instance by having customers wait after initial processing into the service organization (commonly used in hospitals). This effectively hides the extent of the queue from new customers who may arrive.

(b) *Reduce the randomness of the arrival patterns* by appointment systems. The aim of an appointment system for the operations person is to be able to increase the utilization of the service-producing unit while still maintaining high performance for the service. In many cases queues still occur to some extent because of the variability of service times and either the early or late arrivals or non-arrival of customers. There is then the question of the priority for dealing with the waiting customers: whether to serve next the customer who has been waiting longest or the one who is scheduled for the next appointment but has only just arrived. In using appointment systems it is important that the expectations of customers are not raised, so that in the event the customer is then dissatisfied after only a short queueing period. It does seem to be important that the service takes place at the time at which it has been promised. This point applies to the use of appointments for field service operations.

(c) *Make the queue priority fair* in operation. If the customer therefore expects first-come-first-served queue discipline this may be done by physically preventing customers from queue jumping or by the use of numbered tickets given to, or taken by, the customers (this may require some training of the customer) as they join the queue.

(d) *Change the number of serving channels or serving times* to reduce queue length and waiting times as they arise. Increasing the number of channels may be done by switching people from other duties like cleaning in a fast food restaurant or filling shelves in a supermarket. Decreasing the service time is more difficult although it may be done by using more experienced staff (perhaps full-timers rather than part-timers). This is, of course, a feature of capacity management as discussed in Chapter 4.

(e) *Provide different service points* for different categories of customers. This is seen with fast checkouts in supermarkets for customers with a specified low number of purchases and the various customer-operated pay-out and pay-in facilities in banks. All of these measures help to increase the customer's sense of control in the service environment.

6. CONCLUSIONS

The management of queues is one of the most important aspects of service operations management. Many of the queueing systems which develop are complex and difficult to completely predict what is likely to happen, even with the use of mathematical modelling. The service operations manager is often left without any guidance from statistical models to produce an optimum solution, trading off costs of the service-producing unit and the level of the service which is given to customers. There are a number of options which can be used either to make changes to the capacity of the service-producing unit or to change the customer's perception of the queue and the waiting time.

Appendix 1

Analytical Approaches to Queueing

1. SIMPLE QUEUEING MODELS

The classic queueing model is for a single server with a single queue. It assumes that:

(a) Customer arrivals can be approximated by a Poisson distribution.
(b) Customer service times can be approximated by an exponential distribution.
(c) There are no constraints on queue length or service capacity.
(d) A first-come-first-served queueing discipline is followed.

If we define the following variables:

λ = mean arrival rate (number of customers per unit of time)
μ = mean service rate (number of customers served per unit of time)

$\dfrac{1}{\mu}$ = mean service time per customer

then the mathematics of queueing theory give us the following equations:

1. Service utilization (proportion of time the server is busy):

$$\rho = \frac{\lambda}{\mu}$$

2. Mean length of queue (number of customers in the queue):

$$L_q = \frac{\lambda^2}{\mu(\mu - \lambda)}$$

3. Expected number of customers in the queue *and* being served:

$$L_s = \frac{\lambda}{\mu - \lambda}$$

4. Mean time a customer waits in the queue:

$$W_q = \frac{\lambda}{\mu(\mu - \lambda)}$$

5. Mean time a customer is in the system (queueing *and* being served):

$$W_s = \frac{1}{\mu - \lambda}$$

6. The probability of having no customers in the system:

$$P(0) = 1 - \left(\frac{\lambda}{\mu}\right)$$

7. The probability of having n customers in the system (queueing and being served):

$$P(n) = P(0)\left(\frac{\lambda}{\mu}\right)^n$$

Example

What serving rate must we set in a hamburger restaurant if the arrival rate is 120 per hour and we wish to have a mean time in the system of one minute?

$$W_s = 1, \qquad \lambda = 2 \text{ per minute}$$

We must solve equation 5 for μ:

$$1 = \frac{1}{\mu - 2}$$

$$\mu - 2 = 1$$

$$\mu = 3 \text{ per minute}$$

Therefore serving time must be 20 seconds per customer.

The simple queueing theory does not cover more complex situations, such as multi-channel systems and service times following other distributions. For more complex situations or when the assumptions stated above do not hold, simulation modelling can be used.

2. SIMULATION MODELLING

Simulation modelling is a powerful tool for examining the behaviour of more complex queueing systems and the impact of various decision variables on the service level and the cost of providing service. No special techniques are required; standard modelling procedures enable one to simulate complex systems and patterns of variability that are different from the standard Poisson distribution, and different patterns of customer behaviour and queue disciplines.

3.   USE OF ANALYSIS

The two key measures of a system performance in a queueing environment are the service level of the customer and the cost of providing the service. Any analysis of a service system will normally examine the effect of the controlled and non-controlled variables on these measures. Customer service at its simplest is the average queue length. Average queue length is a function of the variability of arrivals rate and of service time, the number and capacity of the service channels, the arrival rate, and customer behaviour. Customer service can be looked at in more details in terms of the service rates of individual groups of customers, the variability of queue length, and the maximum queue length.

A key element of cost is the service facility utilization. This is primarily a function of the queue length and the variability of arrival and service times. For a given queue length, the utilization will fall with an increase in variability. For a given variability, the utilization will increase with an increase in queue length. There is an obvious trade-off between the cost of providing service capacity, the economic benefits of high utilization, and the costs of low customer service if queues are too long.

There are a number of decision areas where analysis of queueing can be of great benefit:

(a) *Service facility capacity planning*. Formal queueing analysis can be of great benefit in helping to decide the required capacity of a service system. Given forecasts of demand patterns and customer behaviour, it is possible to evaluate various possible combinations of capacity and queue lengths. Such analysis may, for example, be used in deciding on the pattern and capacity of new lifts in a ski resort or deciding how much capacity to build into a new hamburger restaurant to ensure that queues do not exceed a certain length at the peak.

(b) *Service facility operational planning*. Many service facilities are characterized by the ease with which short-term capacity can be changed. For example, a supermarket can vary its checkout capacity quite easily to meet changes in demand throughout the day. Queueing analysis can help in determining the best manning schedules to meet customer service levels at minimum cost, and in developing decision rules for increasing and decreasing service facility capacity in the short term.

(c) *Queue discipline and demand management policies*. Once a queueing environment has been modelled, it is possible to consider the alternative queue discipline policies and demand management policies that can be applied to the customers of the system.

Case Study: The Baker Street Branch

In March 1982 Swee Lian Tay and Satome Terabe, Master's students at the London Business School, became frustrated with the slow service at their bank. They decided to study its front end operation. The bank was a branch of one of the Big Four, situated at the corner of Baker Street and Marylebone Road in London. The internal layout of the bank is shown in Figure 1. As an alternative to teller service, two automatic cash dispensers were situated opposite the till.

Figure 1   Layout of the Baker Street branch

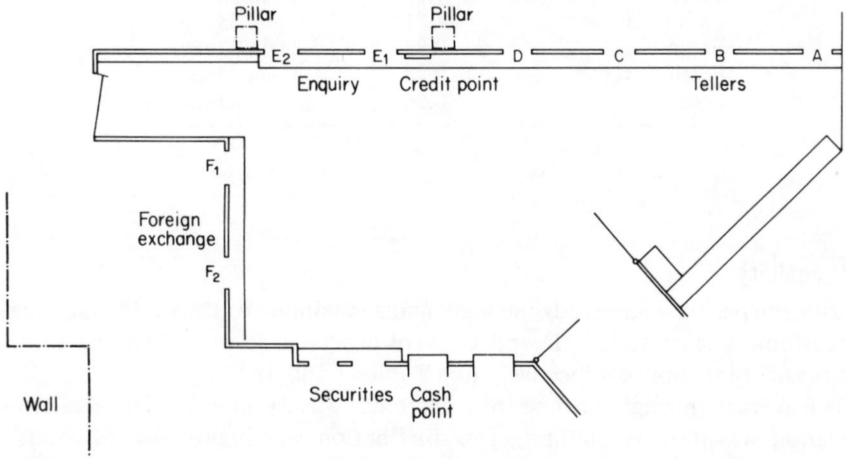

Swee Lian and Satome chose a peak period, from 12:10 to 14:00 on Friday 5th March. They observed and timed every transaction during this period. (A summary of these transactions broken down by type of service is shown in Table 1.)

1.   RESULTS

The bank was visited by 536 people − 481 of these used the services of the bank while 41 were 'friends' of customers. Fourteen people left because the bank was too crowded. Table 2 gives the arrival rate for the various services provided.

This case was written by Dr. C.A. Voss, London Business School. It is intended for teaching purposes only.

Table 1   Services provided

Transactions	Proportion (%)
Withdrawals from current A/C	
Withdrawals from deposit A/C	42.4
Deposit (cc/dep. A/C)	
Transfer/bank giro	
Cash point	41.4
Enquiry	8.7
Foreign exchange	6.0
Others (securities, etc.)	1.5
Total	100.0

Table 2   Arrival rate

	Customer/min	Interval
Tellers	1.85	0 min 32 sec
Cash point	1.81	0 min 33 sec
Enquiry	0.38	2 min 37 sec
Foreign exchange	0.26	3 min 48 sec
Others	0.06	15 min 43 sec

1.1   Tellers

During the period under study the bank had a maximum of three tellers serving its customers. Two tellers, D and C, were observed between 12:18 to 13:07 hours and 14:02 hours respectively (see Tables 3 and 4).

The average throughput time for a customer was $3\frac{1}{2}$ minutes. The standard deviation was also $3\frac{1}{2}$ minutes. The distribution was highly skewed. Some customers had to wait as long as 19 minutes. During this period the tellers were fully occupied and had to do some transactions in parallel. A customer, on average, spent as much time being served as in the queue (1 min 43 sec compared to 1 min 52 sec respectively). Ninety per cent of the transactions could be served within 1 min 22 sec. There was a wide range of service times, however, from 9 sec to 18 min 51 sec.

1.2   Queue Length

When counter D was opened the maximum queue length was eight. After 13:00 hours when counter A was opened and counter D closed, congestion occurred at counter C because the queue at counter C prevented access to counters A and B.

Table 3 Service rate

		Throughput time (sec)	Service time (sec)	Queueing time (sec)
Total (C+D)	n	83	83	83
	$\bar{x}$	215 (3m 35s)	103 (1m 43s)	112 (1m 52s)
	s	214	128	171
Teller C	n	55	55	55
	$\bar{x}$	193 (3m 13s)	74 (1m 14s)	119 (1m 59s)
	s	139	100	97
Teller D	n	28	28	28
	$\bar{x}$	257 (4m 17s)	151 (2m 31s)	106 (1m 46s)
	s	313	219	224

n = number of customers
$\bar{x}$ = mean
s = deviation

Table 4 Service time (C and D)

	Withdrawals from current A/C	Transfer deposit bank giro	Large transactions and withdrawals from dep. A/C	Others (multiple transactions, change, etc.)	Average
Sample size	46	31	4	5	86 (TOTAL)
Average service time	1m 22s	38s	11m 12s	3m 46s	1m 43s
Standard deviation	43s	35s	5m 22s	1m 47s	2m 08s
Range	38s – 4m 10s	9s – 3m 07s	7m 24s – 18m 51s	22s – 6m 15s	9s – 18m 51s

1.3 Cash Dispensing Machines

The queues at the cash dispensing machines moved at a faster rate than those at the tellers. Service time was about one minute per customer. On one occasion the queue built up to seven but this was quickly cleared.

1.4   Enquiry and Foreign Exchange Counters

Only once were there more than three customers at each of the enquiry and foreign exchange counters (at 12:42 hours when there were four customers at the foreign exchange counter). The service rate at these counters varied because of the diversity of the transactions, but customers were few and easily manageable.

2.   OTHER OBSERVATIONS

The pair noticed that the bank faced several problems due mainly to the fact that the bank premises was too small to support the volume of throughput.

2.1   Inadequate Queueing Space at Counter A

Figure 2 shows the queue pattern with counter D opened and counter A closed. As can be seen, the queue was just about manageable. However, when counter D was closed and A opened, congestion began to build up. A snapshot at 13:10 hours 30 sec is given in Figure 3. Customers were confused and did not know which queue to join. Some simply hung around and waited for the queue to sort itself out before joining. Others joined the queue at counter C, then discovered that A and B were open and joined them instead. This resulted in unfair queueing as later arrivals were served first. If the queue at counter C was more than four, customers could not go to counters A and B. The reformation of the queue would lead to later customers being served first.

2.2   Closing of Counters not Brought to the Attention of Customers

The tellers indicated that they were open by lighting up the 'open' sign above their counters. Unfortunately, even when the lighting of the 'open' sign had

Figure 2   Queue at teller D at 1258 hours 30 sec

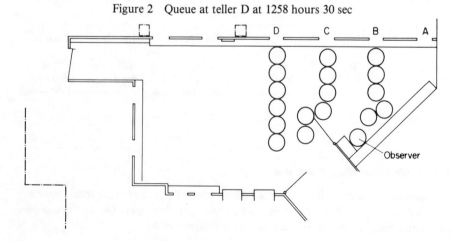

been switched off, customers continued to queue at the counter because the teller was still serving the last customer. These customers were told later to rejoin other queues. This could cause customers to become irritated.

2.3   Forms for Withdrawals from Deposit Account and Transfers Available Only from Tellers

Although the bank had forms for deposits and giro available in the banking hall, the forms for withdrawals and transfers had to be obtained from the tellers. Customers had the problem of having to queue for a form, filling in the form, then deciding where to rejoin the queue (i.e. either at the end of the queue or after the last person being served).

2.4   Withdrawals from Deposit Accounts Require Manual Verification

The need to verify customers' balances when withdrawals were requested added not only to the customers' waiting time but also added to the problem of queueing space. There was no place for the customers to wait for their names to be called. The customers nevertheless had to be near the tellers so that they could hear their names being called. It took about 11 minutes for an account to be verified.

3.   THE BANK'S ATTITUDE

Swee Lian and Satome discussed their results with the manager of the Branch. The manager did not feel that they were of much interest or relevance to him. Operations was the responsibility of head office staff, not himself.

Figure 3   Queue at teller C at 1310 hours 30 sec

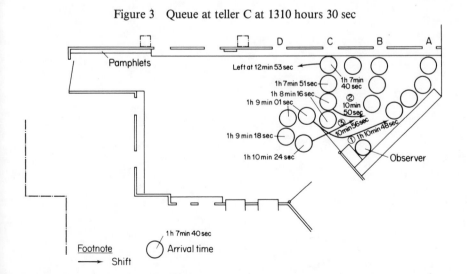

Chapter 9

Material Management

Colin G. Armistead

Material management covers all the activities which are associated with obtaining and looking after materials. As such it will include the processes of purchasing or buying, stock or inventory control, and stores control and distribution. In many service operations, materials do not play a large operational part, e.g. in professional services. However, if the control of information is included in the overall term of materials management then in this context it is applicable to a wide range of service operations. Other service operations such as retailing have materials as one of the most important features; many of the more advanced material control systems are to be found in these organizations. Other services such as banks have a special requirement of security for their materials management control systems (i.e. money). It is only possible in a short text to identify the main aspects of materials management and not to examine individual service operations.

1. THE AIM OF MATERIALS MANAGEMENT

The aims of materials management are:

(a) To supply the service operation with the materials at the specified quality, quantity, at the time they are required
(b) To ensure continuity of supply by maintaining good relationships with existing suppliers and developing new sources
(c) To maintain inventories at a lowest cost while sustaining the required level of service (in terms of availability of materials when they are needed)

2. MATERIALS AND MONEY

Apart from the actual costs of buying materials there are other costs associated with obtaining and looking after materials. The main areas in which costs are incurred are:

(a) Ordering and delivery costs
(b) Carrying costs

(c) Stockout costs

(d) Cost of the stock administration

Each of these will be looked at in more detail:

(a) *Ordering and delivery costs.* When an order is placed there is a cost incurred in placing the order. This will be greatest for the first order, when a number of suppliers have to be contacted, than for a repeat order from the same supplier.

(b) *Carrying costs.* The costs of holding stocks of materials arise from the following factors:

    (i) Money which is used in stocks might otherwise be employed to generate a return.

    (ii) Cost of storage space arising from rates and rent, heating, lighting, materials handling equipment.

    (iii) The loss of stock through deterioration or damage.

    (iv) Insurance charges.

In total the annual carrying cost can typically be 25 per cent of the total cost of the stocks.

(c) *Stockout costs.* The cost of not having materials available when they are required is difficult to calculate as it may result in the loss of a customer's business in the future and has the immediate effect of loss of contribution.

(d) *Costs of administration.* There are costs associated with running materials management systems in terms of wages, office space, and data processing systems.

3. REASONS FOR HOLDING STOCKS OF MATERIALS

Given that there are substantial financial costs associated with holding materials service operations still maintain stocks for the following reasons:

(a) To decouple the service operation from the supplier

(b) As an insurance against supplies being interrupted, e.g. by weather conditions or industrial disputes

(c) To take advantage of price variations which result from fluctuations caused by supply and demand changes

(d) To gain economies by purchasing in large quantities

4. MATERIAL MANAGEMENT DECISIONS

Materials management is a trade-off between the various costs entailed in procuring and holding stocks of materials. The decisions which relate to this trade-off are not taken by one individual in an organization and the separation of the different decision makers can cause problems for the overall management of materials within a particular organization. The sectors who are involved are purchasing (or buying), stock controllers, operations, and marketing. The decisions to be made are:

(a) What to buy (operations/marketing/buyers)
(b) Where to buy (purchasing/buying)
(c) How much to buy (stock controllers/purchasing/buying)
(d) When to buy (stock controllers/purchasing/buying)

4.1 What to Buy

The specification of the items to be purchased may come from the operations people (field service, transport operations) or from marketing (merchandisers in retailing operations). The way in which specifications are presented is important if those carrying out the purchasing process are to be able to obtain the materials at the lowest total cost. If the specification is too explicit it will reduce the flexibility for the purchaser to look at a range of possible suppliers. On the other hand, if the specification is too loosely defined it makes it difficult for the purchasing person to know what is in the mind of the person requiring the materials. It is important that the purchasing section should know which particular aspects on a specification can or cannot be modified.

The specification of what to buy requires good communications between the buyer, the user, and the designer (if they are different people). Good communications and realistic specifications give a greater opportunity for standardization of materials which are bought. This assists in the overall quality control of materials and thus the service package as it reaches the customer; service operations which have a number of different sites often have a centralized system of specifying and buying to gain the benefits of standardization.

The quality of materials which are specified and purchased has other consequences. It may be particularly important in service operations to know that materials received from suppliers meet the buying specifications because the delay in obtaining replacement could mean that customers could not receive the service. Consequently, the quality control tests which are required for the materials are often included as part of the purchase specification.

4.2 Where to Buy

Purchasing should be a dynamic activity with the purchasing people maintaining a continuous assessment of the suppliers who might sell materials needed by the organization whether or not they are currently suppliers. Major suppliers or those who might become major suppliers may be subjected to a detailed assessment with respect to their operational competence and their financial stability (suppliers who cease to trade could put the customer organization at risk). Areas for assessment may include:

- Prices
- Contract terms
- Financial record
- Management structure
- Capacity
- Premises
- Technical competence
- Quality
- Planning and control systems

A less detailed assessment scheme for evaluating existing or past suppliers is that of 'vendor rating', when a number of assessment criteria (e.g. quality, price, delivery lead time, delivery reliability, and customer service) are given a weighting (say quality: 9, customer service: 6, price, delivery lead time, and reliability: 4). Each supplier is given an assessment for each criteria, which is multiplied by the weighting, and the multiplied quantities for all the criteria are totalled for each supplier. For example, if there are three suppliers, X, Y, and Z, for particular materials an assessment can be made of them with regard to past performance on price, quality, delivery lead time, delivery reliability, and customer service by combining a performance rating for each of the criteria on a scale of 1 to 10 with the weighting for each criteria and creating a points total for each supplier. The supplier with the highest points total is the most favoured. This is shown to be supplier Y in the example below.

Assessment criteria	Suppliers		
	X	Y	Z
Price	$2 \times 4 = 8$	$4 \times 4 = 16$	$6 \times 4 = 24$
Quality	$3 \times 9 = 27$	$5 \times 9 = 45$	$5 \times 9 = 45$
Delivery lead time	$2 \times 4 = 8$	$4 \times 4 = 16$	$3 \times 4 = 12$
Delivery reliability	$6 \times 4 = 24$	$4 \times 4 = 16$	$3 \times 4 = 12$
Customer service	$5 \times 6 = 30$	$4 \times 6 = 24$	$3 \times 6 = 18$
Totals	97	117	111

If alternative sources of materials are evaluated there is often the possibility of obtaining supplies from more than one supplier i.e. multiple sourcing. In deciding whether to multi- or single-source a number of factors may be considered:

(a) *The price*. It may be that buying from one supplier allows a reduction in the purchase price to be negotiated because of the quantities. On the other hand, the use of several suppliers may lead to price reductions through competition between the suppliers.

(b) *Supplier security*. Single-sourcing may be easier to organize but it may present problems if anything happens to the supplier and another is not readily available.

(c) *Standing with the supplier*. If supplies are bought from more than one supplier the quantities which are ordered may reduce the priority which an individual supplier gives to the purchaser. It is often useful for an organization to make an assessment of all of its suppliers in terms of the supplier standing/position in the eyes of the organization and the organization's standing/position of importance in the eyes of the supplier. In extreme cases where an important supplier gives the organization a low priority it is time for the organization to identify other possible suppliers.

(d) *Market structure*. Buying from a single source may help to create a monopoly for that supplier with the power to control prices.

4.3 When to Buy

Two factors are important when deciding when to buy: firstly, uncertainty about future requirements and, secondly, uncertainty about the lead time to obtain materials from a supplier.

Uncertainty about future requirements may be quantified by the application of forecasting techniques on the basis of historical demand. Uncertainty about the lead time may be quantified statistically from the variation in lead time for past orders from a particular supplier; alternatively, the longest lead time from the last few orders may be used when placing the next order.

The various stock control systems aim to indicate when orders should be placed for new supplies of materials.

In service operations dealing with food and other perishable items the lead times are often very short. It is the aim of effective purchasing to reduce lead times wherever this is possible, as this allows an overall reduction in the level of stocks which are required.

4.4 How much to Buy

The question of how much to order can be complicated. The decision centres around whether to purchase the whole of the requirements for a particular period in a single order or whether the requirement should be divided in some way into a number of orders. Again it is a question of a trade-off between costs. There are a number of theoretical models which can be used to calculate the size of batches to be ordered; the oldest and best known is the economic order quantity (EOQ) formula which aims to balance the cost of placing an order with the cost of carrying stock according to the formula:

$$EOQ = \sqrt{\frac{2 \times \text{average annual demand} \times \text{cost of placing one order}}{\text{cost of holding one item of the stock}}}$$

The EOQ calculation is generally crude in this simple form, as apart from the difficulties associated with establishing the cost data the other assumptions of continuous demand over a period of time and instantaneous replenishment of stocks are not always met. Instead of being used as absolute statements of order quantities the EOQs in one form of another provide a useful guide to purchasing people on the quantities to include in a single order.

A frequent consideration when deciding on the order quantity for a single order is whether there are discounts offered by the supplier for orders of larger quantities. The decision to increase the size of an order depends on whether the savings given by the discount are sufficient to compensate for the increased costs incurred in having to hold extra stock. This evaluation is incorporated into mathematical formula based on the EOQ formula.

A similar decision to that for discounts may be taken when it is possible to buy a number of different items from one supplier on one order. The question is whether it is less costly to reduce the cost of ordering while increasing stocking costs.

5. THE PURCHASING PROCESS

There are several main ways in which purchases may be made:

(a) *Standard buying* is the type of buying in which a single order is placed for a quantity of goods. This order may or may not be repeated.
(b) *Contract buying* in which a contract is entered into with a supplier for a quantity of goods over a period of time. The phasing of the deliveries may be agreed at the time the contract is placed or order may be made against the contract as and when they are needed. The advantage of this type of buying is that it allows the price of the goods to be fixed for the whole contracted quantity at a lower price than would be possible for smaller orders.
(c) *Sole supplier agreements* are agreements with a single supplier to supply all the requirements for particular goods.

The steps in the purchasing process are:

(a) *Selection of possible suppliers.*
(b) *The enquiry.* Once a number of possible suppliers have been identified an enquiry is sent to each of them which will seek to find out if they can meet the requirement and to obtain details of the terms of supply.
(c) *The quotation.* Assuming there are a number of suppliers who provide a satisfactory source for the goods that are required then the placing of orders will depend on the price and other conditions of supply and sale. A comparison of these factors for the possible suppliers is compiled after asking each of them to provide a quotation.
(d) *Assessment and negotiation.* Once a number of suppliers have submitted quotations these are assessed and alterations in the terms offered can be negotiated with individual suppliers before deciding where to place the order.

(e) *The purchase order*. The purchase order is very often one of a set of five forms. Two are copies of the order itself, one for the buying department and the other for the goods receiving department. Two others are a purchase delivery record card and an acknowledgement of order form (to be returned by the supplier on receipt of the order). The last copy is sent to accounts.

(f) *Progressing an order*. The purpose of progress is twofold: firstly, to check before delivery is made that goods that have been ordered will be delivered on time and, secondly, to chase orders that are late.

(g) *Goods receiving*. When goods are delivered to the receiving department they are checked to ensure that the quantity (and perhaps the quality) is correct. In some cases it may not be possible to inspect goods for quality as they are received and the goods may then be accepted subject to inspection.

(h) *Payment* against an invoice from the supplier after checking the goods received documents.

6. MAKE OR BUY DECISIONS

The decision on whether to make or buy a particular item depends on a number of factors which involve marketing and operations as well as purchasers directly. The decision is often part of the design of the service operation as, for example, a fast food outlet will buy hamburgers ready for cooking whereas a restaurant may make its own hamburgers. Decisions may be made on the basis of:

(a) *Focusing of operations*. On the premise that it is easier to do a few things well within an operation, service organizations usually do not wish to be major manufacturers (field service operations are an exception) and thus for the most part buy from a supplier. However, many service organizations (notably large retailers) will influence the manufacturing operations of their suppliers to ensure quality and delivery standards.

(b) *Quality*. A service organization may choose to make items if it is uncertain about the quality of the items it can receive from a supplier. Alternatively, the organization may choose to buy as the reasons in (a) mean that the quality of materials from a supplier is easier to control.

(c) *Costs* will always be a factor in making an evaluation of whether to buy or make a particular item. A supplier may have economies of scale of manufacture.

(d) *Delivery time and reliability of delivery* may be a factor in deciding to make rather than buy if no alternative sources of supply are available.

7. LOOKING AFTER MATERIALS

Once materials have been delivered there is a requirement to look after them in a way which keeps the quantities at levels which provide the required supply to the operations while meeting financial constraints and gives effective access to the materials as they are needed by the operations. The first requirement is met by using a stock control system and the second by effective stores or wharehouse management, materials handling, and distribution.

8.   STOCK CONTROL SYSTEMS

Stock control systems used in service industries fall into two main categories:

(a) Fixed order point (re-order level) system
(b) Periodic review (re-order cycle) system

Fixed order point systems are based on using a changing level of stocks as the means of deciding when to replenish the stock, whereas periodic review systems are time based using the level of stock at regular time periods to indicate whether replenishments are needed.

8.1   Fixed Order Point

The use of stock and the replenishments for stock items which are used regularly shows the pattern in Figure 9.1 for the fixed order point system. This has the following features:

(a) The stock level is monitored continuously.
(b) When the stock quantity drops below a re-order level an order is placed. The re-order level is a function of the expected rate of demand over the lead time for replenishment (DOLT) with an allowance for errors in estimates (i.e. a safety stock S). Thus:

$$\text{Re-order level} = \text{DOLT} + S$$

(c) The amount ordered is a fixed quantity (often based on an economic order quantity).

Figure 9.1   Fixed order point stock control

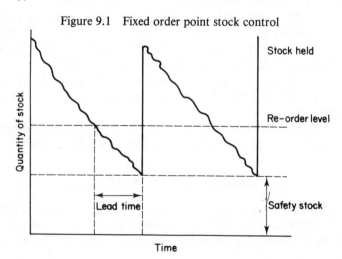

The safety stock level can be calculated statistically to give a particular level of availability of materials (i.e. probability of stockouts) based on the variability in historical data for the lead time.

The fixed order point system is commonly used in computer-based stock control systems which have replaced the stock card systems where records of the quantities of a stock item are kept on a card which is altered as stock is removed or replaced or ordered.

8.2 Periodic Review

The periodic review system does not require the stock levels to be monitored continuously as in the fixed order point system; rather the stock quantities are reviewed at regular intervals of time and if the stock is then found to be below a predetermined level an order is placed to restore the stock to that level (at that time). A typical pattern for the periodic review system is shown in Figure 9.2. The system has the following features:

(a) A fixed interval between reviews. The length of time is a function of the importance of the stock item and the costs of holding the stock item.
(b) A variable quantity is ordered each time to bring the stock level back to a maximum (the system is often called the 'topping-up system'). The maximum level may be calculated as a function of the expected rate of demand (D) over the lead time for replenishment (L) and the review period (P) with a safety allowance for errors. Thus:

Maximum stock level $= D(P+L) + S$

The safety stock may be calculated in a similar manner to that indicated for the fixed order point system.

9. CHOICE OF STOCK CONTROL SYSTEMS

The choice of a stock control will depend on a number of factors:

Figure 9.2   Periodic review 'topping-up' stock control

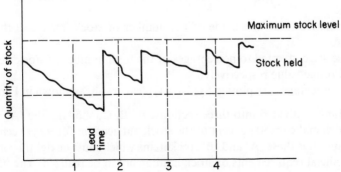

(a) If orders are placed and delivered from suppliers at regular intervals (e.g. daily, weekly, monthly) or a number of different items are ordered and delivered from one supplier the periodic review system is the more likely to be used.

(b) If the stock item is used regularly and does not conform to the conditions of (a) the fixed order point system is more appropriate.

(c) If the stock item is particularly important a manual method of frequent stock checking and ordering may be more appropriate. This requires some form of stock classification.

10. CLASSIFICATION OF MATERIAL STOCKS

The importance of a particular stock item and consequently decisions on which stock control systems to be instituted follow from seeking answers to questions like the following for each stock item:

(a) Why is the item stocked at all?

(b) How critical is the item to the operations?

(c) What is the pattern of demand?

(d) Is the item perishable?

(e) Are there volume constraints on stocking?

(f) Are there weight constraints on stock holding?

(g) Are there security constraints on stock holding (e.g. bonded items or money)?

(h) What is the ease of replenishment?

(i) Where does the item lie in an ABC (Pareto) analysis?

The Pareto (ABC) analysis is a method of classifying stocks according to usage value following the relationship that for most stocks a large proportion of the money spent on materials is associated with a small proportion of the total number of stock items.

The basic steps in the analysis are as follows:

(a) For each stock item the average usage value is calculated in terms of money per unit time (e.g. pounds a year).

(b) A list of all items is made starting with the item with the highest usage value.

(c) Cumulative totals are made of the number of stock items and the usage values.

(d) These are converted to percentages of the total number of stock items and total usage value respectively.

(e) The percentages are plotted to give a typical graph, as shown in Figure 9.3.

The graph is divided into three sections, A, B, C, showing the 'A' and 'B' items which make up 50 per cent of the stock but account for 90 per cent of the usage value. It is these 'A' and 'B' stock items which must be tightly controlled if the financial requirements of stock holding are to be realized. The 'C' items

Figure 9.3   Pareto analysis for stock classification

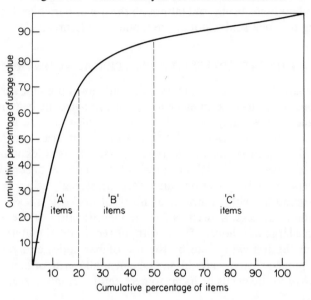

do not require the same degree of control financially although they may still be operationally important. The use of the Pareto analysis allows decisions to be made on which items to stock and the methods of control for each item or classes of items.

11.   ORGANIZATION OF MATERIALS MANAGEMENT

In a large service organization with a number of sites there exists the choice of whether to centralize the procurement process and also to have centralized distribution centres which supply the individual sites. The factors which influence the choice are:

(a) More influence over suppliers from buying in large quantities − centralize
(b) Specialism by buyers − centralize
(c) Standardized materials − centralize
(d) Perishable items − local
(e) Flexibility to move materials − centralize where they are most needed

Service operations which maintain centralized purchasing and distribution are notably the retailers who supply individual stores on a daily to weekly basis from a main warehouse. The growth of computer-assisted stock recording systems both in the warehouse and the stores allows a rapid compilation of the items and quantities which are needed to replenish items in the stores. This allows the level of stocks in the individual stores to be kept to a minimum. Food retailers in particular are able through the use of computer assistance to replace stocks overnight to refill shop shelves. This is achieved by the use of bar coding on shelves and on items being sold (although the use of bar codes for point-of-sale recording of stock sold is not at the moment widespread).

12. COMPUTER-ASSISTED MATERIALS CONTROL

The rapid spread of low cost computers is now making it possible for small service operations which have to manage materials to realize the benefits of computer assistance. These may be simple systems which replace a stock card system with a computer recording system. If this is integrated with financial data it is possible to carry out Pareto-type analysis of the stock items easily.

Those service operations which must have effective material control systems like the retailers and field service operations are increasingly using computers to assist in warehouses with computer control of forklift trucks and other material-handling devices, as well as for the identification of the location of stock items in a large warehouse. Taken with the recording of material used and required from the individual site by the use of bar codes and point-of-sale systems, computer-assisted materials management allows an organization to be more responsive to the needs of its customers and to maintain stocks at a low financial level.

13. INFORMATION AS A MATERIAL RESOURCE

While many service operations do not have physical materials as a large part of their service package they do have to manage information and maintain stocks or inventories of information which are accessible for use by the operations people in the production of the service package. While there are not complete parallels with all the physical stock control systems there are, nevertheless, some similarities:

(a) Accessibility for operations
(b) Security
(c) Need to classify
(d) Need to update
(e) Need to remove obsolete items
(f) A trade-off between the system performance and cost

The biggest difference between information and physical stocks is that information can be sold or given away but still be retained by the service organization.

Service organizations have been some of the major users of information technology to allow the rapid transfer and switching of information between different sites. This process will continue with customers increasingly participating in the process through the use of linked computer terminals in the home.

14. CONCLUSION

In many service operations, materials management forms a large part of the operational activities. These operations have been successful in introducing computer assistance to improve the ordering, stock control, and delivery of materials. Other service organizations may have a low physical materials content but do have a large information inventory, which must be managed in many ways which are similar to physical materials; again computer-assisted systems of information management are increasingly being used.

Case Study: Hospital Stores

John Barnes is the Stores Manager in a hospital stores which serves the main hospital in which it is located, as well as six other hospitals in the group through smaller satellite stores. John is responsible for sixteen people who are all storemen and clerks, with the exception of two who are butchers, and he reports to Mr. Dove, the Area Supplies Officer.

The supplies consist of items in the following main categories:

- Provisions
- Hardware
- Crockery
- Medical and surgical
- Clothing
- Stationery

The main stores are situated in an old building which dates from Victorian times. Several of the storage areas are not at ground level and access to them is by way of lifts.

The stock control system used by John and his people is now computer based, having moved over from a stockcard system during the past few years (although some of the bedding and linen stocks are still controlled by stockcard).

The stock control system is essentially a fixed order point system and was originally developed by the National Coal Board before being adopted by the NHS. The calculation of the re-order point is standard, with the refinement that the lead time for an order to be delivered is calculated on the basis of the longest lead time for the last ten deliveries from a supplier.

In addition to calculating the re-order level the computer programme calculates a value for an order quantity, based on a standard economic order quantity calculation. There is a provision in this part of the programme to examine the cost benefits of buying in larger quantities to obtain quantity discounts.

Until very recently there was no interaction of the stock control system and the financial systems in the hospital. However, recent changes in the computer system now make it possible to produce a printout showing the value of any

This case was prepared by Colin G. Armistead

items of stock. Replacements for stock items are ordered through the purchasing department in the main hospital. Two copies of the order to a supplier are sent to the stores and when the completed order has been received, one of the copies is sent to the finance department to initiate payment. Items are issued from the stores in response to a requisition which must be signed by someone of a required authority. John operates a strict rule with his staff and himself that items should never be added to a requisition, and stores people should not make out requisitions. A requisition should include a description of the item and catalogue number as well as the quantity required.

All additions and withdrawals are notified to the computer by computer operators who receive the goods received note and supply requisitions. John tries to ensure that his staff process all the data within a day of receiving it.

Although the introduction of the computer-based systems has aided the production of information on stocks, John is still wary of the information that appears on the printouts. As he says, 'I can't be sure of the computer information and paperwork causes the problems.'

As a result of the perceived inadequacies of the computer system, John spends a good deal of his time manually checking the system. On questions relating to the operation of the stock control system, John has complete autonomy regarding the layout of the storage area and maintenance of stocks. If adjustments have to be made to the stock records or stock written off, John must refer to Mr. Dove.

Chapter 10

Site Location

C.A. Voss

A large number of service industries involve multiple sites consisting of branches of the operation. Finding the right sites can be a major managerial problem and have a significant impact on competitiveness.

1. SITE LOCATION CONTEXT

Before embarking on selection of individual sites, the context should be examined. As a starting point, a company can ask whether, given the sort of business we are in, how do people travel to and from our branches? For example, if it is predominantly by public transport, the possible location of sites will be limited and certain sites will be better than others. Will people travel specifically to us or is it a more random decision like, say, choosing somewhere to eat, when out shopping? How far will people travel to the business that we are in? What sort of site access is needed?

The context is likely to be very different if we are breaking new ground with a new service rather than filling in the gaps in an existing network of sites. Of particular importance will be the scale economies of the service. What is the smallest economic size of site? How do fixed and variable costs and the breakeven points change with increase in size? This will influence both how densely we choose to build sites and how large a site we need for a particular location.

2. CHOOSING A TOWN

In choosing a town we must distinguish between flagship locations and satellites. We may choose to have a few, highly visible flagship locations whose high cost may be offset by marketing spinoff. Flagship towns or locations need to be evaluated for their spinoff potential.

When building chains of outlets media boundaries – radios, TV, and press – are important factors in choosing terms. Locating multiple sites within a

This was written by Dr. C.A. Voss based on a framework developed by Dr. Charles Baden Fuller of the London Business School.

single media boundary presents opportunities for lower cost and higher effectiveness in advertising.

Knowing the demographic characteristics of a town will provide much useful information as to its suitability. Demographic information includes data on population: size, age, sex, etc., income levels, growth rate, voting patterns, existing outlets, etc.

3. CHOOSING AN AREA

Within any town there are likely to be better and worse areas for locating particular businesses. Two important variables are competition and people. Who are the competition and where are they located? Is it preferable to locate near competition or away from competition? Should we locate where people live, where they work, shop, or visit or on the routes where they travel between these?

4. CHOOSING A SITE

Once an area has been selected, it is important to get to know the area. It is important to know how frequently sites are likely to become available. Much that has been written on site selection assumes that there is an abundant supply of relatively cheap sites (as in much of the United States). In large cities world wide, and most of Europe, this is not the case. When sites arise infrequently it is important to have fast-acting evaluation procedures. It is also important to have well-developed sources of information. Where sites are in short supply, they often change hands without going through estate agents. Estate agents are often left with the dregs of the market.

Knowing the area means knowing the local government and the planning regulations in areas such as town planning, fire and health regulations, and liquor licensing. Knowledge of these before a site arises is important as there is often insufficient time to explore them fully after a potential site has been found. A buyer often has to gamble on the ability to get a site reclassified for a different use.

A major characteristic of an area is its flows of traffic and people. Knowledge of car parks and bus stops, pedestrian flows, and car traffic are important. Data at a microlevel can be important. For example, the location of pedestrian crossings and traffic lights may affect the desirability of a site.

In addition to the above, there may be 'signals' of good sites. For example, a photocopy shop chain found that locations next to betting shops were particularly favourable.

5. SYSTEMATIC SITE SELECTION

In multi-site service industries developing systematic site selection procedures are important. A good procedure can be flow-charted and should identify financial and non-financial criteria for choice. Financial criteria will include at a minimum some breakeven calculation and possibly more sophisticated analysis of cash flows and discounted cash flow analysis.

Non-financial criteria will include those already outlined plus other criteria where necessary. An important part of a site selection procedure is the collection and evaluation of experience so that the knowledge base from which site selection criteria are developed can be refined.

6. BUNDLES OF SITES

A particular opportunity that can arise when searching for sites is buying a bundle of sites, often comprising an existing chain that has been closed. This provides the opportunity for rapid growth. Against this may be set a number of problems. Firstly, not all of the sites in the bundle will represent good sites for your business, even if they were good sites for the previous business. Should unsuitable sites be sold off individually and, if so, what price would they fetch? Secondly, fitting out and starting a large number of sites in a short period may cause considerable strain to both cash and management resources.

This chapter has outlined some of the considerations of site selection; the following case illustrates the specific consideration and procedures used by one large multi-site firm.

Case Study: Wimpy International (C)

In June 1982 Mike Chambers, the Franchise Sales and Planning Director of Wimpy International, was considering whether to go ahead with a site for a new counter service restaurant in Guildford. Sites in Guildford were particularly difficult to find due to the popularity of the town with retailers and lack of properties of appropriate size and location. Since their move into counter service restaurants,[1] Wimpy had been rapidly expanding throughout the country. The counter service restaurants open or under construction are shown in Exhibit 1.

1. BACKGROUND

Wimpy International had been acquired by United Biscuits in 1977. At that time, few of Wimpy's outlets were in prime sites. Moreover, most would be unlikely to be easily adapted for change. In 1977 the Managing Director wrote:[2]

> ... there is hardly a city in Britain in which the size of our outlet, the quality of the management, or the site of the outlet is correct for that city. There are many which are just totally inadequate. This has come about because of:
>
> − the changing rent equation of the High Street
> − re-development of town centres
> − introduction of one way streets
> − because there has been no compulsory renewals of equipment and property.

In 1982, Wimpy International controlled about 400 outlets, 35 of which were modern counter service outlets, the remainder being traditional 'Wimpy Bar' table service restaurants. The company's policy was to expand rapidly its network of counter service restaurants, while maintaining and refurbishing the existing table service network. The majority of the counter service and almost all of the table service outlets were operated by franchisees. For new restaurants

---

This case was written by Charles Pollard and Dr. C.A. Voss, London Business School. It is not meant to illustrate good or bad management practices. Some figures and names have been disguised.
[1] A more detailed background of Wimpy's operations is contained in the Wimpy International (A) and (B) cases.
[2] In 1977 all of Wimpy's sites were table service outlets.

Exhibit 1   Wimpy International counter service store openings

1978	Opened
Notting Hill Gate	12. 7.78 C

1979	
Hempstead Valley	24. 5.79 C
Manchester	25. 5.79 JV (Now C)
Chiswick	1. 6.79 C
Maidstone	26.10.79 C

1980	
Oxford Street	23. 5.80 C
Crawley	12. 6.80 F
Birmingham	3. 8.80 F (Now C)
Piccadilly	1. 9.80 C
Norwich	8. 9.89 C
Putney	22. 9.80 C
Sheffield	4.12.80 C

1981	
Wolverhampton	6. 4.81 F (Now C)
Windsor	25. 4.81 C
Walsall	12. 5.81 F
Bristol	14. 5.81 F
Victoria	22. 5.81 C
St. Helens	28. 5.81 F
Plymouth	8. 6.81 F
Aberystwyth	22. 6.81 F
Woodstock Street	9. 7.81 C
Blackpool	3. 9.81 F
Newcastle	24. 9.81 F
Watford	30.10.81 F
Queensway	4.11.81 F
Lewisham	13.11.81 F
Leeds	24.11.81 F
Birchwood Centre	27.11.81 F
Boscombe	1.12.81 F
Portsmouth	8.12.81 F

1982	
Cambridge	24. 2.82 F
Holborn	2. 4.82 F
Baker Street	8. 4.82 F
Walthamstow	28. 5.82 F
Romford	14. 7.82 F

Key
Company owned C
Franchised .... F
Joint venture .... JV

Wimpy intended to be an operator as well as a franchisor. In counter service they often operated a new outlet themselves for a few years before selling it to a franchisee. They thus maintained a 'rolling' core of company-owned restaurants.

It had been the company policy to expand the counter service outlets in the London TV region. In practice this policy had not always been followed. For example, sites were difficult to find and if a good site became available elsewhere it would be difficult to turn down.

2. SITE SELECTION PROCEDURES

2.1 Finding Sites

The prime responsibility for site selection lay with Mike Chambers. He was responsible for:

(a) Acquiring and managing property
(b) Design and construction of units
(c) Sales and 'propositions' to franchisees

Once a unit became operational it was handed over to the Operations Division.

For some years Wimpy had maintained a national site plan. This plan covered every target town in the United Kingdom. (In general, target towns were those with a population greater than 30,000, or smaller towns with a substantial seasonal influx of visitors.)

For each town a detailed map was prepared indicating which were good, reasonable, and poor locations. This was prepared by the Area Franchise Sales Representative. It was based on traffic counts (car and pedestrian), location of competitors, and major factors which draw customers such as Marks and Spencer stores and other factors such as the location of traffic lights, car parks, bus stations, etc., and the representative's intimate local knowledge of the area. The plan was updated annually.

In 1982 Wimpy were opening counter service sites only. There were two main sources of sites. Site finding was one of the responsibilities of the franchise sales representatives. They were encouraged to search for sites and to take steps such as joining the local Chamber of Commerce. In addition, Wimpy had an Estate Surveyor who was responsible for finding and surveying sites throughout the United Kingdom. He was continually in touch with major estate agents throughout the country. Occasionally, sites were suggested by other sources such as existing franchisees. In practice, 90 per cent of UK property was found by the main London estate agents. Wimpy's normal procedure was to find the site first, then match the franchisee to it. At any time they had a waiting list of around twenty potential franchisees.

2.2 Site Selection

When a potential site was identified the four major questions asked by Wimpy were:

(a) Is it in the right spot?
(b) Are the rent and rates affordable, given the sales potential?
(c) Will the landlord permit the building to be used for catering?
(d) If permission does not exist, will the local planners allow a change of use from retail to catering (such changes typically took many months)?

Wimpy had developed a set of procedures for assessing new sites. A summary of these procedures is shown in Exhibit 2. Mike Chambers had stated that:

> Site selection and site assessment remain an inexact science and there can be no substitute for the experience to be gained by merely opening more and more Counter Service units. However, we must take advantage of every crumb of information acquired along the way in order to give Franchisees and our own operating division the best commercial advice on this subject.

A set of guidelines had been issued to indicate the nature of the information to be collected (see Exhibit 3).

2.3 Pedestrian Flows

One of the major quantifiable factors associated with site location was the pattern and volume of pedestrian flow. It was hoped that data collected from one site could be used in another. Data from two different stores are summarized in Exhibit 4. Wimpy believed that the notional peel-off rate (the percentage of pedestrians entering the store) was about 2 per cent. It was the intention that the store size matched the demand. The cost structure for typical high and low throughput stores are shown in Exhibit 5.

3. THE GUILDFORD SITE

At the end of 1981 a prime site had been located in Guildford; a prosperous town of 56,000, Guildford had two table service Wimpy's, one quite close to the proposed site (see Exhibit 8). A preliminary collection of data (Exibits 6 and 7) indicated that the site was a candidate for a new counter service outlet. It was estimated that the net rates and rent would be about £60,000 p.a. and the gross start-up capital and other costs would be £274,000.

Mike Chambers felt that the rent and rates were £10,000 over the odds for such a site,[1] but it might be profitable. McDonalds had a store in a less favourable location on the other side of town and were reputed to be turning over £15,000 per week. The two table service Wimpy's had a relatively low turn-

---

[1] Wimpy did a rule-of-thumb calculation of maximum affordable rent and rates based on a first estimate of potential turnover. For Guildford the maximum figure was £50,000 p.a.

Exhibit 2   Procedural checklist

Franchise sales division
Form F.S.D.   10A/81

APPLICANTS NAME:

	Franch Sales Exec	Franch Sales Mngt	Franch Plan Comm	Prop Dept	Finance Dept	Ops Dept	Mkting Dept	Project Co-ord	Train Dept	Legal Dept	Buying Dept
1 Initial interview with applicant	A	I									
2 Franchise application completed, applicant approved	A	I									
3 Site feasibility request	I	A									
4 Apply for change of use	A	I									
5 Site located, evaluated and approved	A	C	I	I		C					
6 Site assessment form completed	A	I	I	C	I	I		I			
7 1st year cash estimate completed	A	I	I	I	C	I		I			
8 Conditions confirmed and accepted by applicant	A	I	I	I	I	I	I	I	I	I	I
9 Freehold or headlease offer accepted subject to contract	I	I		A						I	
10 Sub-lease terms accepted by applicant subject to contract	I	I						I	I	A	
11 Exchange of contracts for freehold/leasehold & sub-lease	I	I	I								
12 Payment of non-returnable deposit by applicant	I	I		I	I			I			
13 Product sketch plan	I	I			I	I	A	I			
14 Agree sketch plan with applicant	A	I			C	I					
15 Product detailed plans and specifications	I	I				C		A			
16 Agree detailed plans and specifications with applicant	A			I		I		C			
17 Landlords permission	I	I		I				A			
18 Apply for full planning permission	I	I		I				A			

Activity	1	2	3	4	5	6	7	8
19 Invite quotes from shopfitters	I	I		A				C
20 Establish equipment requirements	I	I		A		I		I
21 Agree appointment of shopfitter with applicant				A				C
22 Agree equipment requirements with applicant	I	I		A		I		C
23 Obtain full planning permission	I			A		I	I	I
24 Confirm starting date and estimated completion date	I	I	A	A	I	I	I	I
25 Instruct buying department to purchase equipment				A			I	I
26 Supervise shopfitter, assist in authorising stage payments in conjunction with applicant				A		I		I
27 Buy equipment	A			A				I
28 Arrange supply of all equipment	A		A	I	I			I
29 Arrange training of applicant and staff				I				I
30 Complete general details form and submit to H.O.						C	I	A
31 Send franchise agreement and trade mark form to F.S.E.			I			A	I	I
32 Sign-up applicant and obtain balance of franchise fee						I	I	A
33 Send signed franchise agreement & trade mark form to H.O.				I	I	I	I	A
34 Arrange store openings						I	A	I
35 Arrange store promotion	I	I	I	I	A	I	I	I

Key : A = Action
I = Inform
C = Consult

Exhibit 3   Site selection guidelines

1. LOCATION
   Population of town
   Population of surrounding district
   Seasonal influences
   General spending power of locals

2. PHYSICAL LOCATION
   Type of shopping area, i.e. prime High Street
   Surrounding buildings, i.e. office − Bedsitters
   Other factors relevant to pedestrian flow, i.e. proximity to:
   1. Post offices
   2. Railway stations
   3. Bus stops
   4. Bus station
   5. Dance halls
   6. Bingo halls
   7. Theatres
   8. Cinemas
   9. Car parks
   10. Any local situations which would influence potential
   11. Cars able to stop within 200 yd of site

3. COMPETITORS
   Position of competitors' sites
   Menu contents of above
   Price structure of menus of above

4. OTHER FACTORS
   Position of pedestrian crossings
   One-way streets
   Pavement width
   Area and size of maximum pedestrian flow on the High Street
   Good visability
   Spending power of public

SUMMARY OF AREA FOR LOCATION
   A good site for a Wimpy will be an amalgam of all of points mentioned above. This can be summarized as good visibility balanced with maximum pedestrian flow, so as to maximize profitability potential.

5. THE SITE
   1. Cost
      Due to high capital cost of freehold property, it is normal practice to secure a lease on property, rather than buy the freehold.
   2. Lease
      The standard term of a lease is ____ years, with rent reviews at ____ and ____ years. The majority of leases are 'full repairing and insuring'.
      − Minimum term acceptable ____ years
      − Offers for a lease should be made subject to:
        Landlords consent
        Planning permission and Wimpy International's acceptance
   3. Rent and rates
      To be within ____% of the turnover potential, i.e. £____ potential T/O per week
      − rent and rates between £____ and £____ per week. Turnover potential to be advised by the Franchise Negotiator.

.4 The Building
Should check on:
1. Wide open frontage
2. Minimum acceptable width
3. Clear open floorspace
4. Split level floor
5. Rear access
6. Ceiling height
7. Minimum structural alteration required
8. Basement or first floor storage space available
9. Columns
10. Ventilation possibilities
11. Age of building
12. Floor loadings, etc.
5. Size
An approximate guide to seating capacity related to square feet of floor space is:
300 sq ft − 20 seats. (This figure will vary depending on the shape of the shop and whether it is for table or counter service.)

over of about £60,000 p.a. each. Despite this, Wimpy were pursuing the matter further and 'change of use' had been applied for in January 1982.

The site had a number of potential problems. The ground floor was of limited size and to get the required number of seats, the basement would have to be utilized. This would give thirty-four seats on the ground floow and forty-five in the basement. There were also problems with getting an even shopfront line because of potential development of the neighbouring shop.

By the middle of June Mike Chambers was being pressed for a quick decision. It would seem that at least two other fast food retailers were interested in the site. However, change of use permission had yet to be received from the council. The council were concerned about a number of issues including the amount and the nature of the delivery traffic, the litter from take-away customers, the prospect of extra cars coming to Wimpy's, overloading the car parks, and whether such a restaurant was needed (see Exhibit 9). Wimpy were using a skilled development planning consultant to try and ensure change of use permission was granted.

On 7th July, Mike Chambers returned from a trip to find the following memo on his desk:

RE: NORTH STREET, GUILDFORD
In your absence negotiations on the Guildford site progressed rather rapidly. The outcome is that the agents have agreed to accept our terms on the basis that we sign a Letter of Intent by close of business today.

This in turn means that we shall not be able to await the outcome of the Planning Committee Meeting this evening and we may well yet find ourselves having to either dispose of this unit as a retail outlet, or go to Appeal.

Exhibit 4 Pedestrian counts at two stores

Site 1. Large city in North West

Pedestrian flow	Number of people passing site in either direction per min during each key hour (on site side of road only)						
Hours starting	M	T	W	Th	F	S	Sun
8:00		20		20		10	
10:00		60		37		25	
12:00	68		82		52		5
13:00	78		140		118		7
14:00	58		124		63		4
16:00		65		54		144	5
18:00		89		72		96	5
20:00		4	4		19	7	
22:00		5	3		23	7	

Site 2. Middle size town in South East

Pedestrian flow	Number of people passing site in either direction per min during each key hour (on both sides of the road)						
Hours starting	M	T	W	Th	F	S	Sun
8:00		30		31		40	
10:00		65		86		110	
12:00	77		73		75		12
13:00	98		89		71		7
14:00	89		52		58		10
16:00		64		70		133	4
18:00		12		19		29	9
20:00		7	7		12	12	
22:00		3	4		7	8	

Daily average net sales

	Site 1	Site 2
Sunday	£ 950	£ 350
Monday	£ 1,450	£ 600
Tuesday	£ 1,500	£ 650
Wednesday	£ 1,400	£ 600
Thursday	£ 1,400	£ 700
Frdiay	£ 1,600	£ 750
Saturday	£ 2,300	£ 1,350
Total	£10,600	£ 5,000

Exhibit 5 Counter service cost structure

Net Sales (Exc. VAT)	*£K250 min.*	*£K600*
Food/paper (inc. waste)	95	228
Royalty	21	51
Management/staff (inc. meals)	52	126
Expenses	21	48
Rent/rates	25	60
Profit (before interest, tax and depreciation)	36	87
Capital invested	£K140	£K271
Years pay back	3.9	3.1

Exhibit 6 Extracts from data collected on Guildford site

IMMEDIATE LOCAL FACILITIES WHERE CUSTOMER COULD SENSIBLY TAKE OUT FOOD TO EAT.

Castle etc

PARK [X]   SEATING [X]   CAR PARK [X]   OTHER [X]   (PLEASE SPECIFY)

CAN CARS STOP WITHIN 50 YDS – DURING SHOPPING HOURS   YES/~~NO~~
                         – DURING EVENING HOURS   YES/~~NO~~

IF NO, HOW FAR AWAY IS NEAREST STOPPING POINT? at Rear C/C .   YDS

LONG TERM CAR PARKING WITHIN 400 YARDS   CAPACITY   1100

SHORT TERM CAR PARKING WITHIN 400 YARDS   CAPACITY   1100

Other relevant data
North Street to be made traffic free in 1983/4.
New Friary Shopping Precinct being developed immediately to the west of proposed site.
McDonalds at the top of High Street/London Road, opened late November/December 1981.

TOWN VIABILITY STUDY

Town ...Guildford...................   Pop ...56000.....................

Town Hall ..0483-71111..............   Influx ....Daily 23000+.........

Industry Main ..."University".........   Working Pop ....42%....

Employment Service Industries......   No. of family ...18000.............

Expenditure Town ....110-1981.......   Expenditure food ...39m 71 & 2.833

Expenditure per head .. ..   Average wage ...132.PW.+.........

Siting Policy...PRIME TOWN....................................

Prime Area FRIARY-NORTH STREET - HIGH STREET.................................

Pedestrian Flows ...Very good at North St. (See form for details)...

Competition National McDonalds at top High St. Not Prime Nr London Road.

Competition Local ...2 T/S WIMPY (Greasy)..............................

Attractions near ...Bus Station & Edge of Friary......................

Residential pop ..56 K Plus University Students 9000.....................

Business pop...= RISING =...........   Office pop ...Phase II 15000....

Numbers of people by age ....   Under 1, ...593   1.06%............

1-4 2564   4.58%............   5-14 ...8,439 15.07%............

15-29 ..12.084 21.58%............   30-44 ..10.628 18.95%............

45-64 ..13.652 24.38%............   65-74 ..5.080 9.28%............

75 & Over ...2.856 5.10%............   Total ...100% = 56,000...........

Detrimental factors ... NONE ....

Local Menu prices ... Higher than average 12% up ....

Council attitude to catering & take away ... Should be OK have allowed McD. ....

Percentage of trading after 6 pm ... 20% Bus Station 50 yards ....

Max. turnover 100% prime Wimpy Counter Service ... 420 k 1981 Prices ....

Rent avge. 2000 square foot prime ...... 45 K ....

Last premium paid prime .... K - Not known - not my area . No Records ....

Recommendation ... 1st class site must try for it (UCO) ....

Zone A Rent ... £18 High St. ....

Cathedral - cobbled High St - Sports Centre - Castle
2 Theatres - University - Lots Historic Builds - xxx
Yvonne Arnaud
      Lido - 1st Class shops - Arts Centre
Bus Station - 3 Cinemas - Market Fri-Sat - <u>Royal Grammer School</u>
Waterside Centre   2 Golf Clubs
Water Sports   X Very conservative - minded council X

Exhibit 7   Pedestrian count — Guildford site, taken in November 1981

	No. of pedestrians passing site per min in either direction on both sides of the road					
	M	T	W	Th	F	Sat
8:00	—	—	—	—	—	—
10:00	—	86	—	—	—	119
12:00	—	104	—	—	—	186
13:00	—	—	—	129	—	—
14:00	—	—	—	106	—	—
16:00	77	—	—	—	—	111
18:00	—	—	68	—	—	—
20:00	—	—	63	—	—	—
22:00						

(— = no data collected)
Market days Fri—Sat
Half day — Wednesday

266

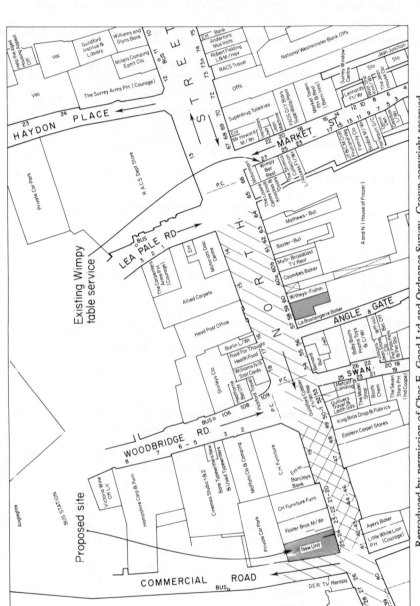

Exhibit 8 Site locations in Guildford.

Exhibit 9   Extract of letter from town planning officer

I refer to your recent planning application in respect of the above mentioned site. I assume that deliveries to the restaurant will be made via the private car park to the rear of the premises fronting Commercial Road and which is owned by Guildford Borough Council. If this is the case then a Notice under Section 27 of the Town and Country Planning Act 1971 will have to be served on the Council and the Certificate B accompanying your application be amended accordingly.

Turning to the merits of the proposal I am sure one of the worries the Council's Planning Committee will express is what steps you propose to take to prevent litter in the surrounding locality. You will be aware that McDonalds Restaurants are already established in the town and the granting of consent for their premises hinged upon assurances given by that Company regarding their efforts to ensure that litter from the restaurant did not cause a problem in the town centre. Accordingly, I would be obliged if you could inform me what steps your Company propose to take to avoid this problem arising.

You will recall when the application was submitted it was indicated that it would be desirable if floor plans indicating seating, kitchen and toilet facilities could be made available prior to the application being considered by the Council. I was wondering whether these plans are now available and ask you to ensure that adequate facilities are made available for the disabled insofar as access to the shop and toilets are concerned.

Chapter 11

Operations Strategy

Robert Johnston

Operations strategy is a set of plans and policies by which an organization aims to meet its objectives. Such objectives may be concerned with maintaining or increasing market share, diversifying, or with meeting any financial, political, or statutory requirements by providing a service to customers. A strategy can define the choice of technology, the degree of usage of technology, the degree of vertical integration, the number, size, and location of units in a multi-site operation, the operations infrastructure, the relative split between front office and back room (Chase, 1978), and can try to describe the quality, availability and flexibility of the service and the costs of providing that service.

1. TRADE-OFFS

Strategy is concerned with matching what the organization is good at, its 'distinctive competence' (Skinner, 1969), with its 'primary task', the reasons for its existence, and the markets that it is there to serve. There is no such thing as a 'perfect' service; it is unlikely that every customer will be completely satisfied with the service that they have received. No operation is going to be able to fulfil every single request and requirement, though some organizations would attempt to do this more than others, e.g. a four star hotel compared with a guest house. Strategy has to deal with the trade-offs between what the operation can/will do and what the customer expects/requires, given the resources available, and any external constraints imposed upon it by a corporate body or by government (Figure 11.1).

Making decisions about trade-offs is difficult in service industries because of the ambiguity in the service itself and the expectations of the customer. The service is not always clearly definable – a good holiday, no more toothache, an enjoyable evening at the theatre – and the degree of quality and resulting satisfaction will be perceived differently for each and every customer. Service organizations need to have a vision of the 'perceived' client and a definition of acceptable ranges of requirements in order that most customers in the particular market can be catered for. The fact that there will always be a dissatisfied customer is more of a fact of life of service industries than it is of

Figure 11.1   Trade-offs in operations strategy

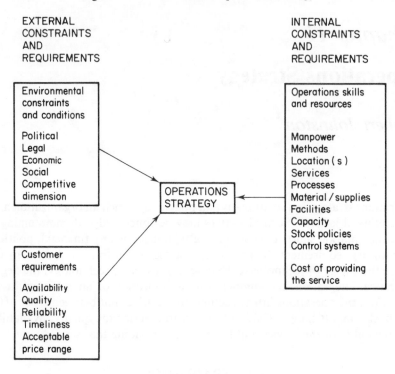

manufacturing, and there is the potential for more direct feedback since it is usually the customer who is being processed (Wild, 1977) in a service operation.

2.   BARRIERS TO ENTRY

In a competitive environment, business strategy has to determine how to gain advantages over competitors (Skinner, 1969) and how to prevent the erosion of market share by new competitors entering the field. Service operations frequently use different competitive strategies from product-orientated companies (Thomas, 1978). There are three main operations strategies available to service organizations: the strategic location of units, the creation of economies of scale, and the development of technology and a differentiated service.

In a non-competitive environment, barriers to entry are usually regulated by legislation. Operations strategy here is usually concerned with maintaining or expanding the services to customers, often without increase in revenue, budgets, or grants. The same strategies can be used to those ends.

2.1   Location and Multi-site Operations

We have seen over the last few years the proliferation of service outlets along the High Street – banks, fast food outlets, advisory services, travel agents, and building societies in particular. Because a service is usually provided by a single unit of people and/or equipment and can be abstract and perishable in nature (Thomas, 1978), it needs to be decentralized and local, so location decisions for multi-site operations are very important. Multi-site operations can benefit from economies of advertising and economies of scale in the back room, and so serve as a barrier preventing organizations without the buying, borrowing, or advertising power from competing in the same geographical area. Investment in many carefully strategically placed units has been a means by which some organizations have achieved spectacular growth.

2.2 Economies of Scale

In product-related companies capital is the most commonly used barrier to entry (Thomas, 1978). With economies of scale a product-orientated company can invest in new technology and research and development to give lower unit costs and more varied or differentiated products. Because a service is usually provided by a single unit of people and/or equipment and is decentralized and local, there is reduced opportunity for developing economies of scale, particularly in the front office. Some organizations do gain economies in the back room, e.g. by centralizing purchasing in catering operations. There are some opportunities for economies of scale at the level of the site, especially in equipment-based organizations. The multiple-unit cinema, for example, has centralized ticket and refreshment facilities in the front office and centralized projection equipment in the back room. Scale can also make regional and national advertising feasible; Berni Inns, Bass public houses, car retailers and building societies for example, all advertise regionally and nationally for the benefit of local outlets. Many small and single unit companies neither have the ability, nor often the need, to mount advertising campaigns, as they are small enough to survive on word of mouth recommendations, e.g. jobbing electricians and plumbers. Some organizations, solicitors, doctors, and dentists, for example, are not legally allowed to advertise.

The small independent unit is now under increasing pressure from conglomerates. Mergers and takeovers are frequent. In recent years we have seen the emergence of the 'Big Four' banks and the 'Big Six' brewers. The squeeze on profit margins on petrol now make the small independent station vulnerable to the giants.

2.3 Technology and Service Differentiation

Service differentiation means that established firms have brand identification and customer loyalties which stem from past advertising, word of mouth recommendation, previous good service, service differences, or simply being first in the market. Such differentiation creates a barrier by forcing entrants to spend heavily to overcome existing loyalties (Porter, 1980). Investment in technology can not only create a barrier to entry but can also develop a degree of service differentiation. One of the largest building societies has recently introduced a cash dispenser, a lead that many of the smaller societies will not be able to match. Another society has linked into a view-data system to give yet another dimension to its service.

Building barriers to entry in service businesses is generally more difficult and has to be done in less traditional ways than in product-orientated companies. Brand identification is still important but reputation, within its own locale, can also play an important part. Economies of scale are still possible in the back room and to a lesser degree in the front office. Development may be sought also through differentiation and technical advancement. Mergers and takeovers may help increase the potential for economies in the back room.

3. SERVICE OPERATIONS LIFE CYCLE

The product life cycle concept (Figure 11.2) has long been used in product-orientated organizations and has only recently been applied to service industries (Sasser, Olsen, and Wyckoff, 1978). As service organizations grow by increasing the number of service units and usually service locations, the management tasks and functions change. Large non-competitive organizations, too, often decentralize some of their operations. Sheffield City Council, for example, has recently split its Housing Department into small units spread across the City to provide a better service to its customers. Other large service organizations grow by creating more units, maybe on the same site, to provide extra or enhanced service to the customer.

Figure 11.2   Service life cycle

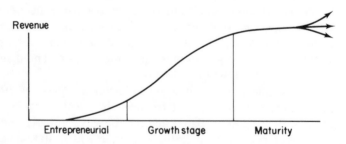

The service life cycle consists of the following three stages.

3.1   Entrepreneurial Stage

In the entrepreneurial stage the operation tends to be a single unit. Any expansion from this base is usually limited by facility/resource availability and market potential. If a nearby market exists, and the entrepreneur has the ability to attract customers, space may be a limiting factor, or if the market is too disparate for the single unit, expansion to a multi-site operation can be an expensive business. Clearly finance, financial acumen, and market awareness are key needs for the entrepreneur. Once these criteria are satisfied there are yet more stumbling blocks. There are many entrepreneurs with good ideas, good financial backing, and respectable markets yet who have considerable difficulty expanding successfully. The reasons often lie in the nature of the entrepreneur. They often have little self-discipline in administration, control of operations, costs, staff, budgets, or cash flow. They need operational and financial help but the operation is not necessarily big enough to be able to support it. Also, very often the entrepreneur is reluctant to relinquish his grip on any part of the organization.

In this stage changes tend to be market-led, as the entrepreneur takes advantage of every market opportunity that appeals to him, often without understanding the full implications for the operation. The operation itself has to be able to adapt quickly to live up to new requirements and expectations.

3.2 Growth Stage

If growth is achieved, it can be by the addition of extra units at the same site or in order to take advantage of a disparate market by turning to a multi-site operation. Back room administrative planning and control becomes an important and distinct function with the additional task of managing several, possibly remote, units. Financial systems will be evident and will be key in supporting decisions to take on new facilities and staff. By this stage much of the operations function has been delegated. The main operational tasks, apart from acquisition, are the running and staffing of operations and troubleshooting as the operations manager moves himself up the learning curve. The pressure is very much on the operation to provide the required service on time without obvious problems for the consumer and to create enough cash to facilitate the growth that the organization is undertaking. Delegation, training, and supervision are therefore vital, but are often overlooked because of the fire-fighting nature of the operation. Over time the operation becomes much more formalized, with a clear structure, and often fast progression through it, formalized training programmes, purchasing, control systems, and procedures.

The key features of this stage are careful strategic location of units, market awareness and penetration, and rationalization of processes, control procedures, and organizational structure.

3.3 Maturity

At some stage the rate of growth may decline, due to several factors, e.g. changing tastes or changes in competition. The original service concept by now may have lost much of its uniqueness and concentrated efforts are needed to increase or even maintain market share. Costly exercises in promotion and advertising reduce margins still further. Any changes tend to be operations-led, as any such changes have to be certain of being cost efficient. If new market opportunities are to be exploited, however, there is also a need for marketing pressure, the implications of which may be resisted by the operation.

By this stage standardized control and administration systems are clearly evident. Maintenance and replacement of facilities becomes increasingly important.

4. SERVICE/PROCESS MATRIX

The link between product and process life cycles has been identified by Hayes and Wheelwright (1979), and can be developed for service organizations as shown in Figure 11.3. This can be a very useful tool to help understand the changes that are taking place in organizations and the strategic implications of those changes.

Figure 11.3   Service/process matrix

	Single service unit, several services (Entrepreneurial)	Several units, several services (Growth)	Many units, few specialized services (Maturity)
Single customer treatment			
Customer/ order batching			
Customer/ order processing			

Natural evolution occurs, either way, along the diagonal, though actual change tends to be market-led (horizontal), then compensated for by operational change (vertical), or vice versa. Any such movement needs firstly to be recognized and secondly to be managed, as the implications for planning, control, and customer handling are different at every stage.

The biggest difficulty in applying this concept to service operations is the problem that the service can be perceived very differently by the people involved in providing and consuming the service. For example, most crematoria would be found in the bottom right of Figure 11.3 as their service is very specialized and very much akin to flow production, yet the customer expects a more individual and personal service, so his perception of the service would be at the top left of Figure 11.3. Some organizations have successfully overcome this difference in perception by the quality and training of the front-of-house staff, who can make the customer feel unique and important despite the 'processing-type' operation. At a four star hotel I visited recently, the head waiter said to his number two, as we were being shown our table, 'stick 'em on number three'. At another similar hotel the waiter treated us as though we were well acquainted and as though there was no-one else in the busy restaurant.

5. SERVICE OPERATIONS AUDITING

Policy and operations audits are desirable for the formulation of strategy and to help understand the implications for the operation of change that has occurred or is planned to occur. A questionnaire approach is shown in Figure 11.4, which can be applied to service organizations. The application of the questionnaire is no panacea nor will it create strategy or formulate policy, but it will

Figure 11.4   Service systems audit questionnaire. (From Chase and Aquilano, 1981. Reproduced by permission of Richard B. Chase and Nicholas J. Aquilano)

Product
1. Ratio of customer direct contact time with system to service creation time (low/medium/high)   A B C
2. Extent of direct labour input in creating service (small/medium/large) A B C
3. Primary service is viewed as (professional/trade/artistic)   A B C
4. Breadth of service (standardized/mixed/customized)   A B C
5. Variability of customer service demands (low/medium/high)   A B C
6. Complexity of service (low/medium/high)   A B C
7. Range of supplementary services (narrow/medium/wide)   A B C
8. Uniqueness of service relative to regional competition
   (little/some/much)   A B C
9. Introduction of major new services (rare/occasional/frequent)   A B C
10. Concern with legal restrictions in performing service
    (little/some/much)   A B C

Technology of transformation
11. Capability to alter service capacity rapidly (little/some/much)   A B C
12. Degree of mechanization of service (little/some/much)   A B C
13. Amount of preparatory work prior to providing a unit of service
    (little/some/much)   A B C
14. Average number of processing stages customer goes through in
    obtaining service (few/several/many)   A B C
15. Emphasis on efficiency in layout of facility (little/moderate/major)   A B C
16. Emphasis on aesthetics in layout of facility (little/moderate/major)   A B C
17. Extent of equipment specialization (little/some/much)   A B C
18. Number of service centres (one/few/many)   A B C
19. Size of service centres relative to direct competitors
    (small/medium/large)   A B C
20. Specific service centres located primarily for convenience of
    (customer/owner/other)   A B C
21. Reliance upon other suppliers (little/some/much)   A B C

Operating-control system
22. Investment in stock control system (low/medium/high)   A B C
23. Extent of use of materials in producing the service (little/some/much)   A B C
24. Primary stock viewed as (space/people/supplies)   A B C
25. Operating level (level/mixed/adjust with demand)   A B C
26. Allowed variability in service scheduling (little/some/much)   A B C
27. Ability to backlog service orders (little/some/much)   A B C
28. Number of supervisory levels (few/several/many)   A B C
29. Number of staff departments to support service (none/some/many)   A B C
30. Method of assignment of service personnel (customer selects/ mixed/system selects)   A B C

Workforce
31. Size of workforce relative to competition (small/medium/large)   A B C
32. Required range of worker skills (narrow/medium/broad)   A B C
33. Use of certified professionals in creating service (none/some/much)   A B C
34. Job content of most jobs (short cycle/medium/long cycle)   A B C
35. Work pace controlled by (customer/worker/system)   A B C
36. Wage payment system based primarily on (fees/hourly/output or sales)   A B C

Instructions for scoring
1. Circle either A, B, or C to identify what you believe to be the correct policy alternative (A, B, and C correspond to the order of the descriptive terms in brackets).
2. Place an X over either A, B, or C to identify what appears to be the policy currently being used.
3. Calculate the percentage of items in agreement out of the total items you were able to score (i.e. the items with both an X and a circle). This gives an alignment percentage.
   General scoring guide: 90−100% = excellent; 80−89% = good; 70−79% = fair; 60−69% = poor; below 60% = very poor.

assist in the understanding of potential mis-matches where trade-offs may have to be considered if change is to occur.

The questionnaire can be applied to either compare current and proposed policies or current policy against how the market would expect the operation to be running. A good application of the questionnaire is the 'Big Jim's Gym' case following this chapter.

REFERENCES

Chase, R.B. (1978). Where does the customer fit in a service operation? *Harvard Business Review*, **56**, No. 4 (November−December 1978), 137−142.

Chase, R.B., and Aquilano, N.J. (1981). *Production and Operations Management*, Irvin, Illinois.

Hayes, R.H., and Wheelwright, S.G. (1979). Link manufacturing process and product life cycles, *Harvard Business Review*, **57**, No. 1 (January−February 1979), 133−140.

Porter, M.E. (1980). *Competitive Strategy*, Free Press, New York.

Sasser, W.E., Olsen, R.P., and Wyckoff, D.D. (1978). *Management of Service Operations*, Allyn and Bacon, Boston.

Skinner, W. (1969). Manufacturing – missing link in corporate strategy, *Harvard Business Review*, **47**, No. 3 (May–June 1969), 136–145.

Skinner, W. (1974). The focused factory, *Harvard Business Review*, **52**, No. 3 (May–June 1974), 113–121.

Thomas, D.R. (1978). Strategy is different in service businesses, *Harvard Business Review*, **56**, No. 4 (July–August 1978), 158–165.

Wild, R. (1977). *Concepts for Operations Management*, John Wiley and Sons, Chichester.

Case Study: Big Jim's Gym

Big Jim has been in the body building business for many years. His gymnasium, originally for men, now consists of separate facilities for men and women, and is located next door to a pizza house in Manchester. Jim sees the primary task of the business as 'providing a full range of body building and weight reduction services for upper and middle class men, women, and children in the Manchester area'.

Currently, he has twenty employees, who work with the customers in designing their health programmes. The gym has separate weight-training and exercise rooms for men and women, a pool, a sauna, and a small running track behind the building. While Jim states that every customer is different, he makes men go through his 23-step conditioning course and women follow the diet in 'Big Jim's Energy Diet' pamphlet. Customers are usually enrolled in a ten week introductory course, and then left to advance at their own pace.

The gym is modelled after the one Jim first managed on an Army base in Aldershot 'right down to olive-green walls'. Jim maintains that the spartan atmosphere is necessary 'to build mental and physical toughness'. With some pride, Jim notes that he has all of the latest barbells and slant-board equipment. Jim has always viewed his major inventory items as liniments and bandages, which are ordered periodically from a wholesaler or are purchased from a nearby chemist if stock-outs occur. Other items are purchased from a local sports goods store.

Jim is very concerned about keeping all of his staff busy and keeping the equipment in constant use, so he requires that customers follow a specific hour-by-hour schedule on equipment. If the equipment is fully booked, he requests that his customers come at slow periods during the day or evening. This procedure has met with some resistance from customers, but Jim tells them that that is the price they must pay if he is to provide the most up-to-date health centre service.

Jim has done a survey of the prices charged by the other four centres in the

Adapted by Barbara Morris and reproduced by permission of Richard B. Chase and Nicholas J. Aquilano.

area[1] and his fees are about average. The other health centres have about the same number of employees, although two of them use licensed beauty consultants. Jim considers this an 'unnecessary frill' and tells all of his customers that anybody who works for him is an expert on all aspects of body maintenance. Jim has instituted a policy of job rotation whereby each member of the staff, with the exception of the clerk-typist, changes activities each hour. Employees are paid by the hour and are primarily PE college graduates who are interested in athletics. Turnover has not been a problem, even though Jim pays only slightly more than the minimum wage.

[1] Within this market segment, Jim is competing with, among others, the Manchester Athletic Club. MAC's facilities include five squash courts, eight tennis courts, a 50 metre pool, sauna, steam rooms and jacuzzi, a weight room with five £2,500 Nautilus weight-lifting machines, and a fully equipped health bar. MAC's staff includes a trainer, five masseuses, five instructors, and ten other staff members.

Case Study: The Chicago Pizza Pie Factory

The Chicago Pizza Pie Factory (CPPF) was one of London's most successful restaurants. Most days of the week, lunch and evening, people queued to get in and at the end of 1979 sales exceeded £30,000 p.w. Its American owner, Bob Payton, had given up his job as an advertising executive with J. Walter Thompson to open a restaurant serving the food he loved from Chicago. The first restaurant in Crown Passage, just off Pall Mall, was opened in 1977. In 1979, following the expiration of the lease, the restaurant moved to Hanover Square. In March 1980 Bob was considering how to capitalize on his success and what role he should have in the management of CPPF.

BACKGROUND

The original idea developed out of Bob's fondness for the deep dish pizza, served in Chicago. Deep dish pizza is described by Bob as 'thick, rich, and gooey', it is normally served direct from the pan. Bob developed a marketing plan for an up-market restaurant, but had difficulty raising finance. He eventually received backing from a small company, Norton Warburg. The first CPPF was opened in Crown Passage, a narrow alley in St. James. Despite its off-the-beaten-track location, it rapidly became one of the 'in' places to go, and was soon very busy and profitable. Peter Burholdt, a catering consultant who had advised Bob before and during the start-up, said, 'Even my optimistic view was pessimistic in reality. The main reason Bob has been successful is that he has a product which enables people to eat relatively cheaply, but allows Bob to make a hefty profit out of it. Bob's biggest contribution to his success is himself.'

Bob was also assisted at the start by Johnny Grant, who had a similar restaurant in the United States. Grant came to the United Kingdom with his wife, who trained the waitresses. At the end of the six weeks Bob offered Johnny a percentage of his share. Johnny accepted and agreed to sell his own business in America and come to London. Johnny said that he was amazed at the price Bob proposed for his UK pizza because it was double the US price. The early stages of the partnership were highly successful as Bob had a lot to

This case was prepared by C.A. Voss, London Business School, and Elizabeth Kennedy. The case, which is not meant to represent good or bad business practice, is intended for teaching purposes only. Some names and figures have been disguised.

learn, but Bob and Johnny were quite different characters, and eventually Johnny couldn't keep up with Bob. Resentment started to creep in, and finally Bob bought Johnny out of the business about a year after start-up.

The Crown Passage restaurant, which could seat about 100 was usually crowded, with long queues. In 1978 a much larger basement site was found in Hanover Square. Hanover Square is off Oxford Street and between Bond St. and Regent St., London's leading shopping area. It is also a busy business area with many offices. There are few restaurants in the area which is about $\frac{3}{4}$ mile from the main West End and Soho theatres and restaurants, thus evening parking was relatively easy.

Early in 1979, shortly before the lease expired, Crown Passage was closed, having reached weekly sales of £11,000, and the CPPF moved to Hanover Square. Here Bob was able nearly to triple his seating capacity to over 250 people while keeping the unique atmosphere he had created at Crown Passage. The new restaurant opened within seven days of Crown Passage closing. A number of operational improvements were made in the new restaurant, but the concept and decor was not significantly changed. The total investment in the new Restaurant was about £220,000.

Like Crown Passage, the Hanover Square restaurant was an immediate success, and was soon very profitable (see Exhibit 1). By March 1980 sales were exceeding £30,000 per week.

THE RESTAURANT

The layout of the restaurant consisted of stairs and a passage leading from the street, a bar and reception area (without seats), a main eating area with a secondary area on one side (which could be closed off), a kitchen, storage, and staff changing rooms (see Exhibit 2). In his original plan Bob had had a clear idea of the image he wanted and had hired Barney Broadbent, an interior designer, who had the experience to turn it into reality.

The decor was simple with natural wood and brick predominating. The colour was red with the tables covered in red oilskin cloths, identical to those in Chicago's original deep dish pizza restaurants, Uno's and Due's. The walls were covered with Chicago paraphernalia, specially shipped from Chicago, ranging from street signs, traffic markers, and the official city seal to old movie posters about Chicago. There was an efficient air-conditioning system with the air-conditioning ducts exposed, adding to the 'factory' image. Barney Broadbent said that a lot of the interior design became a feature by accident; for example, Crown Passage had high ceilings and needed to have lights hanging low to reduce height. Because it was a successful formula, similar features were incorporated into Hanover Square.

All the design from the decor to the toilets reflected great attention to detail both by Bob and Barney. Bob, who was fanatical about music, had ensured there was a sophisticated music system; this had twenty-three speakers placed to achieve perfect balance. Bob had tapes flown in from Chicago's WBBM-FM

Exhibit 1   My Kinda Town Limited accounts —

Month ended 30th June 1979

		£
Gross Sales		88,731
Less: Cost of Sales (Food and Beverages)		28,100
Gross Profit		60,631
Less: Expenses		
Operating Expenses — Payroll, etc.		
Wages and National Insurance	22,378	
Staff Welfare	1,384	
	23,762	
Operating Expenses — Other		
Promotion, Printing, etc.	2,206	
Other	2,762	
	4,968	
Occupancy Costs		
Amortization of Lease	8,000	
Rent, Rates, and Service charge	4,500	
Depreciation, etc.	2,599	
Repair and Renewal	3,247	
Insurance	430	
	18,776	
Total Expenses		47,537
Operating Profit		13,094
Less: Interest and Loan		684
Net Profit		13,410

radio station which played during the day. In the evenings disco music was played, but at a volume that did not totally inhibit conversation. About every hour and a half the theme 'Chicago' sung by Frank Sinatra was played. In the bar/waiting area there was a non-stop video show of American football featuring Chicago teams, which could only be seen by customers waiting for a table.

The clientele came from a wide cross-section, mainly in the age range 18 to 35. The lunch-time trade was usually from local business people, while the evening trade attracted people from all over London. Detailed patterns of trading are shown in Exhibit 3.

Bob had always placed much greater emphasis on the restaurant than the bar as he saw himself primarily as a restauranteur serving good food, not as a cocktail bar owner. He said one of his ambitions was for the CPPF to be the first pizza restaurant in the Michelin Guide. In addition, gross margins (sales—raw material) were higher for food (77.5 per cent) than they were for drink (67.5 per cent).

Draft Trading and Profit and Loss Account

Draft Balance Sheet
as at 30th June 1979

Fixed Assets		
Per attached Note 1 on Schedule 2		180,000
Current Assets		
Stock	6,703	
Debtors (expense)	25,320	
Cash at Building Societies – Excluding		
June Interest	250	
Cash at Bank	33,665	
Cash in Hand	4,273	
	5,056	
	75,267	
Less: Current Liabilities		
Trade Creditors	25,875	
Sundry Creditors and Accruals	46,977	
Taxation	6,250	
	79,102	(3,835)
		176,165
Financed by:		
Share Capital		1,000
Profit and Loss Account		113,665
Deferred Creditors		51,000
Deferred Taxation		10,500
		176,165

CUSTOMER EXPERIENCE AT THE CPPF

Having found the restaurant (the entrance was not actually in Hanover Square, but in a side street, and had only a small, discreet sign), the customer would progress downstairs into the basement. On most evenings, and the busier lunches, there would be a queue. Up to 180 people could be queuing, and a wait of $\frac{3}{4}$ hour to 1 hour was not unusual on busy nights, with a packed bar. In Crown Passage, when the queue became very long, free pieces of garlic bread were handed out to the waiting customers. There was a Front-of-House Manager always on duty, responsible for all the front-of-house staff. The bar area near the entrance was controlled by a Host or Hostess, and people were allowed into the bar as soon as possible, but only after the Hostess has taken the customer's Christian name, party size, and sorted out smoking and non-smoking preferences. There were distinct smoking and non-smoking areas, and pipes and cigars were completely forbidden. Staff were also discouraged from using

Exhibit 2   Hanover Square layout

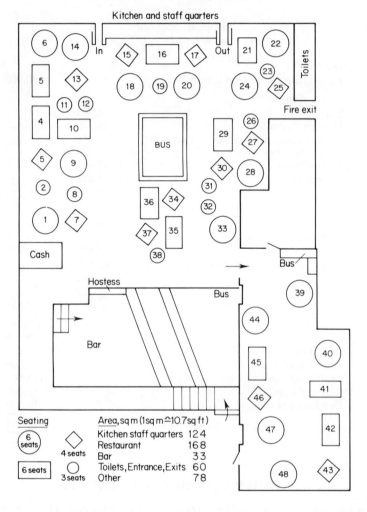

perfume because Bob said he wanted his customers to smell the aroma of the food. Customers in small parties were also asked if they were prepared to share a table. Customers would then wait in the, often packed, bar.

Drinks available at the bar included Coca Cola and American Beer. Coke was served straight from bottles (said Bob 'it tastes better than Coke from cans or the tap') into glasses filled with ice. The only beer available was ice-cold American-brewed Schlitz. Spirits were expensive and only doubles were served. Various cocktails were available including a St. Valentine's Massacre (the CPPF version of a Bloody Mary).

Requests for tables were dealt with strictly on a first-come-first-served basis. When a table was available customers were called on a small public address

Exhibit 3 Chicago Pizza Pie Factory sales pattern for a typical week

		Average spend per cover			Bar revenue	Gross revenue (including bar)
		Total	Food	Beverage		
Monday	a.m.				£ 29.90	£ 1,021.82
	p.m.				£ 172.43	£ 3,124.90
	Total	£ 5.01	£ 3.64	£ 1.37	£ 197.33	£ 4,146.72
Tuesday	a.m.				£ 33.75	£ 915.67
	p.m.				£ 374.83	£ 3,852.81
	Total	£ 4.83	£ 3.40	£ 1.43	£ 408.58	£ 4,768.48
Wednesday	a.m.				£ 71.70	£ 1,155.94
	p.m.				£ 415.25	£ 3,950.36
	Total	£ 5.09	£ 3.63	£ 1.46	£ 486.95	£ 5.106.30
Thursday	a.m.				£ 15.05	£ 1,208.84
	p.m.				£ 540.60	£ 4,585.32
	Total	£ 5.28	£ 3.87	£ 1.41	£ 555.65	£ 5,794.16
Friday	a.m.				£ 165.98	£ 1,648.52
	p.m.				£ 687.83	£ 5,396.33
	Total	£ 5.26	£ 3.74	£ 1.52	£ 853.81	£ 7,044.85
Saturday	a.m.				£ 135.50	£ 2,314.82
	p.m.				£ 896.93	£ 6,563.46
	Total	£ 4.60	£ 3.36	£ 1.24	£ 1,032.43	£ 8,878.79
Total for week		£ 4.97	£ 3.58	£ 1.39	£ 3,534.75	£ 35,738.79

Note
Separate average spend figures for a.m. and p.m. not collected, but evening spend per person is estimated to be 5–10 per cent greater than lunch
a.m. = before 4 p.m.; p.m. = after 4 p.m.

Net sales (excluding VAT)   100%

Food sales	73.0%
Beverage sales – restaurant	14.3%
Beverage sales – bar	12.2%
T-shirts	0.5%

Approximately 5 per cent of sales are 'to go' (take out)

system and shown to their seats by the Hostess. At the table the plates would be piled ready in the centre of the table and the customers would order from the menu (see Exhibit 4). The waitresses were young, friendly, and dressed in a loosely-American style uniform. The first course took about 7 to 10 minutes to arrive; the pizza would be ready about 20 minutes after ordering. The pizza came in the cooking pan and was dished out by the waitress in the appropriate number of sections.

Exhibit 4

The Chicago Pizza Pie Factory

PURVEYORS OF CHICAGO PIZZA — TO LONDON AND THE WORLD

Menu

Stuffed Mushrooms

We stuff 'em with butter, breadcrumbs, sherry, parsley, grated Italian cheeses and more than a hint of garlic. You won't soon forget them. **1.25**

SALAD BOWL

Our salad consists of the best fresh vegetables we could find at Covent Garden this morning. Your waitress will serve you as much as you like, so don't be shy. If you're sharing a salad, we must charge for each refill. If you're having only salad and not our pizza, our chef's salad is £2.45.

1.05 per person

Choice of 1,000 Island, Vinegrette, or House Dressing.

Drinks

Coca-Cola	55p
Juices	55p
Other Soft Drinks	50p
St.Valentine's Day Mass.	1.75
Chicago Blizzard	2.30
American Beer	85p
Cocktails	as charged
Chateau Chicago Vin Red or White	
Large Glass (5oz)	85p
Bottle	£3.70
Coffee	55p per mug

To better serve all our customers, we do not normally serve coffee at the table before 2.15 p.m. and only one cup per person in the evenings.

OUR OWN GARLIC BREAD

It speaks for itself. **60p**

THE PIZZA

Our famous Chicago pizza is more like a quiche than an ordinary pizza. Each one is made to order with generous portions of cheese, whole tomatoes, oregano, and other fresh ingredients. You'll not find another pizza like this anywhere in the world. Please allow us 20-30 minutes to prepare your pizza. It takes a bit longer to make this wonderfulness, but we think you will agree it's worth waiting for.

A regular pizza serves up to two people. A large serves three to four people. Don't worry if you can't finish it all, we'll give you a doggie bag to take home.

(On half and half pizzas, we give a full portion of each ingredient).	Regular 2 Pers.	Large 3-4 Pers.
Cheese	3.75	5.95
Cheese & Mushroom	4.40	6.85
Cheese & Sausage *(our specialty)*	4.65	7.20
Cheese & Pepperoni	4.65	7.20
Each extra:		
Sausage, Pepperoni	.90 *each*	1.25
Green Peppers, Anchovies,	.65	.90
Mushrooms, Onions, Cheese		

DESSERTS

Our cheesecakes are a little bit of heaven. They're made with cream cheese, sour cream, other fresh goodies and lots of love. Then they are topped with honeyed whipped cream and almonds. We serve two forks with each order. **1.05**

Even our ice cream is out of the ordinary. Ask your waitress for today's flavors. **90p**

CARRY-OUT

Carry a pizza (or 2 or 3) home for the freezer. Order from your waitress or phone us for a "go" pizza at least 25 minutes before you arrive (if you don't want to fight the queue).

Special Note

Tables for lunch may be reserved until 12.30 p.m. only. If you're in a hurry, order your pizza when you book. It'll be cooking by the time you arrive.

The atmosphere developed by the CPPF was lively, informal, and friendly (people often shared tables). There was always a 'buzz' about the restaurant. The customers would often see Bob standing and talking with customers or checking that everything was being done just right.

Soon after the customers had finished, or sometimes before, the bill would be issued by the waitress, usually signed by her 'with thanks'. Customers were

The menu

often encouraged to move as soon as their meal was finished. The bill was paid at a cash desk near the exit. Credit cards were not accepted, because no credit card salesmen had ever called. Bob, who said that good waitresses deserved good tips, encouraged customers to tip by making a reference to tipping on the bill and at the cash desk. The departing customer would then go up the stairs by the queue of customers waiting for tables.

PUBLICITY

Bob brought with him from advertising a flair for publicity. He worked closely with Jackie Richardson, a freelance publicity agent who was able to turn his ideas into action. For the opening of Crown Passage Jackie ensured that the editors of newspapers and journals were supplied with good press releases, and through her contacts she was able to secure wide free publicity for the CPPF.

The many little things they developed and did included 'doggie bags' to take away uneaten pizza, heart-shaped pizza cooked on St. Valentine's day, for which the CPPF became renowned, and turkey-flavoured pizzas on Thanksgiving Day, which is CPPF's birthday. Bob had recently sent an open letter to the Prime Minister with his views on the British worker. Bob had written 'A Chicagoan's Tour Guide to London' which was given to visiting Americans. The menu was available to take away from the cash desk. Bob had started a CPPF club with cost members 5 guineas a year. They received a regular newsheet and free garlic bread every time they came to the restaurant. At the last count the membership had reached 400.

Bob had made a special effort to ensure that there was publicity in Chicago about his restaurant. He had already supplied free pizza to the Chicago Symphony Orchestra when they were last in the United Kingdom. Many Chicagoans visiting London paid a visit to the CPPF. Bob claimed that he was the third most famous person in Chicago, but was surprised that he had not achieved the same notoriety in London.

Not everything had been a success. The opening party at Crown Passage with a rockband and a group of show business people nearly wrecked the restaurant, but the damage was quickly rectified after some hard work before the restaurant opened to the public. The CPPF rapidly caught on, and continues to receive massive free publicity. So far Bob had not spent one penny on direct advertising. Other than his publicity activities, he relied on word of mouth to bring his customers.

OPERATIONS

The kitchen was controlled by a Kitchen Manager, and staff started work at 8:00 a.m. preparing food for each day's trading. The raw materials were bought from specific suppliers with particular attention being paid to obtaining high quality cheese and crispy lettuce (which had to be imported). Pizza shells were prepared for cooking later in the day and all ingredients were weighed out. Pizza dough was made fresh all day and any remaining at the end was thrown out. When the order was received in the kitchen the pizza was made up with the required ingredients and baked in the serving dish in ovens. As dirty dishes were returned to the kitchen, members of the wash-up team processed them for automatic washing and drying.

The kitchen quarters were cramped and difficult to keep tidy, although kept to a good standard of cleanliness. The original high-utilization kitchen design and size was already proving inadequate for the level of trade in the new premises. Leading off from the kitchen quarters were small, cramped changing rooms with lockers and toilets for use by the staff.

The restaurant area was controlled by a Front-of-House Manager and was staffed by waitresses and busboys–busgirls who cleared up and laid tables. There was keen competition to become a waitress, and staff oten graduated from one of the other jobs to become a waitress. All the waitresses had to serve Bob once before they were allowed to operate on their own. The waitresses could earn considerable tips, even on a quiet night, and usually managed a minimum of £25 in tips. Having taken orders from the customers, food orders were processed through the kitchen, and beer and wine were ordered from the bar. A central dispenser supplied the waitress with ice, water, coffee, and Coke. It was also a storage for dirty crockery, subsequently collected by Busboys and Busgirls, who received tips from the waitresses.

At the cash desk, the sophisticated cash register not only recorded what had been sold and the amount, but also provided a clocking-in system for the staff and an inventory control system. The cashier also took phone orders for take-away ('to-go') trade and handled various publicity material such as T-shirts. In addition to the waitresses there were receptionists who handled incoming customers. The bar was managed separately by a head barman.

All the restaurant and bar staff seemed to be young, bright, and friendly. Talking to waitresses you discover that the staff get on well. They have few customer complaints and those they receive are usually about not being able to have coffee at the table or about over-ordering, although the waitresses try to advise. Said one, 'The customer is very important.'

Said Maggie Sholegh, a waitress of ten months, 'I enjoy working for Americans, but I preferred the clientele at Crown Passage, because there were more middle class and professional people. It's mostly a fashion clientele at Hanover Square and they are not so appreciative and give less in tips.' Maggie says that each waitress covers a work station of four to six tables (there are eight work stations) and the Busboys cover two or three work stations and get a tip from the waitresses (about 10 per cent of the tips or a minimum of £1 for a day shift and £2.50 for an evening shift). Maggie says that she is paid 85p per hour, but normally manages to take home between £100 and £150 per week. The shifts are from 11:30 a.m. to 3:30 p.m. and/or 5:30 p.m. and 7:00 to 12:00 midnight. 'Most staff work a mixture of day and evening shifts with one day off per week; free taxis are organized to take staff who work after midnight.' Bob has recently started a revenue-sharing scheme.

Arlette has been employed as a waitress since the start of Crown Passage. Her last job was as a waitress with the Hard Rock Cafe, but she prefers working at the CPPF. She says the pressure is less, although she works hard and receives about the same tips as the Hard Rock because the bills are higher at the CPPF. She says the hours are good and because the money is good the staff are happy: 'The staff don't work hard for the money they are making.' She says the Busboys are smashing and the staff facilities similar to other restaurants. On

Exhibit 5   Chicago Pizza Pie Factory manning levels

Employees

Kitchen staff (Cooking and Washing Up)	30
Barstaff	5
Busboys	15
Cashiers	3
Hostesses	6
Waitresses	24

Management, etc.

Floor Managers	4
Food and Beverage Manager	1
Buying and miscellaneous	1
Maintenance	1

Office staff	4

Notes
Waitresses are paid on commission, starting at 3 per cent and rising to 5 per cent after 6 months.
Kitchen staff and Busboys and paid hourly (£1.80 and £1.40 per hour)
Barstaff are paid hourly plus bonus (bonus only paid if end of week stock take reconciles properly).
Two separate shifts are worked, six days a week. Kitchen staff work a 40 hour week, waitresses a 32 hour week.
Waitresses are 'fined' if they make an error on the bill. The fine is the amount of the error.

Bob, Arlette comments, 'He's never been in the business before, but he's learnt pretty fast. Americans treat well. Now he's a giant. He cares about his staff.'

Commented the kitchen staff: 'Bob does not have enough contact with people who work for him; he doesn't appreciate how much the place has expanded, and complains if people are sitting down in the kitchen, even when they have been working hard. Unfortunately the kitchen staff only see Bob complain.' Also, 'It's hard work but fun. There is a good atmosphere in the kitchen, but the wages are not enough.'

The staffing costs (excluding management) were 25.9 per cent of sales for the restaurant and 6.6 per cent for the bar. Details of staffing are shown in Exhibit 5. The figures exclude the management staff. Bob's management team, none of whom has a management background, include the Kitchen Manager, the Bar Manager, and three Front-of-House Managers.

Jane Bridger was originally taken on as a waitress (because she wanted to earn some money for a holiday). She quickly assumed a management role and became a Front-of-House Manager. Jane assumed responsibility for the recruitment and training of waitresses, taking over the role originally played by Johnny Grant's wife. Says Jane, 'In a way I feel I have to make up for Bob's inadequacy with people,' and she says she frequently feels drained by Bob's personality. She believes in his concepts, his beliefs, and admires the way people respond to his personal service, but she says that he intimidates staff. She feels he needs to package his comments in a more positive way. She says that no-one can cope with Bob, and finally she decided that she also couldn't. In February 1980 she left to open up her own restaurant. Bob says Jane was his best and his worst employee, and that she frequently decided to do things in a way that was contrary to his wishes.

Another manager commented, 'The restaurant would run well without Bob provided the management are trained, but the organization needs overhauling, e.g. who instigates orders and who carries them out? There is a weekly management meeting with Bob, and the occasional staff meeting for everyone, but communication is not always good.' Another says, 'The CPPF runs very well considering its size (the staff complement is up to 90), but Bob gets people down. He has an incredible eye for detail which contributes to his success, but he shouts at staff in front of other staff.' Said one, 'The CPPF needs Bob because when he is away little things start to go wrong, and the staff start to slacken off.' Bob's Office Manager manages all the administrative activities, e.g. the payroll, and likes to feel she's an extension of Bob. She's young, rapidly acquiring knowledge, and thinks Bob runs the place well, but says, 'He's incredibly aggressive.'

BOB PAYTON

The larger-than-life personality of Bob is one of the key elements of the CPPF. Stephen Gee, Bob's financial partner from Norton Warburg, felt that Bob's driving personality was the most important factor in his achieving financial backing. Stephen was impressed by Bob's professionalism and said that he always did things properly. 'Bob has made terrific use of his marketing ability; he's a perfectionist and very much his own boss. He always finds the right people to help fill gaps, although he has not yet picked a management team, and he still has to be tested in that area.' Stephen had never had to chase Bob and thought he was quite a good partner and exceptionally good at making money.

Another view was expressed by Barney Broadbent, Bob's interior designer. Frequently Bob has presented Barney with a fait accompli, but Barney said he now questioned Bob closely because 'you have to look behind any statement Bob makes and ask why he's making that decision'. Says Barney of Bob, 'I like and respect him, but I wouldn't work for him directly. He's too irrational on a day-to-day basis. His public image is fantastic, but Bob has moods and is not good at appreciating other people's points of view.' Bob had a reputation for paying promptly, and Barney said he's a good business client.

In the changeover to Hanover Square, which was achieved very quickly, Bob had pushed Barney and his architect hard. The alterations were achieved in record time, with the costing being taken on trust. Barney said he was appalled by this practice, and had vowed not to work under this pressure again, but he appreciated that the extra two months' business achieved at Hanover Square was worth the extra Bob paid to get the place open quickly. Bob had always been forthcoming with his views on a wide range of topics.

Exhibit 6   Comparison of different kinds of restaurants

Examples of restaurant operating expenses, percentage of sales

	Fast food restaurant	Steak house	Coffee shop	Full menu cafeteria	Traditional table service restaurant
Sales:					
Food	100.0	85.0	100.0	100.0	90.7
Beverages	—	15.0	—	—	9.3
Total sales	100.0	100.0	100.0	100.0	100.0
Cost of sales:					
Food, percentage of food sales	42.0	45.0	34.0	38.0	35.0
Beverages, percentage of beverage sales	—	30.0	—	—	28.0
Total cost of sales	42.0	43.0	34.0	38.0	34.3
Gross profit:					
Food	58.0	55.0	66.0	62.0	65.0
Beverages	—	70.0	—	—	72.0
Total gross profit	—	57.0	66.0	62.0	65.7
Operating expenses:					
Payroll and related expenses	19.0	20.0	30.0	36.0	38.5
Advertising and promotion	3.0	2.0	0.5	1.0	1.5
Other operating expenses	9.0	9.0	10.2	9.0	11.0
Total operating expenses	31.0	31.0	40.7	46.0	51.0
Profit before occupancy costs	27.0	26.0	25.3	16.0	14.7

	Fast food restaurant	Steak house	Coffee shop	Full menu cafeteria	Traditional table service restaurant
Occupancy costs:					
Rent	8.0	5.2	15.0	7.7	4.5
Depreciation	2.2	2.5	3.9	4.3	3.5
Insurance	0.6	0.3	0.4	0.4	0.3
Total occupancy costs	10.8	8.0	19.3	12.4	8.3
Profit before tax	16.2	18.0	6.0	3.6	6.4

Adapted from studies by Harris, Kerr, Forster & Co., 1976.

Comparison of profitability and return on investment, selected statistical data for a typical year (figures in £ 1979)

	Fast food restaurant	Steak house	Coffee shop	Full menu cafeteria	Traditional table service restaurant
Total sales, £'000	280	950	270	575	600
Number of seats	80	300	200	300	200
Building area, sq. ft.	2,400	7,000	4,800	10,000	6,000
Average food check, £	0.94	3.85	0.66	1.21	2.64
Average daily seat turnovers	10	2.1	6	4.3	3.3
Sales per seat	3,500	3,170	1,350	1,920	3,000
Sales per square foot, £	117	136	56	58	100
Square feet per seat	30.0	23.3	24.0	33.3	30.0
Rent per square foot, £	9.3	4.4	8.3	4.4	4.4
Total investment (exclusive of land and building-leased), £'000	72	153	83	83	166
Return on investment before tax	62.3%	126.5%	19.3%	10.6%	23.0%
Ratio of total sales to investment	5.5	6.2	3.2	2.9	3.6
Investment per seat – furnishings and equipment, £	624	370	416	648	832

Adapted from studies by Harris, Kerr, Forster & Co. 1976.

THE FUTURE

At the beginning of 1980 Bob was faced with a number of issues concerned with the running of CPPF. First was that of personal involvement. Since the opening at Crown Passage Bob had had a great personal involvement with the day-to-day running of the restaurant. Some of the detailed management had been delegated to Jane Bridger, but Bob was still spending a great deal of energy in ensuring that the restaurant was running *exactly* as he wanted it. He had a strong eye for detail and would quickly note if the ice tray was empty, the tables were not set exactly right, or the waitresses were not friendly and cheerful. Bob had begun to question how long he could continue with this level of detailed involvement.

The other major issue was what to do next, and how to capitalize on his success. The restaurant was profitable and performance compared well with US figures (see Exhibit 6). Bob still rode around London on his bicycle, and apart from buying a property in the country which he visited on most weekends, he showed little enthusiasm for spending his profit on himself. He felt that CPPF could be repeated in the UK and abroad and had looked at sites in a number of big towns in the UK including Edinburgh, Bath, and in Paris. Stephen Gee supported Bob's view on expansion though he was less sure about overseas. Bob had recently became very excited by a site in Bath. The site was slightly smaller than Hanover Square, though large for a town the size of Bath. Bob felt this was important as he could avoid the mistake he had made in the past of having too small a restaurant. Bath had a population of about 80,000 but the surrounding area including Bristol had a population of over 1.5 million. He felt the CPPF concept could transfer unchanged to Bath. Other ideas for the future include pizza by the slice, a spare ribs operation, deep dish pizza straight from the freezer, and a competitive franchise chain of deep dish pizza restaurants.

Case Study: Sheffield City Library

The present Central Library building was completed in 1934. This had been a dream for almost eighty years and the Library Committee now had a building where progressive librarianship could be carried out. Services long required became possible including a separate room for the 'Sheffield Collection' (a special collection of local interest), strong rooms for the correct storage of valuable archive material, a separate Junior Library, and a stack capable of housing all probable accessions for forty years. By 1939 the service had ten branch libraries and a total book issue of 2,668,012.

In 1956 the library service celebrated its centenary and had grown to fifteen branches and a total book issue of 4,507,798. Comparisons with 1856 show a book stock which had risen from 6,000 to over 597,000, an issue figure which had risen from 10,000 to more than 4 million and a library in every school in the City.

The period from 1956 to present, produced with new building and local government boundary changes, a total of thirty-seven branch libraries, a mobile and special services division providing library service to areas without libraries, a schools library section covering over 300 schools, and the Central Library providing reference and lending services. Issues have risen to over 8 million with a total stock of over 1,905,000 books. The service is also changing from the traditional reading service to include the various new technologies for information provision.

INCREASE OF BOOK STOCK

Sheffield spends over £1m on books and materials and purchases some 170,000 volumes each year. Exhibit 1 illustrates the increase of book stock held by the library. The stock continues to grow by about 20 per cent a year as purchases outstrip withdrawals. Over the last nine years 1,472,787 volumes have been added whereas 1,190,436 volumes were withdrawn, a total addition to stock of 282,351.

LIFE OF BOOKS

It is generally accepted that decisions on purchases are much easier to make than those relating to the end of a life for a book, which is usually due to physical wear and tear or lack of interest.

Exhibit 1　Past and projected reference book stock

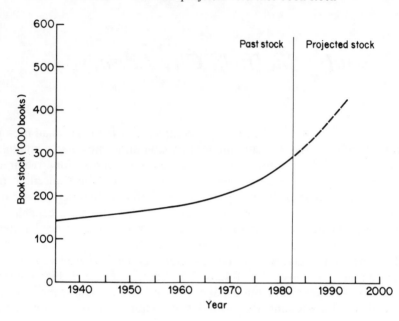

The following criteria are used to help make decisions about stock disposal:

1. Publication date and format. Obsolescence can be a just criterion in some subject areas, science for example. The date of publication can serve as a guideline but complete dependence on this criterion can be a mistaken practice.
2. Recorded uses. If a book has not circulated in the past few years, it is less likely to be requested than another title that has had several recent circulations.
3. Individual selection. Subject biographers or collection department personnel pursue the titles in their field of expertise and make decisions as to the desirability of maintaining individual works in the main collection. The amount of time required to thoroughly review a collection may make this scheme impractical for all but small libraries or those with plans for relatively small storage collection.
4. Duplicate or multiple copies of editions of a title may, in many cases, be removed.

The reference libraries in Sheffield have limited open shelf space and therefore relegation to the stack is a difficult decision. In fact not only do shelf weary items become relegated, but a high percentage of new books are destined to the stack without any shelf life. This is not the case in the lending sector where all new material is given open shelf space. Lending stocks have risen by

117,289 volumes in the period 1975/76 to 1982/83, the increase having been matched by a rise of 492,583 issues in the same period. This would tend to suggest that additional stacking accommodation is not required by the lending sector.

DISPOSAL OF BOOK STOCK

There are two main methods of book disposal; other methods are used but they are only applied to a very small percentage of books:

1. *Sale of books*. Where a book is to be disposed of and is considered to be in a suitable condition it is offered for sale at its service point. The price charged is a reasonable secondhand value and the system is so designed that the Library Licence Agreement is not invalidated. Books remaining unsold will be offered for sale at one-off book sales held periodically in the City Centre. The proceeds of these sales amounts each year to approximately £16,000 and this amount supplements the book purchasing fund.
2. *Discarding*. Books unsuitable for sale are gathered centrally and disposed of at a local waste paper merchants. This method up to 1979 was the main disposal method but following the introduction of book sales, the number disposed of in this way has dramatically reduced.

OPEN/CLOSED ACCESS TO STOCK

Lending Sector

In the main all the stock in the lending sector is on open shelves and therefore available for public borrowing. Certain materials are not available, e.g. the drama collection and central lending reserve stock. These items are obtainable on request following scrutiny of the catalogue, but this reserve stock tends to be little used.

Reference Sector

As the name implies this stock is available for reference purposes and not available for loan in the normal way, although certain materials are allowed out on short-term loan. The stock in the year ending 31st March 1983 in this area amounted to 351,741 volumes which is an increase from 1974 of 93,202 volumes, or 36 per cent. The increase in storage requirements is self-evident when one considers that 90 per cent of the stock is in closed access either in the Central Library or outside stores. There has to be a heavy reliance on the catalogue and on the staff's stock knowledge.

The Central Library stack is of metal construction and of traditional static design made to fit the area allocated. It is on a two-floor basis with the lower stack supporting the upper stock. There is no lift provision to the upper area but book lifts do operate from the lower stack to the Arts and Humanities Library, the Science and Technology Library, the Local Studies Library, and the Central Lending Library.

Outside space, a church hall in Broomhill, St. Mark's, was first purchased in the early 1970s when the Central stack was full. The main hall was converted into a traditional two-storey stack with further space for furniture storage at a point with floor loading problems. Certain branch libraries had space available and stores were made at Hansworth, Greenhill, Manor, Park, and Southey Branches. In 1980 space again was critical and a short life store was acquired in the abandoned Housing Department building in Pond Hill.

STOCK STANDARDS

Open Stock

The actual appearance of the open shelf stock in Sheffield is better than many other local authorities. This has much to do with the maintenance of a good book fund whereas many local authorities have suffered reduced spending in this area. It is worth noting that much time is spent in Sheffield Libraries on repairing and maintaining its open shelf stock and discarding for sale or pulp where the standard falls below that which is acceptable. The professional library staff assess stock standards throughout the system and it is subject to individual interpretation; therefore, standards vary slightly from area to area.

Closed Stock

Closed access stock standards are much lower than those on open shelves. Some 300,000 volumes are held in closed stacks and many volumes are in need of repair. Consideration to conservation of stock is paid only lip service, there being only one conservator on the staff, this person dealing mainly with archival material.

ISSUES FACING THE LIBRARY SERVICE

Library management feel that there are a number of issues currently facing them:

1. There is no written book selection policy.
2. There is no stock management policy.
3. A major proportion of stock is unavailable to the general public because of closed access and lack of suitable subject index.
4. There is no conservation policy for closed access materials.
5. There is no more room for further additions to the stack and little space left on the open access shelves. In addition the Pond Hill store has shortly to be vacated and all other storage accommodation is full. Further complications

Exhibit 2   Costs of storage

A preliminary costing exercise is given below. As the stock is only part of the use the building and staff are put to, costs have been apportioned accordingly.

	Central Library £	St. Marks £	Pond Hill £
Employees			
Professional staff			
Supervision	3,850	1,240	2,232
Maintenance	—	3,800	—
Library assistant	—	—	660
Stack assistants	6,050	—	—
Student vacation work	1,485	—	—
Cleaning staff	9,475	1,000	—
Cleaning supervision	550	—	—
Premises			
Repairs and maintenance	10,725	1,000	200
Lighting, heating, and			
cleaning	8,100	1,630	800
Rates	9,710	2,610	3,810
Furniture and fittings	175	100	—
Supplies and Services	600	100	—
Transport	210	200	—
Overheads	7,480	2,300	100
Totals	58,410	13,980	7,802
No. of volumes	300,000	15,000	9,000
Cost/volume p.a.	0.19	0.93	0.87

are added because of the closure of the Attercliffe Branch Library following the opening of a new Darnall Branch Library in 1981 and the unsuitability of the Park Branch store because of floor loadings (see Exhibit 2 for a comparison of storage costs between the three main sites).

6.   There is one major store with materials almost immediately accessible, but several outside stores where access is limited by the number of visits staff can make to the sites (see Exhibit 3 for the costs of obtaining books from stock):

(a) Obtaining material from the stack takes at least ten minutes using non-professional personnel.

(b) When a search by a professional member of staff is required, the delay may still be in excess of ten minutes. This must also be accompanied by a reduction in services at the enquiry counter.

(c) Stock held at an outside store can only be made available by appointment and therefore customer resistance may be felt.

(d) There is the increased possibility of damage to materials being transported from outside stores.

(e) Staff time is taken by journeys to outside stores.

(f) Much of the material in the stores is not catalogued.

7. Forecasts suggest that the reference book stock will continue to increase (Exhibit 1).

Exhibit 3   Costs of obtaining books from stock

The costs of issuing materials from stock is difficult to ascertain with any accuracy because the number of issues is not recorded. In addition the professional and clerical time spent would require detailed study to determine the exact time spent on these activities. However the following is an attempt to estimate the figures.

	Central Library £	St. Marks £	Pond Hill £
Employees			
Professional/clerical	19,500	2,230	1,232
Stack assistants	6,050	—	—
Van driver	—	560	500
Other			
Transport	—	350	440
Lift maintenance	1,500	—	—
Stationery	500	100	100
Totals	27,550	3,240	2,272
Estimated issues	50,000	2,000	750
Cost per issue p.a.	0.55	1.62	3.03

Case Study: The Malabar Beach Hotel

In early 1981, Craig Barnard, the General Manager of the Malabar Beach Hotel in St. Lucia, West Indies, was considering a plan that he believed would radically change the nature of the product he was offering to the market. The combination of a worldwide falloff in the holiday market, weakening currencies, and hurricane damage had led to a poor season and poor prospects for the tourist industry in St. Lucia. In addition, it looked as if severe price cutting was about to develop on the island. In an effort to try and develop a new product that would prosper in this market, Craig Barnard had developed a no-money concept, whereby all guest expenditure, not just food and accommodation, would be paid for in advance.

THE HOTEL

The Malabar Beach Hotel, a family owned hotel, was situated just outside Castries, the capital city of St. Lucia, a small island in the West Indies (see Exhibit 1). The hotel was opened in 1968 and by 1981 had 86 rooms; eighteen of the rooms were self-contained chalets, the remainder being in a recently built hotel block. The Hotel was situated in six acres of ground on Vigie Beach, a mile long sandy beach containing two other hotels (both of which were well separated from the Malabar Beach Hotel) (see Exhibit 2).

There were two restaurants offering a good choice of courses and wines with meals. There were three bars and the hotel was known for its good cocktails at reasonable prices. The reception facility (which included one of the bars and the offices) was separate from the other buildings and was originally the family home. There was a swimming pool set back from the beach and a watersports facility. Watersports which included windsurfing, waterskiing, and sunfish sailing were provided free to guests. In the evenings there was usually some entertainment, a band, crab racing, or some similar activity. There was little entertainment in Castries, but guests often walked or took taxis to neighbouring bars or hotels. (The Halcyon Beach Hotel, a mile away, had a very lively discotheque.)

This case was written by C.A. Voss, London Business School. It is intended for teaching purposes only.

Exhibit 1   St Lucia (From Pegasus Holidays Brochure 1981)

ST. LUCIA
Unspoilt and friendly

Qariblue
Smuggler's Village
Bois D'Orange
Halcyon Beach Club
La Toc
Castries
Halcyon Days
Soufriere
Vieux Fort

The Caribbean is generally dreamt of as a sun-drenched paradise with exotic plants and flowers and delicate humming birds. And all this is true. Yet within this necklace of islands, each country is totally unique and the product of a whole range of influences. We have been going to St. Lucia now for 7 years and it is still our main choice because it really does represent an unspoilt beauty which has not been tarnished by commercialisation and this cannot be said for all the islands in the Caribbean.

Second largest of the Windward Islands in the Eastern Caribbean, St. Lucia is 27 miles long, 14 miles wide and has a population of around 130,000. Columbus is said to have discovered the island in 1502 and it was alternately under French and British control fourteen times before being ceded to Britain in 1814. (It is now an independent Commonwealth country). This unique mix of cultures is exhibited in its cuisine, place names and local patois.

The capital, Castries, is a bustling market and business town with a large harbour, an open-air market, a number of interesting restaurants and some fine examples of old-style colonial buildings. Nearly all the architecture dates from 1780, when a hurricane destroyed most of the buildings. The former capital, Vieux Fort, is situated at the southern tip of the island and the local market (every Saturday) is worth a visit. St. Lucia is a relaxed, friendly and beautiful island which visually has many contrasts. The east coast, facing the Atlantic, is rugged with a gentle breeze continually blowing from the sea. Then a mountainous backbone cut with deep, lush valleys full of tropical flowers and trees. Travel the west coast, looking onto the Caribbean Sea and experience the thrill of narrow, winding roads which climb and fall through exquisite scenery. Here you will see Marigot Bay, where Admiral Barrington hid the British fleet from the French and which in more recent times was used in the filming of 'Doctor Doolittle' and 'Firepower'.

Visit the small fishing town of Soufriere which boasts the drive-in volcano. Nearby are the bubbling Sulphur Springs, whose waters it is said have curative properties. The Diamond River flows through these springs and there is the beautiful Diamond Waterfall. Just north of Soufriere you can drive through the exotic rain forest. But this whole area is dominated by the 'Pitons'. These twin ex-volcanic peaks rising sheer from the shore, are now clothed with green vegetation and have been called the most photogenic landmarks in the West Indies. Further up the west coast is Pigeon Island, now connected to the mainland. It is a national park but with 17th century ruins and a lovely beach. Around Castries and travelling inland, you can visit Morne Fortune with its ancient barracks and guard room which housed both French and British forces in turn and where you get great views of the island. St. Lucia has much to show off to the visitor, but you can also arrange to visit neighbouring islands, such as the Grenadines.

Welcome to St.Lucia
THE WEST INDIES

8

Exhibit 2   Malabar Beach Hotel – a typical brochure entry (From Sovereign Holiday Brochure)

Malabar Beach Hotel

The Malabar Beach Hotel is just a short drive from the town of Castries. It is ideally situated for those wishing for a beach-side location, with all the fascination of a local town nearby.

Unpretentious, but with comfortably furnished air conditioned bedrooms, this hotel has a casual, relaxed atmosphere. There is a restaurant and a bar beside the swimming pool. Complimentary sports including tennis, snorkelling, sailing and water skiing are an added attraction at this hotel.

The twin bedded rooms are in a garden setting and the cottages are alongside the sandy beach. At night it is pleasant to sit in the beach-side lounge bar, and there is entertainment most nights of the week with a live band for dancing and a weekly floor show and calypso band. The transfer time to the hotel is approximately one hour 30 minutes.

When the Hotel had opened, the Island and the Hotel catered primarily for the 'carriage trade', rich, up-market, usually British clientele who made their own reservations and travel arrangements. They came seeking winter sun and there was very little summer trade.

The development of low cost jet travel and the opening of an airport at the south end of the island, capable of taking the largest planes, had drastically changed the nature of the tourist trade on St. Lucia. The Island moved quickly into catering for package tours.[1] Because of traditional trading ties, the two

---

[1] In a package tour, the clients paid an inclusive price for a travel and accommodation package to a tour operator, an airline, or an agent.

major sources of holidaymakers were Great Britain and Canada. Because there were few holidaymakers from the United States, good air connections with the United States were slow to develop. As a result US package tour operators established themselves on other islands, and by 1981 when air services from the United States had become satisfactory, St. Lucia had not yet become an established destination for Americans.

As a direct result of these changes St. Lucia's clientele had moved down-market, and its image had moved from up-market to a package tour island. The Malabar Beach Hotel's clientele followed the island's pattern closely. In the early 1970s the hotel developed strong links with British Airways with the tour operators using seats on BA, avoiding charter flights. In subsequent years it had developed a flourishing business with the airline and a number of British and Canadian tour operators. The Hotel, because of its location both near the airport and the town, attracted a substantial number of business travellers. The British Market was strong all the year round, enabling the hotel to run with fairly constant levels of occupancy throughout the year. The Malabar Beach Hotel had found it difficult to break out of St. Lucia's down-market trend. The management had taken a number of steps to move more up-market in relation to other hotels on the island. For example, they had changed their Canadian agents, who had been at the bottom end of the market. They also had a positive drive to build up US business from a level of about 0.5 per cent of customers.

THE COMPETITIVE SITUATION IN 1981

The Malabar Beach Hotel was one of a number of hotels on St. Lucia. Craig Barnard felt that these hotels fell into three segments: luxury hotels, middle of the road, and inexpensive. The luxury hotels were typified by the Cunard La Toc Hotel (see Exhibit 3). This had a high standard of room, service, and facilities, set in 100 acres with a nine-hole golf course, floodlit tennis courts, and comprehensive watersports facilities, all of which were free to guests. In addition it had a number of shops including a boutique, a travel agent, a hair-dressing salon, and a souvenir shop. There was a secluded, though not private, beach (all beaches in St. Lucia were public property, with right of access to all). The hotel facilities included two swimming pools, two restaurants, a coffee shop, three bars, and a varied programme of nightly entertainment.

The Malabar Beach Hotel was firmly in the middle segment. Hotels in this segment were modern, well equipped with restaurants, bars, water sports facilities, and a swimming pool. They were generally on a smaller scale, less luxurious, had fewer staff, and had a narrower range of facilities than the luxury hotels.

Hotels in the inexpensive segment tended to be older or simpler, with less well-equipped rooms often lacking major facilities. Typical of this segment was the East Winds Inn. This had ten beachside cottages in a secluded bay. Free watersports were available, but there was no swimming pool. It was described

Exhibit 3   La Toc (From Pegasus Holiday Brochure, 1981/2)

Exhibit 3 contd.

CUNARD LA TOC
HOTEL & VILLAS
ST. LUCIA, W.I.
SUMMER TARIFF
April 16, 1981 — December 20, 1981

Daily Rates — European Plan

Category	Twin	Single
Standard	$ 80	$ 70
Superior	100	90
Third person	35	

Daily Rates — European Plan — Full Maid Service

Category	
Superior Villa — Two Bedrooms	$125
Deluxe Villa — Two Bedrooms with private plunge pool	155

Child under 12 Free in room with parents
MAP supplement daily
Adult $28   Child $14

WINTER TARIFF
December 21, 1981 — April 18, 1982

Daily Rates — European Plan

Category	Double	Single
Standard	$149	$137
Superior	193	176
Third person	55	

Daily Rates — European Plan — Full Maid Service

Category	
Superior Villa — Two Bedrooms	$195
Deluxe Villa — Two Bedrooms with private plunge pool	220

Child under 12 free in room with parents
MAP supplement daily
Adult $30   Child $15

All prices quoted in U.S. dollars
Add 10% Service and 7% Government tax to all prices.

Christmas Supplement — $10 daily per room or villa will
be added from December 24 through January 1.

For reservations call:

Europe
Windotel 01-730-7144
LRI, Inc. 01-486-3213
Cunard Crusader World Travel
Bristol, England 02-7224386
London, England 01-7411767
Utell International:
U.K. 01-741-1588
Germany 0211-365233

North America
Cunard
555 Fifth Avenue
New York, N.Y. 10017
Phone (212) 880-7390
Cunard
1 Dundas St. W., Ste. 2500
Toronto, Ont. M5G 2B2
416-598-8133
LRI, Inc.
Utell International

5/81   T121

Exhibit 3 contd.

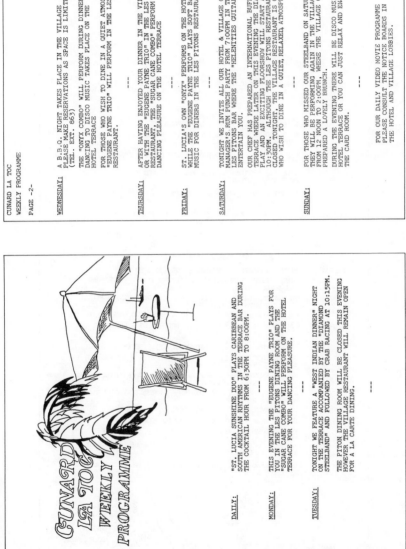

CUNARD LA TOC WEEKLY PROGRAMME

DAILY:
"ST. LUCIA SUNSHINE DUO" PLAYS CARIBBEAN AND SOUTH AMERICAN RHYTHMS IN THE TERRACE BAR DURING THE COCKTAIL HOUR FROM 6:30PM TO 8:00PM.

MONDAY:
THIS EVENING THE "EUGENE PAYNE TRIO" PLAYS FOR YOU IN THE LES PITONS DINING ROOM AND THE "SUGAR CANE COMBO" WILL PERFORM ON THE HOTEL TERRACE FOR YOUR DANCING PLEASURE.

TUESDAY:
TONIGHT WE FEATURE A "WEST INDIAN DINNER" NIGHT ON THE TERRACE ACCOMPANIED BY THE "DIAMOND STEELBAND" AND FOLLOWED BY CRAB RACING AT 10:15PM.

THE PITON DINING ROOM WILL BE CLOSED THIS EVENING HOWEVER THE VILLAGE RESTAURANT WILL REMAIN OPEN FOR A LA CARTE DINING.

CUNARD LA TOC
WEEKLY PROGRAMME
PAGE -2-

WEDNESDAY:
A B.B.Q. NIGHT TAKES PLACE IN THE VILLAGE RESTAURANT PLEASE MAKE RESERVATIONS AS SPACE IS LIMITED (TEL. EXT. 863)

THE "ONYX COMBO" WILL PERFORM DURING DINNER WHILE DANCING TO DISCO MUSIC TAKES PLACE ON THE HOTEL TERRACE

FOR THOSE WHO WISH TO DINE IN A QUIET ATMOSPHERE THE "EUGENE PAYNE TRIO" WILL PERFORM IN THE LES PITONS RESTAURANT.

THURSDAY:
AFTER HAVING ENJOYED YOUR DINNER IN THE VILLAGE RESTAURANT OR WITH THE "EUGENE PAYNE TRIO" IN THE LES PITONS RESTAURANT, THE "SUGAR CANE COMBO" PERFORM FOR YOUR DANCING PLEASURE ON THE HOTEL TERRACE

FRIDAY:
ST. LUCIA'S OWN "ONYX" PERFORMS ON THE HOTEL TERRACE WHILE THE "EUGENE PAYNE TRIO" PLAYS SOFT BACKGROUND MUSIC FOR DINERS IN THE LES PITONS RESTAURANT

SATURDAY:
TONIGHT WE INVITE ALL OUR HOTEL & VILLAGE GUESTS TO THE MANAGER'S RUM PUNCH PARTY FROM 7:00PM IN THE LES PITONS BAR WHERE THE "HELENITIES GUITAR TRIO" WILL ENTERTAIN YOU.

OUR CHEF HAS PREPARED AN INTERNATIONAL BUFFET ON THE TERRACE WHERE LATER ON THIS EVENING THE DIAMOND STEELBAND PLAY AND AN EXCITING FLOORSHOW WILL START AT APPROXIMATELY 10:30PM. ALTHOUGH THE LES PITONS RESTAURANT WILL REMAIN CLOSED TONIGHT, THE VILLAGE RESTAURANT IS OPEN FOR THOSE WHO WISH TO DINE IN A QUIET, RELAXED ATMOSPHERE.

SUNDAY:
FOR THOSE WHO MISSED OUR STEELBAND ON SATURDAY NIGHT THEY WILL BE PERFORMING AGAIN IN THE VILLAGE RESTAURANT FROM 12 NOON TO 2:00PM, WHERE THE VILLAGE CHEF HAS PREPARED A LOVELY BRUNCH.

DURING THE EVENING THERE WILL BE DISCO MUSIC ON THE HOTEL TERRACE OR YOU CAN JUST RELAX AND ENJOY A MOVIE IN THE CARD ROOM.

FOR OUR DAILY VIDEO MOVIE PROGRAMME PLEASE CONSULT THE NOTICE BOARDS IN THE HOTEL AND VILLAGE LOBBIES.

Exhibit 3 contd.

CUNARD LA TOC SPORTS

DAILY:	MASSAGE AND SLIM MASTER TREATMENT.INFORMATION AND INQUIRIES AT CARIB TOURING OFFICE BETWEEN 9:00 - 10:30
DAILY:	GAMES ROOM (6) OPEN 8:00AM - 11:00PM ELECTRONIC GAMES AND TABLE TENNIS
	WATERSPORTS (4) 9:00AM - 4:00PM SNORKELLING, WIND SURFING, SAILFISH, WATER SKIING
	TENNIS (5) 7:00AM - 9:00PM FULLY STOCKED SHOP TUITION - RENTALS
	GOLF (1) 8:00AM - DARK - FULLY STOCKED SHOP TUITION - RENTALS
	SWIMMING POOLS - 24HRS. VILLAGE (3) HOTEL (7)
MONDAY:	GOLF CLINIC BY P.G.A. PROFESSIONAL STUART WOODMAN GOLF COURSE (1) - 11:00AM
	GYMNASTICS AND SUNSET JOGGING - ASSEMBLE AT GOLF CLUB HOUSE 5:00PM
	TODAY THE WATERSPORTS OPERATION IS CLOSED
TUESDAY:	WATER GYMNASTICS - VILLAGE POOL (3) 7:30 AM
	WIND-SURFING EXHIBITION AND INSTRUCTION - WATER SPORTS (4) 12:00 NOON
	TENNIS CLINIC BY U.S.P.T.A. PROFESSIONAL FINBAR WILLIE TENNIS COURTS (5) 4:00 PM
	CALCUTTA GOLF AUCTION 7:15 PM AT "CALYPSO COCKTAIL PARTY"
WEDNESDAY:	18 HOLES - PRO-AM BEST BALL GOLF EVENT - ENTRY FEE U.S. $4 (1)
THURSDAY:	WATER GYMNASTICS - VILLAGE POOL (3) 7:30 AM
	GOLF CLINIC BY P.G.A. PROFESSIONAL STUART WOODMAN GOLF COURSE (1) 11:00 AM
	MID-WEEK STABLEFORD GOLF EVENT - 9 HOLES ANYTIME DURING THE DAY, ENTRY FEE U.S. $1
	GYMNASTICS AND SUNSET JOGGING - ASSEMBLE AT GOLF CLUB HOUSE (2) 5:00 PM
FRIDAY:	WATER GYMNASTICS - VILLAGE POOL (3) - 7:30 AM
	NATURE WALK - GOLF SHOP (1) 12:00 NOON
	MIX-IN DOUBLES, TENNIS COURTS 1, 2, & 3, AT 4:00 PM (5)
SATURDAY:	18 HOLE GOLF EVENT - SIGN UP AT GOLF SHOP (1) BEFORE MID-DAY FRIDAY
SUNDAY:	WATER SKIING - INSTRUCTIONS AND EXHIBITION - WATERSPORTS (4) AT 12:00 NOON

Exhibit 4   Malabar Beach Hotel guest statistics

	1979/80	1980/81
Arrivals	5,428	4,981
Bed/nights	53,135	36,263
Occupancy	84%	58%

Origin of guests

Great Britain	14,520 bed/nights
Canada	8,100 bed/nights
USA	2,800 bed/nights
Caribbean	4,200 bed/nights
Other	6,600 bed/nights

Note
British guests typically stayed for two sometimes three weeks; Canadian and US guests for one sometimes two weeks. Caribbean and other guests included a considerable amount of commercial, short stay business.

by a well-known guide book as 'very casual with upkeep somewhat ditto, but with devoted island savvy clientele'.

In the middle of 1981, the hotel business in St. Lucia was not good, with the general worldwide depression having led to a reduction in the tourist trade. Craig Barnard believed that the Malabar Beach Hotel had higher occupancy levels and was weathering the depression better than other hotels, but business was down on previous years (see Exhibit 4).

The depression had led to a bout of savage price cutting on the island with even the luxury hotels undercutting the Malabar Beach Hotel in selling rooms to tour operators.[1] The Malabar expected to get $US 90 a day for a double room (excluding meals) from a UK tour operator, during the high season. The Cunard La Toc was believed to be offering surplus rooms to operators at a high season rate of $US 22 per day and the St. Lucian Hotel to be offering surplus rooms at a low season rate of $US 10 per day.[2] (Hoteliers and agents were understandably reticent about actual contract rates.)

MANAGERIAL CONTROL

The Malabar Beach Hotel was family owned. Craig Barnard had recently taken over the management of the operation from his father, who though in his seven-

---

[1] In the United Kingdom and Canada, tour operators bought rooms at a fixed price from hoteliers; then they added their own markup to the room prices to arrive at the price shown in their brochures. There was no standard markup. The system in the United States was different. Rooms were offered by hotels at the price they were to be sold to the consumer, the rooms were bought by wholesalers (who received a commission of about 20 per cent), who in turn sold them to retailers and other agents.

[2] The currency in St. Lucia was East Caribbean Dollars ($EC). It was linked to the $US. In 1981, $EC 2.50 = $US 1.00 = £0.50.

Exhibit 5   Malabar Beach Hotel, Staffing 1981

Bar	12
Dining room	22
Kitchen	21
Food and beverage	2
Store room	2
Transport	3
Housekeeping	18
Watersports	3
Bell boys	4
Maintenance	4
Gardeners	7
Security	13
Reception	12
Laundry	4
Total	122

ties was an active member of the board. The staffing of the Hotel is shown in Exhibit 5. Craig Barnard ran the Hotel using a tight financial control system. The Hotel was divided into four profit centres: hotel, bar, kitchen (and restaurant), and laundry. Management attention was focused on maximizing the profitability of each profit centre (except the laundry which was expected to break even). Revenues were allocated to each profit centre. For example, if guests had paid for meals in advance, these revenues were allocated to the kitchen. Guests could charge for meals or drinks against their room numbers; the accounting system enabled all tills to be balanced at the end of the day, to be controlled against a particular section or profit centre, and to be posted to guest folios. Craig Barnard believed that a tight profit centre control system was important, not only for profit maximization but also to control shrinkage of bar and kitchen stocks and cash losses from tills.

Staff were paid on a fortnightly basis made up of a base rate plus service points (staff were paid $EC 80 per service point in the high season and $EC 35 in the low season). A new member of staff would be paid $EC 90 per fortnight plus two service points, an established receptionist would be earning around $EC 300 per fortnight plus service points, and a department head around $EC 1,000 per fortnight.

GUEST EXPENDITURE PATTERNS

Guests could book in advance using different plans, depending on their needs.[1]

[1] The plans were: American Plan (AP), all meals; Modified American Plan (MAP), bed breakfast and dinner; European Plan (EP), no meals; and Continental Plan (CP), bed and breakfast.

The choice of plan varied with country of origin. The British usually chose MAP, Canadians EP, Americans EP or MAP, visitors from the Caribbean CP, and other visitors MAP. Visitors who had not prepaid their meals could purchase meals at the Hotel or each at other restaurants. For guests paying for meals the Hotel charged $US 4.00 for breakfast and $US 16.00 for dinner. There was an *à la carte* buffet lunch with the average spend per guest taking lunch being $US 4.00. The revenue and expenditure in the restaurant in an average month is shown in Exhibit 6.

Guests drinking at the bar normally charged their drinks to their rooms. The average expenditure per guest in the bar was $US 3.00 per day. Cost of sales (excluding labour) was 30% of revenue. The overall extras bill of MAP clients was between $US 28.00 and $US 32.00 per week and of EP clients about $US 52 per week.

Exhibit 6   Malabar Beach Hotel restaurant expenditure
in a typical month in the high season 1981

$US

Revenue allocated from	
pre-paid plans	56,400
Meals paid for	6,000
Total revenue	62,400
Food cost	28,000
Guest nights	4,100

THE NO-MONEY PROPOSAL

Over the year Craig Barnard had been devoting considerable thought to the problems facing the Malabar Beach Hotel. As well as the problems outlined previously, he was worried by overdependence on Great Britain and Canada. He felt that the economies and the currencies of both these countries were likely to decline against the US dollar. (The Eastern Caribbean dollar was linked to the US dollar.) He therefore wished to increase his US clientele. He had retained a firm of marketing advisors in the United States who had advised him that the US holiday market could be considered as three segments: singles, couples, and families. Craig Barnard had rejected the singles market as it had connotations that he was unhappy with, but had decided to consider the implications of the other two segments further.

In his search for ways of developing the hotel he had visited one of the Club Mediterranee complexes. Club Mediterranee was founded in 1950 in France, originally running 'Polynesia'-style village resorts in the Mediterranean. In 1981 they ran a wide range of holiday facilities around the world. There were three Club Mediterranee villages in the Caribbean (two on Guadaloupe, one on Martinique). The Club villages were all very French in character. There is a

Exhibit 7   Popular tours taken by holidaymakers in St. Lucia[1]

                                                           Cost

1. *Round the Island Tour* $US 17
   A one-day bus tour round the island, visiting various towns, bays, and beauty spots and visiting the 'drive-in volcano' at Soufriere.

2. *Barque Voyage* $US 30
   A one-day sailing trip in the *Barque Buccaneer*[2] or the Brig Unicorn to Soufriere. Includes a visit to the volcano, lunch, swimming off the boat, and free rum punch throughout the voyage.

3. *Martinique Visit* $US 90
   Fly from Vigie Airport at 7:00 a.m. to Martinique. Full-day tour round the island with time for shopping and beach visit. Quality lunch provided. Return 7:00 p.m.

4. *Grenadines Visit* $US 130
   Fly from Vigie Airport to Grenadines. Full-day sailing through the Grenadine Islands (including Mustique where Princess Margaret stays), return to Vigie in evening.

[1] Craig Barnard owned St. Lucia Representatives which would organize these tours.
[2] Craig Barnard owned the *Barque Buccaneer*, one of the two boats making day voyages to Soufriere.

strong emphasis on informal open air atmosphere. Guests live in 'huts' and are encouraged to wear 'polynesian' clothes. All drinks are paid for with beads, with are bought in advance and worn as a necklace. All food and wine with meals are included in the package. There is a strong emphasis on sports, with ample facilities and all provided free of charge. He had been impressed by the operation, but realized that the concept and scale would not transfer easily to the Malabar Beach Hotel. However, from these various discussions and visits he developed the belief that a substantial segment of the market would buy a comprehensive holiday package. He had developed a proposal that he believed would radically change the nature of the product being offered by the Malabar Beach Hotel. His proposal was to do away with money in the hotel and sell holidaymakers a package that included everything. They would use no money during the holiday, and have no bills to settle at the end. He felt that such a range would be very attractive to a substantial number of holidaymakers.

   To turn the concept into reality, he faced a number of difficult tasks and decisions. The first was to sell the concept to the board. The board, not unexpectedly, had strong reservations about the concept and questions were asked about how the concept could operate in practice. The no-money concept would need clearly defining. It was proposed to include all meals, drinks (at the bar and wine with meals) and cigarettes in the cost of the holiday. A key question was what other services would be provided free. In addition to hotel expenditure, holidaymakers typically spent money on telephone calls home, local tours (a list of popular tours is shown in Exhibit 7), visited the town of Castries ($US 4.00

taxi ride), and bought souvenirs. Another element of the no-money plan was its price and how the price should be stated in relation to existing plans.

Another issue facing Craig Barnard was, given that he could sell the concept to the board, how should the concept be implemented? There would be changes in the way in which the Hotel was marketed and in the Hotel operations. He felt that he had two alternatives, either to decide on a changeover date and introduce the package on a large scale from that date, or to introduce the concept incrementally over a period of six to twelve months.

Name Index

Subject Index